TRUCKS
in GARDEN
the
of EDEN

'This other Eden, demi-paradise... this blessed spot... this England.'
William Shakespeare, *Richard II*

'The road to hell is paved with good intentions.'
An old Portuguese proverb

TRUCKS
in the GARDEN
of EDEN

IN SEARCH OF BRITAIN'S UTOPIAS

VITALI VITALIEV

AMBERLEY

To Vitaly Grazutis

First published 2024

Amberley Publishing
The Hill, Stroud
Gloucestershire, GL5 4EP

www.amberley-books.com

Copyright © Vitali Vitaliev, 2024

The right of Vitali Vitaliev to be identified as the Author of this work has been asserted in accordance with the Copyright, Designs and Patents Act 1988.

All rights reserved. No part of this book may be reprinted or reproduced or utilised in any form or by any electronic, mechanical or other means, now known or hereafter invented, including photocopying and recording, or in any information storage or retrieval system, without the permission in writing from the Publishers.

British Library Cataloguing in Publication Data.
A catalogue record for this book is available from the British Library.

ISBN 978 1 3981 0024 4 (hardback)
ISBN 978 1 3981 0025 1 (ebook)

1 2 3 4 5 6 7 8 9 10

Typesetting by SJmagic DESIGN SERVICES, India.
Printed in the UK.

Contents

	Acknowledgements	7
	Confessions of an Anglophile: Instead of an Introduction	8
Chapter 1	No Place Like Utopia	16
Chapter 2	My utopian Neighbourhood	33
Chapter 3	The utopian Province of Hertfordshire	51
Chapter 4	Tavi and Chucho	70
Chapter 5	St Evenage, aka Silkingrad	90
Chapter 6	Motopia, or 'Let's Kill the Car'!	107
Chapter 7	Utopias in the Time of Pandemic	118
Chapter 8	Arcadia and the Real Estate	135
Chapter 9	Ornate Doors to Nowhere	152
Chapter 10	The Bridge that Crosses Nothing	170
Chapter 11	'Do Not Tell Titus!'	185
Chapter 12	The Case of Negative Nostalgia	202
Chapter 13	Per Insulae Ad Astra!	222
Chapter 14	In The Eye of The Beholder, or My Utop Ten	239

Trucks in the Garden of Eden

'Malice in Wonderland' Instead of an Epilogue	262
Notes and References	266
Appendix 1: Incomplete Angler	271
Appendix 2: Utopias: an A to Z Primer	277
Other Books by the Author	287

Acknowledgements

I am grateful to:

Charles Dark of Cardiff
Connor Stait of Amberley/Icon Books
Councillor Rex Shayler of Newtown, Wales
Dominic Lenton of Hitchin
Duncan Folkes of MWT Cymru, Wales
Eileen Rainsberry of Visit Southwest Scotland
Frangelica Flook of Aurora Expeditions
International Travel Writers Association
John Spillets of Port Sunlight, Wiral
Josh Tidy of Letchworth Garden City
Kirsty Rose of Rockhall Tower, Dumfries, Scotland
Magdalene College, University of Cambridge
Magnus Llewellyn of Times Scotland
Royal Literary Fund

And, above all – to my beautiful wife and partner Christine, the love of my life, without whom this book would not have been written.

Confessions of an Anglophile: Instead of an Introduction

> 'I had a dream that whatever I thought was a dream was reality, and whatever was reality – a dream.'
>
> Anton Chekhov

Of all existing definitions of Utopia, I prefer one, coined by the young Cambridge-based historian Anna Neima, who described it in one of her books as 'a kind of social dreaming'.[1] Human nature is such that we tend to get used to good things easily and are quick to start taking them for granted. Therefore, a Utopia, like a much-coveted fantasy land, or indeed a sweet, even if 'social', dream, is probably best appreciated from a distance – before you had a chance to visit it for the first time, or – on the contrary – after you got fed up and left it for good!

It is all nicely summed up in a concise Russian proverb '*Tam khorosho, gde nas niet*!' which can be roughly rendered in English as 'The grass is always greener on the other side of the fence'. Word-for-word, it translates as 'The good life (read Utopia) is wherever we happen not to be.'[2]

Britain had been my beloved Utopia since early childhood. when I started learning English (at the age of 7), without the slightest hope of ever visiting the UK, and remained as such until fairly recently, when having lived in the UK for over 30 years, I started noticing the country's less appealing features, not limited to Europe's worst and priciest trains; football hooligans; ridiculous TV tax, known as 'TV licence'; the ugly Dystopian 'New Towns', full of Soviet-scale poverty, crime and despair; chronically littered forests and motorways; sewage-polluted rivers; council tax; class system; increasingly inefficient NHS, etc. etc...

Confessions of an Anglophile: Instead of an Introduction

I learned about such shameful episodes of Britain's modern history as the forced repatriation of Russian POWs to Stalin in 1945; the incarceration of refugees from Nazi Germany, branded 'enemy aliens' (to echo Stalinist 'enemies of the people'?) in the internment camps on the Isle of Man; dispatching the WWII refugees to Australia on board HMT *Duneira* in 1940; 'model occupation' of the Channel Islands; invasion of Iraq in 2003, and so on and so forth...

The more I think about it, the more I come to the conclusion that there are several areas in which Britain – for reasons which are hard to pinpoint – is simply unable, or possibly unwilling, to excel: trains; clean streets, roads and public toilets; manufacturing of anything, except perhaps for Dyson vacuum cleaners, and so on... Interestingly, in some of those areas, like, say, railways and manufacturing, this country used to be one of the most successful global trailblazers while still an empire, but has since somewhat lost the knack. As well as the plot.

On the other hand, there are areas in which Britain remains successful and can even be called the world leader: ales, cider, high teas, Cornish pasties, female binge drinkers (if we believe an OECD report, published in November 2023). And I nearly forgot: vacuum cleaners, of course! So impressed I became with their unfading perfection that I made a heroine of my fantasy novel *Granny Yaga*, a dedicated London witch called Melissa, fly 'the latest Dyson vacuum cleaner, with GPS and solar panels', instead of a traditional antediluvian broom!

What else? League football, tabloid newspapers, spy thrillers... that's about it, I guess.

No one is perfect, least of all countries... Apart from Utopias! The moment the country where you live loses the glamour of perfection in your eyes, it stops being the shiny Utopia of your dreams, and instead becomes your Motherland (sic), whether you were born in it or not. It is then and only then that you start maturing into a proper citizen, even a patriot. for patriotism is not about eulogising a Utopia. What can be easier? It is the intention to make your country better, and such a mission cannot be constructive if you ignore your land's less attractive sides.

In many ways, Britain still remains my most desired country, my 'other Eden', to quote Shakespeare. Thirty odd years ago, I consciously gave up my Australian fame and material well-being to live in it. As they say, I voted for Britain with my feet.

Trucks in the Garden of Eden

And, yes, for me it is still a Utopia of sorts. A poor man's, perhaps, yet still a caviar!

A Garden of Eden with trucks, so to speak.

Of all anniversaries, memorable dates, jubilees and birthdays, I never forget to mark one – the 8th of October 1988. It was on that warm autumn afternoon that at the tender age of 34, I arrived in Britain – and in the West – for the first time.

As a romantic, travel-hungry boy in the dusty and long-suffering Ukrainian city of Kharkiv, I often dreamt of a trip to Britain. I imagined that I would start in some godforsaken Ukrainian hamlet with a silly Soviet name (like Red Excavator, say – there was such a village on the outskirts of Kharkiv). First, I would travel on a cart, dragged by a tired horse; then on an equally fast *elektrichka*, a squeaky electric shuttle train. 'Where are you going to, boy?' the red-nosed residents of Red Excavator would ask. 'To London,' I would answer matter-of-factly. No, to puzzle them even more, I would rather say 'To Shrewsbury' or, better still, 'To Bourton-on-the-Water'.

I wanted my imaginary journey to Britain, my childhood Utopia whose language, literature and history I had been studying assiduously since the age of eight as an antidote to the all-permeating Soviet dogma, to be long and unhurried.

If the Soviet stretch of my imaginary pilgrimage was more or less clear to me, the British part was clouded in mystery. The problem was that my armchair traveller's impressions of Britain were thoroughly utopian and mostly grasped from the books of Dickens, Thackeray and Conan Doyle (more modern authors were too politically explosive to be published in the Soviet Union at that time), so the only picture of London I was able to drum up in my fevered imagination was that of moustachioed Victorian gentlemen in bowler hats feeding pigeons in St James's Park.

As for the countryside, one of the few sources I could rely upon was Conan Doyle's *The Hound of the Baskervilles*, which described (among other things) a turn-of-the-century train ride from Paddington to Devonshire, undertaken by Dr Watson and Sir Henry Baskerville. I knew the passage almost by heart: 'The journey was a swift and pleasant one. In a very few hours the brown earth had become ruddy, the brick had changed to granite, and red cows grazed in well-hedged fields where the lush grasses and

Confessions of an Anglophile: Instead of an Introduction

more luxuriant vegetation spoke of a richer, if a damper, climate.' In my daydreams, I could easily visualise myself, in a bowler hat, next to a simnilarly bowler-hatted Dr Watson, smoking a pipe and looking at the well-cultivated pastoral landscape unveiling beyond the window.

'The train pulled up at a small wayside station and we all descended. Outside, beyond the low, white fence, a wagonette with a pair of cobs was waiting. Our coming was evidently a great event, for the station-master and porters clustered round us to carry out our luggage.'

At this point I, too, had to descend – from cloud-cuckoo-land – to look up the word 'cob' in my dog-eared English-Russian dictionary. The only meaning given was 'male swan'. A wagonette drawn by swans? It sounded straight out of Grimm's Fairy Tales, which perfectly matched my perception of Britain as a kind of fairyland...

Uncharacteristically, I chose to travel to the UK by train, in a Moscow-Hook of Holland Soviet carriage (built in East Germany) which kept being attached to different trains (Moscow-Brest, Brest-Warsaw, Warsaw-Berlin and so on) during its 40-hour long journey, and then by ferry to Harwich. It was my first ever trip outside the USSR, my first ever contact with the long-forbidden Western world and my first introduction to the then mysterious and alien Western way of life, of which the impressive Dutch ferry *Queen Beatrix* was the first shining example. But let's come back to it, or rather to her (I mean the ferry), a little later.

I decided to take a train for one simple reason: I wanted my long-awaited journey to the West to be as long as possible, just to be able to savour it quietly, without a rush.

Even when already on the train, I was still finding it hard to believe that the journey, which, as I had always thought, would never take place, was actually happening. But the fact remained: as a well-known Moscow journalist I had been invited to England by the *Guardian* newspaper and its then Moscow Correspondent, my friend Martin Walker.

It was still over two years until, under growing pressure from the Soviet authorities, I'd have to defect, i.e. to leave the USSR for good. The first of the couple of trips prior to the ultimate defection, that initial one was very special, albeit I didn't know then that it would herald the beginning of my new life...

The truth was that I was not at all sure what to expect and had to rely on the advice of my omniscient friends, who had either been to Britain or, more likely, knew someone who had. They told me never to declare my Russianness – let alone 'Ukrainian-ness' – in public ('They don't like Russians and have probably never heard of Ukrainians'); always to check the billboard with today's prices before venturing into a cafe ('They will rip you off otherwise'); under no circumstances to use taxis ('They will take you for a ride around the block'); to do all shopping in charity shops ('They sell the same things as the plushest boutiques, only much cheaper'); to have *matrioshka* dolls and other cheap Russian souvenirs handy in order to bribe discounts out of shop assistants (they assured me that a customer was always meant to bargain in shops); and lots of similar expert tips, which I dutifully recorded in my notebook.

The reality of my first-ever trip to the West, however, proved much more puzzling. I remember popping into one of the lavatories on board the *Queen Beatrix* Cross-Channel ferry, which took me from the Hook of Holland to Harwich. Overwhelmed by the mirrors and the smell of deodorants, I rushed straight out again, convinced I had wandered into a hairdressing salon by mistake. I stood dumbfounded at the entrance to the ship's small and poorly stocked (as I soon realised) duty-free shop, not daring to step inside. It seemed to have many more goods on display than all of Moscow's stores put together.

In Harwich, it took me half an hour to drag my abnormally heavy bags, full of tins of preserves (to minimise food expenditure) and souvenirs-cum-bribes, to the immigration area near the railway station. To my disappointment, there was no stationmaster, nor anyone else, to greet me by tipping his bowler hat, and porters were not in a hurry to help with my luggage.

Sweating profusely, I probably looked as if I had just robbed a brick factory. That was almost certainly why I was led aside by a buxom female customs officer, who was not wearing any hat, but wore a nasty sadistic grin instead. She asked me to open my suitcases and, when I failed (out of embarrassment) to find the keys, she simply hara-kiried them with a penknife – the last thing I expected to happen during my long-awaited first moments in the free world.

Despite this initial shock, I thoroughly enjoyed my first trip to Britain. I remember being dazzled by all the comforts of my first-ever British hotel, where I was put up by the *Guardian*: a spare television set in the sterile bathroom, snow-white bathrobes, a vast double bed, although I was on my own (sleeping in it alone felt like a minor offence), and not a sign of previous tenants' pubic hair on

Confessions of an Anglophile: Instead of an Introduction

the bathroom floor – a constant feature of an average Soviet hotel, of which I have seen hundreds in my capacity as a roving Special Correspondent of the satirical magazine *Krokodil*.

The well-stocked mini-bar was a special attraction, for I firmly believed that the price of all drinks in it was included in the price of the room (I knew that breakfast was). I was in a Utopia, after all! When it was time to go, I thought it would be a shame to leave behind all those nice-looking miniatures, so I relocated them in my suitcase.

'Have you used anything from your mini-bar, sir?' a reception clerk asked me when I was checking out.

'Yes,' I answered, trying to hide my surprise at another blatant intrusion of my privacy.

'What did you use?'

'Er ... everything, actually.'

He gave me the special sort of a 'Stuff you' look that, as I learnt later, British hotel receptionists and waiters are so good at (you can get a similar stare from a Harrods shop assistant if you ask for a pound of used nails), but didn't say anything. I suddenly realised that I had done something wrong and could feel my face acquiring the colour of the cherry brandy in one of the bottles in my suitcase.

I had done all the sights of London, except for the shops which I was trying to avoid. With the exception of bookshops. You will never guess what my first ever purchase in Britain (and in the West) was. A compact *Roget's Thesaurus*!

During those magic three weeks that to me seemed to have stretched for decades, I visited Oxford (thrice), Cambridge (twice) and Rye (once). The latter sounded precisely like the word for 'paradise' in Russian – *rai*. 'Rye Humour' was the title of my first article for *Punch* magazine which I wrote right there, in my hotel room. The rai-paradise double-entendre was exhilarating – if only to myself...

During those three life-changing weeks, I published five features in the *Guardian* and two in *Punch*. I attended a football match at the Arsenal stadium, a famous *Punch* lunch and the launch of *Soho News*, a glossy magazine that collapsed after the first issue. I was invited to a couple of posh Pall Mall clubs. I went on the beat with London and Oxford policemen researching a feature for *Krokodil*. I interviewed the son of Alexander Kerensky, Russia's first prime minister of 1917, and was myself interviewed by the BBC World Service, London Television and LBC. I took part in an *After Dark* live TV show, where we drank and talked in front of the camera into the early hours of the morning.

I got a contract for my first book from a prestigious London publisher and a literary agent (she was AP Watt's Clarissa Rushdie, Salman Rushdie's first and by then estranged wife). I earned quite a bit of money (by Soviet standards), which allowed me to buy not just all the intended presents and souvenirs for my Moscow friends and colleagues, but also a coveted video player.

I shocked my wife by calling her up in Moscow from the car of a new London friend of mine – a true miracle at the time (later she told me that she didn't believe I was calling from the car and thought I'd had one too many). I wrote to Prince Charles inviting him to come and stray with me in Moscow (he never came but did respond to my letter very warmly). In short, I had a ball.

I fell in love with London and with England, which proved to be exactly what I had dreamt they would be – and even better. As my friend Martin Walker later recalled in an interview:

> When he came to London, I met him [off the boat train] at Liverpool Street station, drove him around the sights, took him to his first supermarket and [a day or two later] down to my parents-in-laws' place on Church Square in Rye. It was like watching someone fall in love: the old town, the medieval church, the cobbled streets and teashops, the shops in general, and visiting the *Guardian*. He was spectacularly happy.

The small seaside town of Rye, with its cobbled streets and toy-like Tudor cottages had indeed become my little paradise, read Utopia, reincarnated!

On my last morning in the UK, I decided to do some sightseeing and went to watch the changing of the guard at Buckingham Palace. Standing behind a massive railing huddled together with hundreds of other onlookers, I was peeping from behind someone's back and vainly trying to see what was happening. The only thing I could discern, however, was the fluffy top of a Scottish guardsman's hat. There was no chance to get nearer as policemen were blocking the way.

'I am with the press,' I told them. 'Can I come closer?'

'Sorry, sir, the rules are the same for everyone,' I was told.

Suddenly the massive palace gates slid apart to let in a white mini-bus. A dozen people got out of it and started watching the ceremony from inside the courtyard – a luxury vantage point. I

Confessions of an Anglophile: Instead of an Introduction

felt furious. My perverse Soviet sense of social justice, moulded by thirty-odd years of almost incessant queuing, was deeply insulted. What kind of big-shots were they to have blatantly jumped the waiting line?

I then had a better look. These were not big-shots but small teenage kids with Down's syndrome. Holding hands, they were looking at the guards pacing across the yard. The policemen were smiling at them. I was ashamed of my fury and moved almost to tears...

In the USSR, one rarely bumped into a disabled person in the street, and yet there were of course millions of them around. Most of them lacked sympathy and help and had to stay at home (if any), too embarrassed and often simply physically unable to go out. The thing that struck me most on that first visit to Britain was not the well-stocked shops and restaurants but the sheer number of disabled people in the streets, where traffic would often stop to let them cross, as well as in museums, stadiums and supermarkets where they enjoyed special toilets, lifts and ramps to allow them to move around freely. Unlike their Soviet counterparts, they didn't look miserable or deprived and were no less smiley, self-confident and free than their able-bodied compatriots.

How could one fail to fall in love with a country like that?

Yes, many dreams came true and many illusions were shattered since that first visit to Britain. And yet, wherever in the world I travelled ever since, I kept subconsciously looking for my late-Victorian utopian dreamland, with its 'swift and pleasant' trains, helpful porters, respectable stationmasters – and, of course, swan-drawn carriages. At times, I could see it behind modern façades, at times I could not, but this constant quest for a Utopia made my eyes sharper and my perception of the confusing late 20th- and then 21st-century reality paradoxically more acute.

I've tried to preserve that kind of vision while researching this book, too.

Yet, there is another perspective which I couldn't – and didn't want to – avoid. Searching for my British Utopia, I couldn't help by keep one eye on my Soviet past: drab and Dystopian, and yet – eventful (if not to say tempestuous) and therefore instructive and worth remembering!

Chapter 1

No Place Like Utopia

A map of the world that does not include Utopia is not worth even glancing at.

                                                                                Oscar Wilde

We all need a bit of Utopia in our lives. Particularly in the middle of a nasty pandemic, when life as we knew it had all but come to a stop, frozen in a seemingly endless lockdown. I spent those couple of years searching for a Utopia. Not any kind of Utopia, but – conveniently for the time when foreign travel was all but banned – a domestic, read British, one, for that is what my quest was about: the utopian communities of Britain, of which, by some estimates, there have existed over 4000, including historical and still functioning ones: Garden Cities, Garden Suburbs and 'model' towns and villages, 'New Towns', colonies, religious, artistic and other communities, 'intentional' (e.g. naturist, vegan or 'green'), low-impact-living and other settlements, etc.

In a specially acquired second-hand campervan, I've managed to visit about 50 of those – a drop in the ocean, but a meaningful drop, or so I hope.

Now it's time to share my discoveries with you.

What is Utopia?

Lexically, it is a 'no place'(from Greek 'topos' – 'place' and 'u', or 'ou; – 'no'), the place that does not exist. Curiously, No Place is also the name of a small village in county Durham. I sympathise with the villagers, who when asked where they live, have to respond 'In No Place'.

No Place Like Utopia

This oxymoron immediately brings back memories of the first three years of my life, spent in a 'secret' Soviet town near Moscow (I will describe it in detail later), to where my parents, young scientists (Mum – a chemical engineer, Dad – a nuclear physicist) and newly married graduates of Kharkiv University, were dispatched in the early 1950s to work at a top-secret Soviet government facility developing nuclear and hydrogen bombs. The town of 40,000 people, unmapped and unnamed (it was referred to as 'Military Unit BA/48764', or something similar) officially did not exist.

Was that a Utopia, I mean a 'no place', then? Well, despite the superior, compared to other Soviet cities and towns, food supplies it enjoyed, I don't think so. It was rather a relatively small, yet highly irradiated (with the background radiation levels hundreds of times higher than the accepted minimum) dystopia, or an anti-Utopia, if you wish, inside the much larger giant dystopia of the USSR, the totalitarian state, which, incidentally, was itself formed (in 1921) as a Utopia of sorts! At times, I used to jokingly decipher the now-defunct country's crudely abbreviated name as 'Utopian Soviet Socialist Republic'.

Indeed, the difference between the two directly opposite concepts, utopias and dystopias, is sometimes negligible, or even entirely non-existent. Most social utopias inevitably evolve into dystopias with time. Moreover, a place that may appear utopian to some, is likely to look utterly dystopian to others.

In the words of Gregory Claeys, Professor of the History of Political Thought at Royal Holloway, University of London, and my favourite writer on things utopian, 'Dystopia is a 'Malice in Wonderland'. As you see, the 'Wonderland' bit still stands. It is significant that in the much-quoted description of Utopias by the great Irish writer and wit Oscar Wilde (in his anarchist essay 'The Soul of Man under Socialism'), the second part routinely gets omitted (see the epigraph to this Chapter) – probably because it may sound a bit confusing:

> A map of the world that does not include Utopia is not worth even glancing at, for it leaves out the one country at which humanity is always landing. And when humanity lands there, it looks out, and seeing a better country, sets sail. Progress is the realisation of Utopias.

To me, Wilde very clearly points out that rather than being an abstract idea and a cliched euphemism for a 'heaven on earth',

Utopia is a dynamic socio-political concept, prone to change and constantly in flux.

A good example of that is Suffolk's Hollesley Bay, which began in 1887 as a sanatorium-style utopian colony for the London unemployed, but with time evolved (or shall I say 'mutated'?) into a Category D HM Prison for adult males and young offenders. At the same time, it remains a Utopia for some. This is what one of the former Hollesley Bay inmates writes in his five-star (!) review of it (yes, prisons get routinely reviewed online – just like restaurants and hotels on Tripadvisor): 'I went there for non-payment of fines. Great thing is fine was for £250. I spent three days there and came out fine free... Would of (sic) liked to stay longer to be honest, because I was having a ball.' To reapply a popular truism, Utopia (like beauty) is very much in the eye of the beholder.

There is an old Soviet joke about an American and a Russian who agree over the phone to meet in their dream city, Paris, where none of them had been before, but by mistake they end up in Warsaw. After a quick look around, they both decide that they had reached their destination, Paris!

When I was about 12 or 13 years old, my mother – a distinguished chemical engineer, with a number of inventions on record – was magnanimously 'allowed' to travel as a tourist to the GDR (East Germany). She came back ten days later full of admiration for the prosperity and luxurious lifestyles led by the 'Ossies' (I learned that somewhat derogatory term much later of course). To crown it all, she brought me several packets of chewing gum, the first I ever laid my caries-ridden Soviet teeth into. There was no question for me (and for my Mum) that the earthly paradise was called the GDR – German Democratic Republic. We knew nothing about the Stasi of course.

However, my British friends who had happened to visit the same GDR roughly at the same time, were shocked by its poverty, dirt, inefficiency, poor quality of food and lack of basic consumer items (they didn't mean the chewing gum, I am sure). Another good proof of Eistein's relativity theory...

Yes, Utopia and Dystopia are siblings, with the same parents (Good Will and Some Imagination?), yet with different lifestyles and hence mutually opposing life principles. Like your average modern family – close-knit and dysfunctional in equal measure.

No Place Like Utopia

As I have noted already, the term 'Utopia' was invented by Sir Thomas More (1478-1535), who, in his eponymous book, first published in 1516, described a fictitious near-ideal country on an island, an imaginary state where everything was perfect, or near-perfect.

While the word 'Utopia' was coined by More in the early 16th century, the idea of it had already had a long history – from the time of Plato's Republic to the Sumerian 'earthly paradise' and the biblical Garden of Eden, people had been mesmerised and enchanted by the image of a 'perfect place'.

Perfect? But isn't perfection itself a Utopia of sorts? It sure is! Nothing and no one is perfect, asserts an anonymous piece of folk wisdom, thus closing the circle: a real Utopia is in itself a Utopia! A four-angled triangle. A contradiction in terms. An oxymoron. A heaven on earth.

In my travel features and books, I used to refer to Switzerland as a 'perfect country'. Indeed, it strikes a visitor as a spotlessly, almost lifelessly, clean land, where everything works with the precision of an expensive cuckoo clock. (Contrary to popular belief, most cuckoo clocks are actually made not in Switzerland but in Germany.) Trains are always on time, and there isn't an inhabited place in Switzerland that cannot be reached by some sort of public transport. The federal law and the Swiss Constitution stipulate that every village with a population greater than 40 is entitled to regular and punctual (!) train and/or bus services. The frequency of these services is in direct proportion to the population density. Timetables are put together four years in advance. They tend to be rather conservative and seldom change. If a new route is to be introduced, the population of the area affected is invited to have a referendum. It was in one Swiss railway stations that I once heard the loudspeaker announcement: 'The train due to arrive at platform ten is running ten minutes late due to an incident in another country.'

Most Swiss cities and towns go dead after 7 pm (particularly in winter) – a living proof of an old truism that all the Swiss do outside money-making hours is sleeping. Don't get me wrong. I admire Switzerland: its beauty, its precision, its international spirit, its neat and geometrically correct, as if regularly recycled and repackaged, mountains; its cleanliness. ('Littering the territory of this rubbish dump is punishable by fine!' read a sign I once spotted at a tip, or in modern PC-speak, recycling facility, near Sargans.) I admire its Alpine horns, its mature cheeses, its blue-eyed cows, etc, etc. But

Trucks in the Garden of Eden

I also understand a 1920s Russian traveller who branded Swiss hotels 'suicidal' (due to the all-permeating boredom) and am ready to repeat after Henry Lord Brougham, who wrote (hyperbolically) about Switzerland in 1816:' 'It is a country to be in for two hours and a half, if the weather is fine, and no longer. Ennui comes on the third hour, and suicide attacks you before night.' But even in the last, rather unlikely, case, you may have a chance to take your life peacefully and painlessly, by way of another highly commendable Swiss innovation, Dignitas Clinic.

The problem is that everyone has their own Utopia, or 'paradise', craved but seldom seen and, to be absolutely honest, best avoided. For a glutton, it is a free smorgasbord, an 'eat-as-much-as-you-like' buffet, for an alcoholic – free beer (that was actually one of the official demands of the striking builders in Melbourne, Australia, in 1990), for a swindler – a free lunch, for a writer – a limitless deadline, and so on. Even my dog Tashi, a fluffy Tibetan terrier, has his own Utopia: our lounge-room sofa, from which he is barred, while still stretching on it clandestinely of an evening.

Most Utopias are temporary and tend to disappear entirely with time. My very first one was ... a book. Yes, Utopias come in all kinds of guises: theories, plans, dreams, towns, communes and even leisure pastimes (see Appendix One), and ever since Thomas More's *Utopia*, books have been among the most popular.

The book was given to me as a birthday present by my Dad at the age of 4. It became my own little Utopia long before I learned how to read, for it was enough just to look at the pictures. I am talking about *Kniga o vkusnoi I zdorovoi pishche*, 'The Book of Tasty and Healthy Food', published in Moscow in 1952. It is one of the two or three of my childhood books that has miraculously survived and withstood all my life's wanderings: Kharkov (now 'Kharkiv')-Moscow-Melbourne-London-Melbourne-Edinburgh-Folkestone-Dublin-London-Letchworth etc.

That weighty, dog-eared, and yet well-preserved and readable, or rather 'perusable' (for 'peruse' was what I used to do to it frequently at the age of 5 or 6) still stands on a shelf in my Hertfordshire house. I remember leafing through its glossy pages with coloured pictures of alluring and not necessarily 'wholesome' Russian foods – never seen in reality and therefore exotic – in bed

No Place Like Utopia

when suffering from a cold or flu, or more frequently when feigning them not to go to school.

Later, I was told that the book had been banned in the 1960s USSR for two reasons: first, because it opened with and was full of quotes from Stalin, whose very name was then temporarily unmentionable in the Soviet Union (after his crimes were publicly – and no-less-temporarily – exposed by Khrushcvev in 1956). Secondly, because the 'subversive' cook book carried recipes and pictures of the dishes, with the ingredients (meat, caviar, cheese, smetana, fish etc.) that had become all but imaginary in the semi-starving country, where even white bread and butter were rationed and took hours of queuing to buy (my parents used to take me out queuing with them, for in the strict per capita food rationing, my little 'caput' also counted). 'One of the peculiarities of our revolution was that it had given the Soviet people not just freedom but also material well-being and a possibility of a plentiful and cultured life,' was the quote from Stalin, typed in huge mournful letters on the flap jacket.

My parents and grandparents, like most ordinary Soviet citizens, were unable to get hold of any of those wonderful delicacies and wines, shamelessly depicted on the book's countless coloured photos and drawings. The only time my mother managed to get some beluga caviar at our local Intourist Hotel for foreigners (the only place in our city where it was at times on sale) when my granny wad dying of cancer and the delicacy, featuring prominently in the utterly utopian 'Book of Tasty and Healthy Food' was offered to her as her life's final treat. No need to say that my granny had never tried caviar before, not counting its aubergine variety, the so-called 'poor man's caviar'.

Of course, for a little boy like me, the lying work was a book of wonderful fairy tales, alongside my other favourite – 'The Bumper Book of Russian Fairy Tales', featuring the crafty witch Baba Yaga, Koshchei the Deathless, a three-headed snake, Horinich, and my favourite – the invariably ingenious and quick-witted peasant youngster, Ivanushka the Fool.

As I was growing up, however, the social 'fairy tales' we were all bombarded with daily from radios, newspapers and later from the match-box-sized black-and-white screens of the first-generation Soviet KVN[3] TV sets (we used to cover their tiny screens with a transparent blue-red-green film to create an illusion they were in colour) were appearing more and more deceitful and therefore annoying; for how many times a day can a child be

Trucks in the Garden of Eden

told that he or is so very lucky to be living in the 'workers' and peasants' heaven'?

I remember how in the early 1960s (I had just started school then), our then 'great and dear leader' Nikita Sergeyevich Khrushchev solemnly declared at a Communist Party Congress that 'the present generation of Soviet people will all be living under Communism!' He even gave us a date – in exactly 20 years' time we would be happily residing in a truly utopian (I didn't know that word then of course) world, where there would be no money and everybody would be able to have anything he or she wanted.

'You mean, I'd be able to have any toys I want?' I asked my mother. 'Yes, of course,' she would smile ruefully.

And once, as I remember very clearly, I was stopped on the way to school by two navvies – both in flat grey caps and dirty overalls – digging a trench in the middle of our street.

'How old are you, young lad?' one of them asked.

'Seven!' I replied proudly.

'So, you will be 27 years old when Communism comes!' the second navvy told me sticking his spade into the ground furiously. The following day, I saw them again in the same spot hastily filling up the same trench, which, as they explained to me angrily, no one needed in the first place.

In Russia, the Utopia-forming tradition of window-dressing and throwing dust in the eyes of the West and its own citizens alike (in the Soviet Union it was known as *pokazukha*) predated the foundation of the USSR by hundreds of years.

What is *pokazukha*? There is no direct English equivalent, the closest synonym being perhaps 'window-dressing'. I would render it in English as 'boasting of non-existing achievements'.

The first historical example of it goes back to the 18th century when Prince Grigory Potemkin (1739-91) constructed fake cardboard villages on the banks of the Volga to impress Catherine the Great. The decorations were painted in bright colours and were designed to mislead the notoriously short-sighted Empress when she sailed down the Volga to inspect her dominions. Behind the cardboard walls there was famine and extreme poverty, but from the river it all looked nice and prosperous. Catherine was impressed and gave Prince Potemkin a promotion. Since then, the phrase 'Potemkin Villages' has been used to denote pulling the wool over the eyes of the rulers to misinform them about the real order of things. The word *pokazukha* (from Russian *pokazivat* – to show) appeared much later, under the Soviet regime, as an updated synonym to 'Potemkin Villages'.

Life in the USSR was full of fake breakthroughs and simulated Utopias, to which we were exposed daily. In Moscow, I had lived for several years next to the 'USSR Exhibition of Economic Achievements' (or the VDNKh) – a utopian town in its own right, or even a mini-state within a state.

It was a functioning model of the whole country, with its own 'Council of Ministers', masquerading as a board of directors; its own ministry pavilions; its own public transport – draughty open-plan minibuses, popularly known as 'sandals'; even its own police force. The VDNKh was actually more than just a 750-acre model – it was a symbol of the Soviet Union exalting the nation to the shining heights, where cramped communal flats and squalid five-story prefabs, the so-called *Khrushchiobi* – a merger of Khruschev and *trushchiobi* (slums) – were transformed into splendidly sculpted palaces; where instead of the real-life queues for dirty-pink sausages which you wouldn't give to a cat, we saw a rich abundance of veal and sturgeon; and where antediluvian educational aids of the type of a good old wooden abacus, still widely used in both shops and schools in the late 1980s USSR, were replaced by the gleaming electronic miracles of scientific and technological progress – of strictly limited availability, of course,

How sweet it was to wander around that fantasy world, blissfully murmuring to oneself: 'We can do it if we want to...' Few used to doubt the ennobling power of that utopian lie and even fewer paused to think that all such lies were degrading both sides – the liars and the lied-to alike.

I was the first journalist in the USSR to expose VDNKh publicly as the utopian 'exhibition of non-existing achievements', first in *Krokodil*, then in *Ogonyok* magazines in the late 1980s. But it was in the year 1980 that I was able not just to witness but to become part of a full-scale state-engineered Utopia, if only for about three weeks.

Some of you might have guessed already that I am talking about the disgraced Moscow Olympics.

Yes, in the summer of 1980, Muscovites (and I was among them) were suddenly granted three weeks of Communism, the Soviet

Trucks in the Garden of Eden

regime's greatest ever show: the Olympic Games, boycotted by a number of Western countries due to the ongoing Soviet invasion of Afghanistan. No participation records were set in Moscow because of the boycott, yet we were warned never to come close to foreigners, who, in the words of one local party official (I was at that briefing myself), might try to inject the unsuspecting Muscovites' buttocks with poison on crowded buses and Metro trains.

Prostitutes, criminals, homosexuals – and, for some obscure reason, schoolchildren too – were temporarily evicted from the city, which was also closed to any Soviet visitor lacking Moscow *propiska* (registration). An unprecedented window-dressing exercise (or *pokazukha* – see above) was in progress. For three weeks only, the normally bare shops were stuffed with the never-before-seen-in-Moscow mutton and butter from New Zealand, canned beer from Finland, and chicken drumsticks, nicknamed 'Jimmy Carter's legs', from the US, among other things. Queues disappeared and the normally rude and uncouth saleswomen had to learn to smile and to memorise such previously unfamiliar phrases as '*Spasibo*' (thank you) and 'How can I help?'

The uncharacteristically polite militiamen in white uniforms were swarming all over the city. Ice-cold Pepsi was sold from the street stalls, and special American-made trucks commuted between them with loads of ice; all of it to impress the foreigners, of whom there weren't that many around due to the boycott.

The biggest shock came with the Olympics' closure three weeks on, when the cynically staged 'Utopia' came to an end. One fine morning the shop assistants became rude again, delicacies disappeared from the counters, and militiamen – with relief – put on their habitual grey uniforms. The slick American trucks no longer brought ice to the Pepsi stalls, and the famous American soft drink was sold tepid. As for the ubiquitous queues, they were longer than ever before: the whole country, whipped up by the rumours of unseen abundance, rushed into the reopened capital... But the abundance was no more. Only the empty Finnish beer cans were dragged along the habitually dusty (from too much dust thrown in our eyes?) streets by the playful wind of an early Moscow autumn...

That sudden 'de-Utopisation' – a transition from a fairy tale back to the gloomy reality – was carried out with unparalleled cynicism towards the people. The Soviet powers-that-be did not even try to conceal the meanest act of duping the whole world in the presence of seven million (the population of Moscow not counting the temporarily resettled 'ant-social elements') silent witnesses. The only feelings those fraudulent Olympics caused in us were those of bitterness and shame.

As if instead of a promised gourmet meal, we all had to stuff our bellies with the glossy pages of the deceitful 'Book of Tasty and Healthy Food'!

Lying, in lieu of dreaming, has been a long tradition in Russia – the character feature and the trend, both social and artistic, that outlived both the Russian Empire and the USSR (where it was known as 'socialist realism') and has firmly established itself as the main approach to life in the 21st century under Putin's regime. Never before had the world had been exposed to so many blatant and cynical lies as it was since the start of Russia's brutal invasion of my native Ukraine on the 24 February 2022, when Russian mass media began pouring out tons of dirty fakes – the more incredible and grotesque – the better.

The picture a gullible Russian citizen could get out of all that torrent of untruths about the war is roughly as follows: Ukrainian neo-fascists had been tormenting their country's Russian speakers for years until the valiant Russian army decided to protect them from 'genocide' and oppression by sending a limited contingent of its troops to Ukraine. Ukrainians, having lost control of their country, started shelling indiscriminately and razing their own towns and villages, with peaceful civilians in them. And so on. No exaggeration here. Russia's UN Ambassador Vassily Nebenzya was recorded claiming publicly at the UN Security Council on 7 March 2022 that Ukrainians must be 'shelling themselves'. So deeply did he immerse himself into the sticky bog of fabrication that I then suggested in one of my columns a new measuring unit for lying – one 'nebenzya'. Then, the statement about Ukrainians targeting their own civilians would probably amount to 10 nebenzyas, and the affirmations about Ukrainian army soldiers hiding inside the bombed maternity home in Mariupol, or, say, the claims that Ukraine had been secretly developing chemical weapons, would amount to 100 nebenzyas each.

The fact that some people inside Russia, including several of my (now former) friends, chose to believe such crude and primitive disinformation, could only be explained by the persisting Soviet mentality, multiplied by fear.

Indeed, life in the former Soviet Union, of which Russia had constituted by far the largest part, was characterised by constant lying on a national scale. Starting from kindergarten we were led to believe that our country was the greatest, the freest and the largest in the world. The latter was true, by the way, and that added a touch of authenticity to all the other nonsense, including numerous lies about technology. At school we were taught that Russia always conducted only just wars and always won; that everything – from the wheel to the electric bulb – had been invented by the Russians.

The first powered aircraft, of course, was a steal by Wilbur and Orville Wright from the Russian scientist Zhukovsky. Wireless telegraph was discovered not by Guglielmo Marconi, but by Alexander Popov. The steam engine was a creation of Ivan Polzunov's genius, and James Watt simply nicked his idea. And so on and so forth. The country's main daily newspaper *Pravda* – 'The Truth' – routinely brimmed with the most outrageous lies on the scale of up 1000 nebenzyas per page. It took some courage and strength to resist that all-permeating deception, with black officially branded white and vice versa.

I myself had to grow up with two undisputable dictums from my well-wishing parents and grandparents: 'Never say what you think if you want to survive' and 'Walls have ears'. I remember being particularly impressed by the latter, but no matter how hard I searched the walls of our bed-room-cum lounge at the age of 6, no matter how thoroughly I probed them, there were no signs of any ears growing through the wallpaper, not even in those multiple spots where it got unstuck from the wall to reveal bald patches of peeling stucco.

I remember thinking how nice it would have been to find somewhere on the wall a pair of pink and soft piglet's ears – for some reason I was sure that the wall's ears, if any existed, should resemble those of a pig – stirring and rotating, like two tiny radars, as if conversing with each other.

Conversely, I used to stubbornly disregard the former parental valedictory: to hold my tongue and never voice what I thought without thinking about it first. To think before thinking? How foolish was that! The price I (and my parents) had to pay for trying to be honest in the suffocating atmosphere of constant lies was high.

The only cry in the wilderness in my memory came from the dissident writer Alexander Solzhenitsyn. On 12 February 1974, he released the text of 'Live Not by Lies', an essay in which he urged Soviet citizens as individuals to refrain from cooperating with the regime's lies. Even the timidest, he wrote, can take this least demanding step toward spiritual independence. If many march together on this path of passive resistance, the whole inhuman system will totter and collapse.

His call fell on deaf ears. The dirty torrent of all-encompassing lies could not be curtailed. It was too powerful, too common and too-much engraved into the very nature of the Soviet – and prior to that, Russian – society. The book by E.B. Lanin, *Russian Traits and Terrors. A Faithful Picture of Russia of To-Day*, published in Boston, Mass in 1891, listed those 'traits' in the following order: Lying; Fatalism; Sloth; Dishonesty...' According to Lanin, 'Whatever the causes of this unveracity, it has struck deep roots in the Russian character, and it would need the Herculean labours of many generations of earnest men to eradicate it.'

Prophetic words! And here's another prophecy – this time from within Russia itself. When Russian 19th-century satirical writer M. E. Saltikov-Schedrin (1826–1889) was asked in an interview to describe future life in Russia in just a couple of words, his answer was: 'If I fall asleep, wake up 100 years later and somebody asks me, what is going on in Russia, my immediate answer would be "P'yut i voruyut!"... "They drink and steal!" A century and a half later, I would readily add to this: "They drink and steal and lie!"'

Lying in Russia has become a substitute for Utopia. Indeed, to create the latter, one needs at least some ideas and imagination, whereas to lie – either out of fear, as they did in the USSR, or out of sheer laziness ('sloth'?) – is much, much easier. 'The utopian fight against the limits of possibility, especially combined with statist faith in "the civilising role of force exerted from above", can produce its own dystopian leap into a new darkness,' noted Mark D. Steinberg, an American scholar, in his 2021 book *Russian Utopia*.

'The new darkness' that has enveloped Russia since 24 February 2022, the day it treacherously invaded Ukraine, is just another proof of the fact that a Russian Utopia has always been and still remains a lie.

Trucks in the Garden of Eden

Another utopian book that I adored as a child was Nikolay Nosov's *Neznaika* ('Dunno') trilogy. It consisted of three beautifully illustrated and charmingly written parts: 1. Dunno and his Friends in Flower Town; 2. Dunno in Sun City; and 3. Dunno on the Moon. I absolutely adored the book's heroes: a cheerful bunch of jolly *malishi* (mites, or little boys) and *malishki* (little girls), living in Flower Town, flying balloons, playing games, travelling, and particularly their indefatigable ring leader, nicknamed Dunno yet always smart as a whip – a cross between Ivanushka the Fool a popular and invariably quick-witted hero of Russian folk tales – and a children's version of Hodja Nasreddin, a legendary Turkish satirist, famous for his sharp 'in-passing' comments. I laughed out loud at their adventures and knew the books almost by heart.

Little did I know then that, in fact, I had been reading not just a funny children's book, but –. wait for it – a 'socialist anarchist utopia' and 'one of the paradigms of social relations', to quote a grown-up US scholar, who wrote a doctoral thesis on the Dunno trilogy. I came across their learned conclusions only recently when researching this book and was amazed to discover that the favourite read of my early childhood 'raises questions of self-subsistence and hierarchy ... science and technology, conscience and society', whose 'structure and social organisation reminds one of the communist state'.

The respected scholar's scientific ardour reaches its crescendo when describing the final book of the trilogy, the funny and beautifully phantasmagorical *Dunno on the Moon*. See for yourselves:

> ...Nosov tickles (sic, she probably meant 'tackles') the scientific debates and institutions of knowledge, and he sees technological advancement as both problematic yet offering possibilities to travel and face the harsh realities of the capitalist society on the moon. Nosov depicts ... the plight of the poor who toil for industrial enterprises owned by the rich – a reality that only exacerbates (sic) in our time and despite the seeming invisibility of the David Copperfields of our day because they have been moved to the so-called 'third world' which I know only too well but with which most 'first-worlders' do not identify themselves and hence dismiss as fickle of (sic) post-industrial imagination and paranoia.

By the end of that tirade, I got sick of inserting 'sic's in the ramble, for the respected scholar (whose name I withhold) – carried away by the passion of their own argument – had completely given up on style, grammar and punctuation.

Please forgive me for quoting so extensively from that 'thesis'. I would have never exposed you to such a barrage of pretentious nonsense, had it nor represented a very common 'scholarly' trend, particularly prevalent in the US, of labelling all kinds of books, movies, buildings etc. as 'utopian' (or 'dystopian' (which is basically the same – see above), and thus opening the floodgate for pseudo-scholarly and pseudo-scientific articles and monographs, shamelessly exploiting the fact that all existing definitions of 'Utopia' (or 'dystopia') – literary or other – are extremely vague, and no one seems to know for sure what 'utopian' (or 'dystopian') actually means.

In his short book *utopianism. A Very Short Introduction*, Lyman Tower Sargent quotes another incomprehensible (from my point of view) definition of literary Utopia by 'literary theorist' Darko Suvin: It is

> ...the verbal construction of a particular quasi-human community where socio-political institutions, norms and individual relationships are organised to a more perfect principle than in the author's community, this construction being based on estrangement arising out of an alternative historical hypothesis.

He continues, with the meanings getting more and more obscure, and the author turning quickly from a 'literary theorist' into a 'literary terrorist'. In my writing tutorials at Cambridge University, I teach students to avoid such 'literary terrorism' at all costs and always opt for clarity and brevity over protracted pseudo-scholastic gibberish.

Mind you, the concise and clear definitions of 'Utopia' do exist. A favourite is another from Gregory Claeys book mentioned earlier, *Utopia. The History of an Idea*: '... utopia explores the space between the possible and the impossible.' Nice and clear, if somewhat indirect. I would only add in the end: '...from a personal point of view and at the given moment in time'.

Another concise and daring definition comes from a modern spiritual preacher Raymond Williams, according to whom Utopia is but 'the hell, in which a more wretched kind of life is described as existing elsewhere'. That can pass for a fairly precise description of

Trucks in the Garden of Eden

the USSR, where official propaganda endlessly lamented the horrible plight of oppressed workers and peasants in the capitalist West.

As I said earlier, many Utopias are also strictly personal and prone to changing with time. And such 'personal' Utopias are not limited to books. One of my life's biggest 'Utopias' which had led to one of my life's biggest s mistakes was a movie. A mediocre, if not to say outright awful, 1977 'mocumentary' called ABBA, in which a hapless Aussie hack receives an assignment to interview the members of the Swedish pop group during their tour of Australia.

I watched that tacky movie in the plywood shed of the shabby 'Park Cinema' in my native Kharkiv. The plot (if any) was simple, if not to say primitive: it was just the footage of Abba's tour of Australia, hastily edited into a 90-minute-long melodrama. What struck me most, beyond the permanently sun-drenched land- and cityscapes, was the Australian crowd that consisted exclusively of leisurely and scantily dressed suntanned people, with open friendly faces, carrying the famous 'no-worries-mate' expression, as if they didn't have a single care in the world.

'This is paradise on earth, a Utopia that has become reality!' I thought then... The rest, as they say, is history.

Monica, the young woman clerk from the Australian High Commission in London, confessed to me later that she immediately recognised me as 'Clive James's Moscow man' when – still under the Abba movie spell – I muttered into her window: 'I need an informal approach!'

And I got it. 'Special status' residence visas were presented to us (my wife, my son and myself) in London, inside the imposing Australian High Commission building in the Strand by the High Commissioner, in the presence of multiple Australian media reps and Clive James himself. 'Top Soviet Journo Opts for a Land of Smiles' – such were the headlines of Australian newspapers the following morning.

My post-defection Utopia continued for some time down under, albeit I was deeply shocked by the unexpectedly drab, rain-soaked and ungraceful outskirts of Sydney, where we landed in the middle of a wet Australian winter. And then a choice of jobs on arrival; a nice cottage in a leafy suburb of Melbourne, with an indoor swimming pool and Jacuzzi, one year later; popularity of my *Melbourne Age* weekly column which had made me a household name in Victoria...

And the ever-growing spiritual heartburn of nostalgia which had become unbearable by the end of my first year down under.

No Place Like Utopia

I had come to understand T.E. Lawrence, who missed London so much when in Arabia that on his return, he was ready 'to eat the pavement of the Strand'. Like him, I was desperately – almost to tears – missing the big world outside Oz – Europe and, particularly Britain – the country that was the first to open for me a window to the West, the very window that was all but closed in Australia of the early 1990s. The local pre-Internet media was insular and provincial, and just like I did in the USSR before defection, I would spend nights trying to tune to the crackling BBC World Service broadcasts, jammed by the sheer 'tyranny of distance', if not by the KGB's bespoke jamming devices on those occasions. And travel to Europe, of whose old stones and grey satin skies I kept dreaming almost every night, was prohibitively expensive.

With awe, I was coming to realise that defecting from the USSR and ending up down under was in a way like swapping an awl for a soap, as we used to say in the Soviet Union, for, in effect, I had found myself facing the same – equally impregnable – Iron Curtain, made of dollars, not of the stale and crumbling Soviet dogmas. By the end of my second year in Australia, my long-cherished, yet infantile and movie-inspired personal Utopia had turned into dystopia.

In October 1992, I was back in the UK – my next 'paradise on earth' – renting a small room in North London and feeling happy.

I am still here 32 years on, and naturally, do not perceive Britain as my ultimate Utopia any longer (see 'Confessions of an Anglophile'). Utopia, as we have agreed earlier, is rather a category of dreams than of reality. But seeing all the downsides of today's Britain, I am still in love with this country and willing to make her better. To me (and I stress, just to me personally), her main difference from the lush and hedonistic Australia, or, say, from the dynamic US, is that Britain has got her own large and mysterious soul – the soul that I am still trying to understand, this book being just another go at it.

Before we start our search for Britain's Shanrgi Las and El Dorados (if any), I have a confession to make: I did experience a full-blown and full-scale Utopia just once: on the day when – after years of suffering and months of the KGB persecution – I left the USSR (read defected), the vast and oppressive land of my youth and the world's largest cage, never to return. That amazing blissful feeling lasted only for very short while- a couple of minutes at the most. But it was so strong and acute that I will not forget it for as long as I live.

Trucks in the Garden of Eden

To mislead the persecutors, we had told all our friends and contacts over our KGB-bugged phone that we would be leaving the USSR by plane. We crossed the border by train several days prior to our confirmed flying date. Until the very last moment, I was not sure it was going to work.

You can find the details of that escape in my book *Dateline Freedom* (Hutchinson, 1991), but here I can reveal one thing: whereas the Soviet bank of the river was still dotted with dirty snowdrifts and firmly in the grips of winter, the Polish side was in the middle of spring, with blue skies, green grass and the invisible birds singing for all they were worth. Until now I can't quite comprehend how it happened: deep winter on the Soviet bank and spring on the Polish side across the river. It looked as if nature itself was welcoming us to freedom. I opened the window, and pungent smells of the sun and young grass, mixed with those of smoke and tar, burst into our compartment. The smell of the long-awaited travel and adventure, the smell of new life, the smell of liberty itself! Birds were chirping like mad in the tress near the track. 'Free birds,' I muttered to myself and smiled. 'Free trees... Free flowers... Free mile posts...'

My life ever since then has been a quest for that particular feeling of freedom, which, as I realise now was itself a Utopia, because freedom, just like Utopia, is a destination you may never reach but have to spend your whole life trying to come closer to. It is like that beautiful sense of a 'flow' that writers experience from time to time when putting words on paper– a semi-blissful sensation that you are about to create something marvellous. That utopian feeling is highly addictive and makes you crave it for years to come in the hope that it will return one day.

It may come back indeed. Or it may not. But you have to keep trying.

Chapter 2

My utopian Neighbourhood

I don't know another country/Where a man can breathe so freely.
                                                A popular Soviet song

By a lucky coincidence, I was able to start my quest for Utopias from my own backyard, or to be more exact, from a peculiar mini-enclave, called Letchworth Garden City, the town where I live. Letchworth, bizarrely, combines it itself the elements of an idealistic urban dream (Utopia) and the painfully familiar (to me) features of a Soviet-style totalitarian conurbation (dystopia).

Let's take a walk around it.

'Hello, dog walkers, bike riders, exercisers, strollers and all fellow-isolators! Please help yourself to the rhubarb and enjoy cooking it at home! Be safe and well!'

Such was the handwritten sign on a makeshift billboard in one of the quiet and leafy streets of Letchworth Garden City, made even quieter by the pandemic's first lockdown. Right underneath the sign, there was a capacious cardboard box, half-full of freshly cut pink rhubarb stalks, asking (almost audibly) to be picked up and put in a crumble. On the ground right next to the box, stood a small bottle with an anti-bacterial hand gel, thoughtfully provided by the anonymous rhubarb grower.

To me, that sign came to symbolize the irrepressible creative spirit of Letchworth Garden City, one of Britain's youngest and quirkiest towns – the town where I happen to be living – and its unique community feeling.

The moment I first stepped onto Letchworth Garden City's asphalt about 16 years ago, I experienced an acute pang of recognition. Initially (only initially, I stress), it felt as if I had been

Trucks in the Garden of Eden

teleported back to the USSR, which I left for good in January 1990 as one of the Soviet Union's last political defectors. Well, to a somewhat neater and leafier version of the USSR perhaps... It took me a while to understand what made me feel that way. The explanation lay in the town's social and architectural history, which I will try to recount below.

Let me tell you straight away that, despite some architectural and planning likeness, Letchworth is an incomparably better place to live than the very best towns of my Soviet childhood and youth. As one current resident and a neighbour of mine put it: 'Letchworth town planning is all about freedom: broad streets, squares and green spaces. The moment you walk out of the house, you feel like you are out in the open – you can breathe.'

At the same time, its strict grid system, its enormous and often unnecessary public spaces, its turret-like church spires cannot help but evoke the memories of my Soviet past. My Hertfordshire town does not try to hide that obvious dichotomy. On the contrary, it brandishes it in your face.

Letchworth is indeed like no other place on the planet. Branded 'the world's first garden city', it is the brainchild of Ebenezer Howard, an idealistic (read utopian) thinker of the Victorian era, a flamboyant revolutionary, a dreamer and a visionary, whose aim was to build an ideal settlement, a so-called 'Garden City', with the comforts of a town and a countryside lifestyle. His ultimate goal was a totally new and highly liveable 'industrial town with an agricultural belt' as a positive alternative to the slums of post-Victorian London and other major British cities.

> There are in reality not only, as is so constantly assumed, two alternatives – town life and country life – but a third alternative, in which all the advantages of the most energetic and active town life, with all the beauty and delight of the country may be secured in perfect combination; and the certainty of being able to live this life will be the magnet which will produce the effect for which we are all striving – the spontaneous movement of the people from our crowded cities to the bosom of our kindly mother earth, at once the source of life, of happiness, of wealth, and of power.

He wrote this poetically and prophetically in his ground-breaking book *To-morrow: A Peaceful Path to Real Reform*, first published in 1898 and reprinted four years later – one year before the world's first 'garden city', Letchworth, came into existence – as *Garden Cities of To-Morrow*.

Howard's book was written as a response to Edward Bellamy's utopian romance, *Looking Backward*, which told of a socialist society as seen by a Rip van Winkle who awakes after years of sleep and discovers a manuscript explaining how it came about. William Morris also read Bellamy. He wrote *News from Nowhere* in response to its message. Both Howard and Morris objected (rather naively, if you ask me) to the centralised, authoritarian character of the socialist society as described by Bellamy. Each of their books centred around federations of small, self-governing communities, in which the benefits of both town and country living could be realised. However, while Morris's book is purely visionary, Howard's is a textbook for how such a society could be built. The term 'Garden City' was likely to have been chosen by Howard to make his project echo The Garden of Eden – the world's most ancient and most persisting Utopia...

In 1903, architects Raymond Unwin and Barry Parker (both of whom were members of the Socialist League and who later, after the success of Letchworth, went on to design Hampstead Garden Suburb in London), started to build Letchworth on Howard's principles on the 3,818 acres of wasteland bought by the specially created Garden City Pioneer Company.

Letchworth was laid out with its public buildings and shops in its centre, with industry separated from dwellings and the whole urban area surrounded by farmland, later turned into a 13-mile green belt where the town's residents could stroll, ride and cycle. Its population maximum was set at 32,000 (it is 32,000 now!) living in conjoined neighbourhoods. Land was to be owned in common, with ground and building rents paying back the capital borrowed for its construction before funding municipal expenses and social welfare.

Howard's principles were outlined in a poster promising potential buyers of cheap (£150 on average) Arts & Crafts cottages the 'health of the country and comforts of the town'.

To attract the new settlers, Ebenezer Howard organised two pioneering public exhibitions in 1905 and in 1907. They both resulted directly from a campaign for affordable rural houses led by J. St. Loe Strachey, then editor of *The Spectator* magazine (he was also the proprietor of *The County Gentleman* and *Land and Water* magazines), who published an article 'In Search of a £150 cottage' (in the October 1904 issue), in which he wrote of the necessity to utilise 'new constructional techniques'.

The 1905 Exhibition attracted over 60,000 visitors (by some estimates 80,000) to the fledgling Garden City, including reporters from every corner of the land curious about modern and innovative types of housing construction and also about the strange new Garden City idea being pioneered there. The success of the Exhibition persuaded the GNR to build a temporary station in the town, so in that sense it literally put Letchworth on the map.

All 130 cottages built for the First Exhibition were sold. Thousands of Londoners travelled by cheap day returns from Kings Cross to have a look at the exhibits. The appetite for affordable country housing was such that it was decided to have another exhibition a couple of years later. Held under the title 'Urban Cottages & Small Holdings', it was sponsored by the *Daily Mail* newspaper, a precursor of its ever-popular Ideal Home Exhibition, an annual event running until the present time and now known as the Ideal Home Show.

The 1907 exhibition was smaller than the first one and, according to Josh Tidy, a Letchworth historian, 'focused much more on groups of houses while its architect entrants were much more local, resulting in a more sensitive approach to the cottages' "look and feel", fitting in with the now-established design aesthetic, or "Letchworth Look"'.

With 120 of 130 First Exhibition Cottages and nearly all of the Second Exhibition ones still around and populated (many – like mine – display memorial plates confirming their participation in the Exhibitions), no wonder that the peculiar 'Letchworth look', with its characteristic roughcast render, red roof tiles, gables, dormer windows and green doors, is still very obvious to any visitor to the town.

Another pioneering trait of Letchworth was (and still is) that it became the world's first – and so far the only – town fully administered not by a town council, but by the Heritage Foundation – a charity that reinvests all the profits it makes directly back into the community and has overall control of the town's cultural and environmental issues. In Letchworth, the Foundation is responsible for the preservation of the town's unique Arts & Crafts architecture, its impressive parks and its 13-mile-long 'Green Belt'. It also runs all local museums, libraries and the notable Broadway Cinema, designed by architects Bennett and Bidwell – one of the country's first Art Deco movie houses, built in

1938. Similar arrangements had existed in Welwyn Garden City, Howard's second utopian creation, until 1969, when the latter was bought by a development corporation and stopped being a 'Garden City' by definition.

As the new settlers moved into Letchworth through the 1920s and into the 1930s, Howard was pushing his utopian 'socialist' ideas further and further. In accordance with his wishes, the town was declared both vegetarian, with no meat served or sold anywhere, and entirely teetotal, with only one strictly non-alcoholic pub, The Skittles (now housing a popular adult learning centre, the Settlement), served herbal-based soft drinks and fruit juices.

Interestingly, resembling a typical Pharisee-like communist leader of the future, Howard himself was neither a Quaker nor a teetotaller and, reputedly, enjoyed his daily shot (or three) of whisky, for which a servant would be sent to the nearest 'non-teetotal' village of Norton. Letchworth stayed alcohol-free until 1958, and even now it only has five pubs, compared to nearly a hundred in neighbouring Hitchin. Letchworth is also home to the UK's only vegetarian public school – St. Christopher's.

Within 10 years of its foundation, Letchworth's account books showed it to be a financial success, as did the growth of industry, public building, housing and population. Businesses big and small kept emerging in the town's thoroughly detached industrial area like mushrooms after rain. Among them were printers, carmakers, small steel factories and engineering workshops. Most employees were able either to walk or to cycle to their workplaces, and special pedestrian pathways connecting residential areas with the industrial zones were built. One example is Common View, with its rows of Arts & Crafts workers' cottages and tree-lined pedestrian shortcuts to the Business Park.

In 1920, the UK branch of the American Spirella Corset Company opened in Letchworth. The Spirella Arts & Crafts Building was designed to provide workers with a highly productive and pleasant environment that focused on the comfort of factory employees. Referred to as the 'factory of beauty', it offered a wide array of employee amenities including 'baths, showers, gymnastics classes, a library, free eye tests and bicycle repairs'.

The company's most popular corset was the Model 305, but Spirella products were not sold in shops. Instead, female staff, the corsetières, were sent to customers' homes. During the Second World War, the Irvin Air Chute Company expanded its production of parachutes into the Spirella building, and women working

Trucks in the Garden of Eden

for the British Tabulating Machine Company on Icknield Way, Letchworth, secretly produced the decoding machines, called Bombes, used at Bletchley Park and elsewhere.

The resounding success of Letchworth Garden City couldn't have failed to impress Russian 'socialist democrats' who had been watching its progress with interest from the very beginning. They included Lenin who, reportedly, stayed in Letchworth overnight in 1907 as a guest of religious minister Bruce Wallace, the man who had rented his Brotherhood Church (see Chapter 14) in London to the Fifth Congress of the Russian Social Democratic Labour Party (RSDLP), and even (again, reportedly) gave a talk there.

Also associated with Letchworth was Vladimir Semyonov, a Russian architect who fled with his wife, an active RSDLP member, to London only steps ahead of the Tsar's Okhranka (secret police) in 1901. Having settled in Britain after a brief spell in South Africa helping the Boers in their rebellion against 'British imperialism', Semyonov practised as an architect, but, most importantly, made a special study of Howard and his Garden City as it developed.

Returning to Russia in 1912, he approached a railway cooperative to allow him to build a village on Garden City principles at Prozorovka, near Moscow. with the idea of a Howard-style settlement for its workers. He got the permission, but then the First World War put a stop to the project.

After 1917, Semyonov and other Russian supporters of the Garden City movement became key players in building a 'socialist' society in the USSR. They designed the industrial city of Stalingrad and parts of my native Kharkiv, then the capital of the Soviet Ukraine, on Letchworth Garden City principles. City ownership of land, however, with its democratically controlled revenue based on co-operative principles, was excluded as the centralist command structure became operative throughout Soviet society.

In 1935, Stalin appointed Semyonov the Chief Architect of Moscow. As such he promptly came up with a draft to redesign the Soviet capital (for a maximum population of two million!) along the Garden City lines. That, however, was not to be. Gigantism and the so-called 'Stalin Gothic' were the order of the day at the peak of the Great Purge. After that, the essential communal core of Garden Cities was lost forever in the USSR – although the form of a Garden City layout still characterises a number of post-Soviet urban

My utopian Neighbourhood

settlements in Russia, Ukraine, the Baltic Republics (I recently spotted a smaller replica of Letchworth's Broadway Gardens in Tallinn, the capital of Estonia, which had been part of the USSR until August 1991). Those included Sokol, a district of Moscow, where I had lived in the 1980s.

This explains why I immediately felt 'at home' (in my case, not necessarily a pleasant feeling) when first arriving at Letchworth in 2006!

While researching this book, I discovered another 'shadowy' figure behind the Letchworth project, Frederic Osborn, one of Howard's closest supporters and a convinced socialist who became Secretary of the Howard Cottage Society in 1912. A Soviet sympathizer who had outlived Howard by many years, he was approached by the Soviets in 1953 and asked 'to advise on the organisation and design of a prototype new town' using Letchworth as a model.

In his groundbreaking book *House in the Country*, with the self-explanatory subtitle *Where Our Suburbs and Garden Cities Came from and Why it's Time to Leave them Behind* (Oldcastle Books,2022), in the concluding section, 'When Osborn went to Moscow', Simon Mathews chronicles Osborn's frequent visits to the Soviet capital during the 1950s. He succeeded in convincing some Moscow city planners to create more open spaces, boulevards, flower beds and other purely 'Letchworthian' features, designed to impress, but he himself fell under the influence of Soviet residential architects, who liked to refer to Le Corbusier in defence of their brutalist housing blocks crammed with people, with none of the multiple storage spaces and leisure areas characteristic of Le Corbusier's style.

It is still a mystery (to me at least) how the Soviets persuaded Osborn to like those new architectural practices and to openly praise then the largest housing construction project in the world – the Moscow suburb of Cheryomushki – one of the most horrible and dehumanising residential areas to be found anywhere. How do I know? Because I lived there myself in the late 1970s.

German writer Karl Shloegel in his weighty 900-page tome *The Soviet Century* refers to similar Soviet housing projects as 'Sublime Vistas of the Prefab Mountains'. As for Cheryomushki, he aptly describes that housing development as 'a showpiece project consisting of five-storey residential blocks of prefabricated apartments built on former kolkhoz fields'. I had the misfortune to reside in one of those human beehives, in the company of ubiquitous cockroaches and permanently drunk neighbours.

Trucks in the Garden of Eden

Despite its Letchworth-like grid layout, with wide streets, boulevards, fountains and plenty of unnecessary open spaces (space was one commodity the USSR was never short of), the factors explaining my strong déjà-vu feeling during my first visit to the 'World's First Garden City', Cheryomushki's closest architectural relatives in the UK were probably the (deservedly) much-maligned 'New Towns' like Stevenage, Corby, Slough or Hemel Hempstead – the symbols of yet another urban Utopia that had degraded into yet another Soviet-style Dystopia. I will talk about the New Towns later.

But here and now I hurry to agree with Simon Mathews, who concluded that if Osborn did indeed like what he saw in Moscow, 'he was breaking the habits of a lifetime.' From what I know about the lSoviet system's modus operandi, however, Osborn could have been forced to deviate from some of his old Letchworth ways in peril of having not just his habits but his limbs broken, too...

With all the unwelcome Soviet associations in mind, I was not particularly surprised to learn through the grapevine that, allegedly (and I stress, allegedly) the UMO Tractor importers in Blackhorse Road, Letchworth, were in fact a base for Soviet secret agents from both KGB and GRU (military intelligence) in the early 1970s. To monitor them, again allegedly, a UK Special Branch office was operating clandestinely from Letchworth Police Station!

After the 'end' of the Cold War, the UMO office (allegedly) lasted a few years, until 1992, as a Belarus-run company, but nobody wanted their tractors in the UK any longer, so they closed.

No matter how attractive the idea of a tractor-importing company operating as a front for Soviet spies and Letchworth having a Special Branch office to keep an eye on it sounded for this book in general and for the story of Letchworth's gradual 'Sovietisation' in particular, it has to be taken with a pinch of salt, for I have so far been unable to find any solid proof of something fishy and sub-rosa happening behind the unpretentious facade of the UMO Tractor importers in the early 1970s.

Paradoxically, the only indirect proof of the above is the sheer size of the disproportionately huge (for a relatively small town) Letchworth Police Station in Neville Road. The oblong 1970s building stays unoccupied most of the time and looks permanently abandoned, with no cars parked around it. From what I know, Letchworth police station is now part-time: 'The office is open 24 hours, dependent on officer availability' (which can easily mean never), according to an online explanation. The occasional

My utopian Neighbourhood

policemen you see on the beat in its streets would, most likely, be visiting from the nearby larger towns of Hitchin or Baldock. So, the excessive size of the station building could have indeed be due to having to accommodate numerous MI5 operatives at some point in time.

Pity, for having convincing proofs would have been enough to justify altering this book's title to a better (and louder)-sounding 'Tractors in the Garden of Eden'. But as a conscientious researcher, I have to stick to bare facts, although, as I have said already, I wouldn't be greatly astonished, if one day it turns out that the Soviet spy nest did exist and thrive in the World's First Garden City in the 1970s. What could they be spying on is, of course, anyone's guess.

Modern Letchworth, with its vaguely Stalinist church spires, its jolly fountains ('from where happy workers' laughter can often be heard', to quote a North Korean propaganda magazine), its reassuringly large public spaces and its cosy residential areas combines the best and the worst of modernist architecture. It comes as no surprise therefore that the young Le Corbusier was hugely influenced by Ebenezer Howard. But if Howard's ultimate aim was to take London workers out of the late-Victorian slums and resettle them in the countryside, Le Corbusier, who hated the very concept of a conventional urban dwelling aspired to build 'a garden city in the sky', and realised that idea in his controversial 'Unité d'Habitation' in Marseille (see Chapter 6), of which the low-built and resolutely non-Brutalist Letchworth is a direct opposite.

A very good example of that highly eclectic architectural mix is Broadway Gardens, doubling as Letchworth's central square – a spacious and disproportionately large 'urban space', lined with Arts &Crafts buildings, and with a large fountain in the middle. Driving through the centre of Letchworth along a wide, tree-lined boulevard called Broadway towards Broadway Gardens always makes me think of Paris. This beautiful wide street leading to the vast square with a fountain in the middle has an uncanny resemblance to a particular stretch of the Avenue des Champs Élysées adjacent to the Place de la Concorde.

Every time I walk across Broadway Gardens, I also remember the brilliant book *Across the Plaza. The Public Voids of the Post-Soviet City* by Owen Hatherley, my favourite writer on modern architecture, who regarded huge public spaces (or, public voids') as sure signs of totalitarianism (read dystopia):

> In East Berlin, in Warsaw, in Kiev, in dozens of cities east of the Elbe from Sverdlovsk to Belgrade ... the long, wide boulevard, the gigantic square ... were invariably reproduced in some form or another, only bigger, grander and more overwhelming that ever before... Local scorn has it, 'the steppe starts here'. These are the poles of East European square, between Prussianism and Tsarism, or later, more horrifyingly, between Stalinism and Nazism.

The similarities with Paris were not purely coincidental; when Letchworth's founder Ebenezer Howard set about laying out his 'utopian' teetotal and vegetarian town, the world's first Garden City, he was very much under the influence of Baron George Eugene Haussmann, the famous town planner, who was behind the spectacular renovation of Paris between 1853 and 1870. Haussmann's vision had transformed the French capital from a messy, polluted city of slums into a sparkling metropolis – a 'City of Light' with vast squares, wide boulevards, parks and posh apartment blocks. Howard's aims in Letchworth were pretty much the same – to create a healthy and aesthetically attractive living environment for English workers who were being resettled to the country from the disease-ridden slums of Victorian London.

Unlike Haussmann, however, who enjoyed full creative and material support from the Emperor Napoleon III, Howard soon ran out of funds. His ambitious plan to construct eight wide boulevards radiating from Letchworth's central square as they do from Haussmann's Place de L'Etoile (now the Place Charles de Gaulle) had to be curtailed and reduced to just one leafy boulevard, the Broadway – an unmistakably Parisian street in the middle of North Hertfordshire.

Another innovative architectural feature of the 'World's First Garden City' is much less known, and I am proud to claim priority in discovering and naming it – 'the Sleeping Towers of Letchworth'. Why 'the Sleeping Towers'?

Well, sleeping porches, balconies and colonnades were parts of the first Garden City's architectural design. In accordance with Victorian beliefs, sleeping in the open air was good for one's health. Several bespoke 'sleeping towers' were therefore added to the town's most eclectic Cloisters building, whose architect, William Harrison Cowlishaw, took the 'sleeping porch' concept one step

My utopian Neighbourhood

further to allow the School of Psychology students, the Cloisters' first tenants, to maintain excellent physical health by sleeping inside spacious, castle-like, open-air turrets. The ensemble also boasted a swimming pool in the courtyard – a rather unusual feature for 1907. Interestingly, the bizarre design of the Cloisters, with its towers, turrets and *trompe l'œil* windows, came to Quaker Miss Annie Jane Lawrence, the building's first owner, in a dream!

It is interesting to note that sleeping porches and sleeping balconies (if not quite the 'sleeping towers') have become habitual terms of the real estate scene in the US (living in the States in the late 1990s, I used to come across them in numerous property listings). They can also serve as an adequate metaphor for utopian thinking. Dreamers, idealists and revolutionaries of sorts see the world differently to 'normal' people. They are often airy-fairy and detached from reality, as if indeed dwelling in a tall tower – a cloud-cuckoo land high above the ground. When one sleeps in the open air, dreams are bound to be vivid and colourful, if at times a bit weird, due to the increased supply of oxygen to the brain... Sleeping towers in general are a good metaphor for Utopia as a whole and the urban Utopia in particular.

One of Letchworth's best-known landmarks is the UK's first traffic roundabout. It is duly commemorated with a memorial plate in its middle that reads: 'UK's first roundabout, circa 1909'. I was told that the plate had been installed by the Roundabout Appreciation Society of Britain, with headquarters in Poole, Dorset. I also found out that until the 1930s, a different sign used to adorn this truly historic site in Sollershott Circus. It simply said 'Keep to the left' – not so much a political statement as a reminder to confused motorists who were unsure how to negotiate the roundabout.

A living – and fast-moving – feature of Letchworth is the proliferation of black squirrels (or 'super squirrels' as they are sometimes called), the aggressive testosterone-loaded mutants who have forced out grey squirrels in the same manner the latter had come to replace the red ones. They are endemic to Letchworth Garden City and can be easily spotted in the town's numerous parks and green spaces. The first sightings of black squirrels in the UK can be traced back to the Letchworth in 1912. It is thought they were brought over there from America by the Duke of Bedford for his estate at Woburn in Bedfordshire. A study carried out at Anglia Ruskin University showed that a molecular switch in DNA was the reason some grey squirrels mutated to have black fur instead.

Trucks in the Garden of Eden

Letchworth also boasts of its own endemic sort of apples – Young's Pinello. Raised in 1935 by Miss E.L. Young, one of the Garden City founders, the fruits have firm, fairly tender white flesh with a sub-acidic to sweet aromatic flavour. According to Ebenezer Howard's initial design, the backyard of every 'cheap cottage' was supposed to have at least one apple tree in the middle.

It is not common knowledge that Letchworth Garden City became an inspiration for hundreds of innovative settlements all over the world, such as Canberra in Australia, the New Towns in the UK and the US, and hundreds of urban communities and suburbs in South Africa, France, Germany, Czech Republic, Brazil, Canada, and, more recently, in China and Japan – all parts of the growing International Garden City Movement of which Letchworth is an indisputable flagship.

Outward similarities aside, the totalitarian USSR is no more, but Letchworth Garden City is thriving like never before. 117 years after its foundation, it remains a great, if somewhat peculiar, place to live.

Some utopian dreams do came true, after all...

※※※

As we have already concluded, Utopias and Dystopias often go hand in hand. At times, as in Letchworth Garden City, they merge.

George Orwell, the author of the 20th century's two greatest literary dystopias, *Animal Farm* and *1984*, lived for several years (between 1936 and 1942) in the village of Wallington 3 miles away from Letchworth. Those were the happiest and the most productive years of the writer's short life. Here he ran a grocery store, got married, and wrote a number of his best essays and novels. It was there that he got the idea for both *Animal Farm* and *1984* – the latter, I have reasons to believe, was largely triggered not by the Soviet Union, which Orwell had never visited, but by 'the World's First Garden City'. he went there frequently to stock up his store and to work in the local public library, particularly after his return from Spain, where he fought with the Red Brigades in the Civil War, was wounded in the throat and became deeply disillusioned with socialist ideals.

The reason for Orwell's dislike was that Letchworth appeared too 'socialist' (read totalitarian) to him – in its architecture and in the character of its founder, Howard, whom Orwell scathingly characterised as 'the typical Socialist ... with vegetarian leanings'

My utopian Neighbourhood

whose doctrines attracted 'every fruit juice-drinker, nudist, sandal-wearer, sex-maniac, Quaker ... quack, pacifist, and feminist in England'.

And here's how Orwell described (in *The Road to Wigan Pier*) a pair of 'socialists' he once came across in Letchworth:

> One day this summer I was riding through Letchworth when the bus stopped and two dreadful-looking old men got on to it. They were both about sixty, both very short, pink, and chubby, and both hatless. One of them was obscenely bald, the other had a long grey hair bobbed in the Lloyd George style. They were dressed in pistachio-coloured shirts and khaki shorts into which their huge bottoms were crammed so tightly that you could study every dimple. Their appearance created a mild stir of horror on top of the bus.

Each January, on my birthday and according to a long tradition, I drive to Wallington to say hi to George. It is less than a ten-minute drive from Letchworth. The bushes, the fences, the haystacks in the field and the green holly leaves in George's front garden are all beautifully glazed with frost as if nature itself has baked me a giant snowy birthday cake. The old village pond is frozen and a couple of puzzled ducks are waddling about on the ice. A lonely fiery pheasant, looking so outrageously ostentatious on the snow, is the only living creature (except the ducks) I come across.

Wallington is tiny, pristine and perennially quiet. If I stare at Orwell's cottage's low and narrow front door for long enough, I can almost discern a tall, dishevelled man emerging from it (he has to bend down to fit through the door). He is holding a letter which he carries across the road to the village's only pillar box before disappearing inside the cottage again...

I first read *Nineteen Eighty-Four* in Moscow in the late 1980s. A tattered and soiled paperback was lent to me for one night only, and next morning I was to pass it to the next person in line.

The book, like all other works by George Orwell, was strictly banned in the USSR. A huge scandal erupted when an American publisher tried to display it on his stand during the International Book Fair in Moscow in the early 1980s. I worked as an interpreter at the Mitchell Beazley stand and remember an irate Soviet official shouting at the hapless publisher: 'Take this book away from your stand this very moment! You can display anything – even bloody Golda Meir if you wish, but not Orwell – this anti-Soviet filth!'

The punishment for being caught in possession of *Nineteen Eighty-Four* could be a prison term. That only added to the clandestine pleasure of reading it. I was savouring the book until dawn, and by the time the last page was turned, I was close to tears. How could someone who had never been in the Soviet Union and had never lived in a totalitarian state, describe our life with such poignant precision?

It would have certainly been banned in Brezhnev's times when the names of Stalin or Khrushchev were not supposed to be mentioned in print in any context. My mother told me how, in the early 1950s when the head of the Soviet secret police and Stalin's henchman Beria was exposed as a 'British spy' and subsequently shot, all subscribers of the multi-volume 'Great Soviet Encyclopedia' received in the post several printed sheets to be glued into the letter 'B' volume where the article on Beria was printed. The enclosed instruction requested that all the Beria pages be cut out of the book and the new ones, with a disproportionately lengthy article on the Bering Strait inserted instead. Special Glavlit inspectors would conduct random house checks to make sure everybody had complied.

Wasn't it precisely what Orwell's O'Brien meant when confiding in Winston Smith during the latter's Room 101 interrogation that if a single mention of a person or event could not be found in print it was as if they had never existed or taken place? No wonder 'Nineteen Eighty-Four' was one of the Soviet system's biggest bugaboos: it explained the technology of totalitarian power.

Amazingly though, those who controlled the printed word found it quite proper to read the banned books themselves (remember 'All animals are equal but some are more equal than the rest'?)

Not too many people in the West know that, in a brilliant case of Orwellian doublethink, all major Soviet publishing houses had secret departments producing limited editions of prohibited books for the elite's exclusive consumption. I've seen such books (each individually numbered and with the word 'Classified' prominently stamped on the cover) a number of times thanks to a friend's mother-in-law who worked in the CPSU Central Committee library. One of them was *Nineteen Eighty-Four* – in impeccable Russian translation. The number on the plain white cover was '59', and underneath it the word 'Sekretno' ('classified') was printed.

Another 'special edition' that I saw was *Secrets of Eternal Life* by C Northcote Parkinson (again, conscientiously translated into Russian). The senile octogenarians who ruled our poor country were naturally – and exclusively – curious about the secrets of 'eternal life', since it was they – not the oppressed voiceless crowds they controlled – who were supposed to live forever.

By the year 1984, Orwell's dystopian *Nineteen Eighty-Four* had been all but translated into reality in the once-utopian Soviet Union...

> We knocked on the door of a little cottage, and it was opened by a tall figure, face and clothes covered with coal smuts, who peered of us through the billowing cloud of smoke; Blair had been trying to light his first fire of the season, to find that the chimney was in some way defective.

That was how writer Mark Benney (quoted by Bernard Crick in *George Orwell. A Life*) described his visit to Wallington in 1936. This is probably why whenever I try to visualise George emerging from The grocer's cottage in 2009, I see him 'with coal smuts' smudged all over his face.

Orwell was happy in Wallington clattering away on his typewriter (he was finishing *Road to Wigan Pier*) when there were no customers in his cottage-cum-shop, which was for most of the time. For some reason, the shop was not very popular among the locals. Were they somewhat put off by Orwell's refined and aristocratic – even if occasionally coal-stained – face, his posh Etonian accent and his 'classy' lanky frame? Then there were the pilfering village children (to watch them Orwell had to drill four holes in the door!), and the shop soon had to be closed down.

George/Eric went on long walks around the village, and the very few descriptions of nature in his books (he was hardly a lyricist) can be easily traced to Wallington, like this one from *Nineteen Eighty-Four* describing Winston's secret pastoral tryst with Julia:

> Winston picked his way up the lane through the dappled light and shade, stepping into pools of gold whenever the boughs parted. Under the trees to the left of him the ground was misty with bluebells... It was the second of May. From somewhere deeper in the heart of the wood came the droning of ring doves.

Trucks in the Garden of Eden

Most rural landscapes hardly change with time.

It was probably during one of these walks that he spotted the dark wooden buildings of the nearby Manor Farm that he used as his model for the Animal Farm in the eponymous classic novella, set, incidentally, near the fictitious village of Willingdon, where the Farmer kept the pigs. The large black sheds and barns of Manor Farm are still there. Looking at them, I don't stop praising fortune for the mere fact that no enterprising developer had yet come up with the idea of digging up the uncomplaining Hertfordshire countryside and building an 'Animal Farm Theme Park' on that spot... Such an 'oversight' is surprising if we remember that *Animal farm* is one of the best known, most loved and most prophetic books in human history.

We did, however, conduct the First (and, alas, so far the last) George Orwell National Festival around Wallington and Letchworth in 2011. It was a great success, and I am proud that I was a member of the Festival's Steering Committee. It was good to see the pristine and ever-so-deserted Wallington coming back to life again, if only for a couple of weeks.

How ironic it is that having come from history's bloodiest real-life communist dystopia, I ended up living in the world's first 'utopian' Garden City, next to the former abode of the author of the world literature's most powerful fictional dystopia!

It was here, in Wallington, that Orwell married Eileen Shaughnessy in the old and eternally open parish church of St Mary. I like visiting the village church – permanently empty and freezing inside in winter – to read the new entries to the Visitors' Book that always surprise me with their geographic versatility. When do all these people come here, I wonder? Outside the Orwell Festival, I had always been on my own inside the church.

On the table next to the Visitors' Book is a pencil holder with reading glasses which suit my slightly presbyopic eyes perfectly – as if left there specially for me. There's also the first scary sign of a potential Animal Farm Theme Park – a stack of photocopied George and Eileen's marriage certificates – two pounds fifty each.

One of the most treasured books in my collection is *The Penguin Essays of George Orwell*.

And not just because Orwell's essays, to my mind, are unsurpassable in their originality, clarity of thought and lucidity of language. This book was given to me as a gift in Moscow by my first ever British friend Martin Walker, then *the Guardian's* Moscow correspondent. 'For Vitali. My favourite journalist of all time, Orwell, to the first Soviet investigative journalist,' reads a faded dedication.

It was 1988 and I had just been voted the Soviet Journalist of the Year for my investigations into the Soviet Mafia. I met Martin, who had just been voted the British Journalist of the Year for his emotional, at times poetic, and yet precise and instructive (Orwell-like?), reports from the USSR, at a British Embassy do, and we immediately clicked. It was Martin who later that year arranged for my first ever visit to the West and to Britain on a short journalistic attachment to *The Guardian* during which I wrote and published my first ever articles in English.

I was delighted to find several Orwell poems in the book. Until then I was unaware that Orwell was also an accomplished poet. The poems were part of some of the essays and I translated a couple of them, including the bitter, poignant and romantic 'The Italian Soldier Shook My Hand' from the essay 'Looking Back on the Spanish War', into Russian: 'The Italian soldier shook my hand/ beside the guard-room table; the strong hand and the subtle hand/ whose palms are only able...'

It was from Wallington, by the way, that Orwell went off to Spain to report from the civil war in early 1937. In May he was hit in the neck by a sniper's bullet and while recovering in a field hospital developed an obsessive fear of rats, which he later 'passed on' to Winston Smith. I read and re-read the collection a number of times, and, like every great book, each time it revealed something knew.

One day I discovered a 30-odd-year-old Moscow bus, tram and trolley-bus ticket ('Valid for one trip. Price 5 kopecks; 89903 AY 21; Invalid without a stamp') hidden behind its spine which came unpeeled. I touched the tiny piece of yellowish paper, and that very moment was miraculously transferred to the dark, dirty and crime-ridden (but not yet openly fascist, as it is now) Moscow of 1988 when I was reading Orwell's essays during an underground journey from Voikovskaya station, where my Mum then lived, to Babushkinskaya, where I resided.

To get to Voikovskaya station from Mum's street, I had to take a tram – a normal Czech-made red-and-yellow Moscow tram – where the ticket had been bought. You would toss a 5-kopeck coin into a metal box from which a ticket paper roll would be sticking out and tear one off. You could of course tear off the ticket without putting the coins into the box (no one was likely to check), but the sum was so ridiculously negligible that very few people were tempted to cheat.

Trucks in the Garden of Eden

By 1988, it was already quite safe to be reading Orwell (particularly in English) in public (in Moscow, at least, it was). In 1984... Well... I wouldn't have travelled far with an Orwell book in my hand.

With my English wife Christine, who also loves Orwell, we once went to Wallington for a barn dance. Why? Perhaps we were hoping against hope to bump into George whose presence is always so strikingly real – almost palpable – in the village. Or at least to have a chat with the people who now live in the cottage. It was a cloudy autumn night. We left our car at an impromptu parking lot off Manor Farm and in pitch darkness made our way to the barn.

We saw ordinary country folk: men, women, children – all with the open, wind-beaten faces of country dwellers. The food was fresh and local, the wine – Australian.

George was nowhere to be seen.

Chapter 3

The utopian Province of Hertfordshire

> Nowadays, quests for utopias make us uncomfortable.
> Dr John Callow FRSA, Director of Archives and
> Librarian of Marx Library 2005-2013

Britain was never short of Utopias.

Mainland Britain's first 'properly' utopian settlement – and I am talking here about social, agricultural and industrial communes, not religious ones, which, of course, appeared much-much earlier – was probably the Diggers Colony of George Hill, Surrey, the origins of which go back to the 1 April 1649, when William Everard, Gerald Winstanley and 15 others, at the risk of being dismissed as a bunch of April Fool jokers (yes, the tradition of April Fool's Day had existed since the times of Chaucer) began to dig and fertilise the waste land on that hill. They were soon joined by 30 more volunteers, who eventually chose to settle there. It was agreed among the colonists that all the benefits of their collective work would be equally shared. Both rich and poor would work on the land together, without divisions into masters and labourers.

The term 'Diggers' originated in 1607 during the Midland peasants' rising against the growing number of enclosures in the countryside, and the Diggers of 1649 saw themselves as proponents of freedom, which they defined in their Manifesto, written by Winstanley, as equal access to land. 'Take notice that England is not a free people till the poor that have no land have a free allowance to dig and labour the commons and so live as comfortably as the landlords that live in their enclosures.'

Trucks in the Garden of Eden

The Manifesto ended on a truly utopian note:

> ...all the commons and waste ground in England and in the whole world shall be taken in by the people in righteousness, not owing any property, but taking the earth to be a common treasury.

Tacitly approved by Cromwell and his colleagues, the Diggers of George Hill (they also liked to call themselves 'levellers') eventually fell victim to the local landlords, who mercilessly harassed them as 'trespassers', and the envy of the neighbouring peasant communities, peeved by the colonists' success and well-being: their crops were uprooted, tools smashed and houses burnt down. And because the Diggers did not accept violence of any kind and offered no resistance to the attackers, they were very quickly overwhelmed. At the end of March 1650, less than a year since its foundation, the last Diggers were driven off the land, and the Colony ceased to exist.

It was not by accident that I referred to the above-described Colony as probably the first Utopia on the British mainland: if we take into account the islands, and the Scottish Islands, in particular, then the oldest and by far the most 'utopian' settlement in British history was probably the amazing and the fairly little-known community of the island of St Kilda, which, by some estimates, had existed there – in total obscurity and isolation from the rest of the world – for about 2000 years, until the remaining 30 or so if its members were resettled on mainland Scotland in 1930. That extraordinary 'mini-society', which in its utter reclusiveness and isolation could perhaps be best compared to Tristan da Cunha, a small archipelago in the South Atlantic with a current population of about 270 and a 'capital' with the alluring name Edinburgh of the Seven Seas. Officially, the most remote community in the world, it was a frequent object of my childhood armchair-buccaneer dreams (until now, I haven't quite lost hope of visiting it one day).

Until the date of their final resettlement, the St Kildans remained the most properly 'utopian' community in human history. They knew nothing about money, but lived off seabirds, fish, crops and sheep, with all members enjoying equal rights. The island had no crime and was ruled by a truly democratic little 'parliament'. I'd better stop here, for by an unexpected stroke of luck I had a chance to visit St Kilda and several other Scottish islands (Foula, Iona, Fair Island etc.) that used to house – and

The utopian Province of Hertfordshire

some still do! – some fascinating utopian communities to be described later.

To come back to the Diggers of George Hill, the noble cause of the 'people in righteousness' did not vanish without a trace. Nourished with the ideas of Robert Owen and later Leo Tolstoy, the Diggers' movement these days comprises hundreds of communes, living independently and listed in a regularly updated directory. I came across several of those in my search for Britain's Utopias.

※○※○※

One thing I noticed shortly after beginning my quest was not just that utopian communities were prone to repeating the same mistakes over and over again, but also that they had (and still have) a tendency to grow in clusters.

Surrey, for example, apart from being the birthplace of the Diggers, at different times was also home to Cokelers – 'The Society of Dependants' who ran a chain of co-operative shops in late 1800s; Jezreelites – an offshoot of the Christian Israelites, who built a huge temple, 'Jezreel Tower' on Chatham Hill near Gillingham; and Lady Henry Somerset's Colony for recovering women-alcoholics (founded in 1805) near Duxhurst; plus a number of Victorian writers' settlements on the hilltops around Haslemere and Hindhead – to name just a few.

Numerous utopian communities were (and still are) to be found in Yorkshire, in Wales, in the Cotswolds, in Northumberland, in Scotland, particularly, on its islands, and in some other areas. Though very few – if any – were located in Berkshire, Herefordshire, or in Country Durham, say.

This book of course doesn't aim to survey all of the 4000-odd past and present utopian/dystopian settlements and communities of Britain. My intention is to introduce the reader to just a handful of hand-picked 'Utopias', interesting and not all well-known. For example, tons of both praise and scorn have been poured onto Milton Keynes, formerly a 'model town', now one of the UK's newest cities. Admiring its parks, lakes and greenbelts, but taking the Mickey out of its endless wind-swept open air car parks, underground shopping malls, countless roundabouts and numbered gridline streets has become a cliché in its own write (pun intended).

Reams have been written about the peculiar garden suburbs of London (Brentham, Hampstead, Ealing, Bermondsey etc[4] and Welwyn Garden City – Ebenezer Howard's second creation (after Letchworth) which all but lost its 'utopian' status in 1949, when it was sold to a corporation and became an 'ordinary' (read unremarkable) English town, with a somewhat bizarre architecture, a mixture of traditional Garden City-style arts-and-crafts with the brutalist monster buildings, multi-storey car parks and chaotic layout of a New Town. On top of it all, Welwyn is now run by a town council, as opposed to Letchworth Garden City, still administered and owned by the Heritage Foundation. 'A Garden City owns itself,' is the Garden Cities' movement main – and pretty much only! – mandatory principle and distinctive feature, with all the rest: green belts, public spaces, architectural uniformity, open community etc. being 'optional', so to speak.

Ironically, Letchworth is much less known in Britain (unlike in Japan, China, US, Australia etc. – see Chapter 2) than Welwyn, possibly due to the latter's proximity to London, and therefore fits in this book well, not just because I am living in it (in an email, a sentence like that would normally be followed by a 'smile' emoticon).

In this chapter and in all the subsequent ones I will be mostly considering the less-known Utopias of Wales and the Cotswolds, Scotland, the Midlands, North West and South East.

As far back as 1919, C.B. Fawcett, an all but forgotten writer and geographer, published *The Provinces of England*, in which he suggested a new administrative division of the country – larger, economically and demographically defined provinces, instead of the smaller and industrially amorphous and archaic counties. Among a dozen or so 'provinces' he drafted were the Province of North England, the Province of Peakdon ('the central and southern Pennines ... the largest coalfield of Britain'), the Bristol Province, the London Province (a bit of an oxymoron) and even a stretch of territory with the intriguing name 'The Anglo-Welsh Boundary'. For better or for the worse, that – purely utopian – idea didn't take off, as we know.

Following in Fawcett's footsteps, I have drafted (if only in my mind) a new 'utopian Map of Britain' to point out the most Utopia-prone 'provinces' through most of which I will travel and from which I will report. I will conclude with listing and briefly describing my own, personal, British Utopias.

Utopias come in all shapes and sizes: big and small; thriving and struggling; real-life and fictitious (i.e. created by dreamers, artists,

The utopian Province of Hertfordshire

writers and architects); past and present. I was lucky to have lived in some and visited some others. But most of all, while researching this book, I kept my eyes (and my heart – complete with its recently replaced bovine valve) open for any, even if minuscule, likenesses to history's biggest (so far) Utopia, the USSR, where I had the misfortune (or possibly, in relative terms, was lucky enough) to be born and to spend half of my life.

'Nobody will embrace the unembraceable' in the words of a fictitious (created by a group of 19th-century Russian writers) spoof 'thinker' and home-grown 'philosopher' Kozma Prutkov, whose other truisms and pseudo-aphorisms included 'Look in the root!' and 'Even an oyster had enemies!' Very true!

And here comes another of my spontaneously born definitions of a Utopia – 'a place, a theory, an ambition (plan) or a tale which tries to embrace the unembraceable'. It could be attributed to both Kozma Prutkov and Vitali Vitaliev, or, if you wish, to a new semi-fictitious utopian writer – 'Prutali Vitkov'.

Is there something in the water that defines utopian ambitions of this or that area or country? I don't think so. Behind them are history and traditions, as can be seen clearly in my 'native' Hertfordshire – the county where I have been living and working since 2007.

One of the smallest, Hertfordshire is also one of the oldest and hence one of the historically richest. Convenient in its proximity to London for those who wanted to flee from the urban dystopias of the capital, the county has witnessed lots of attempts at Utopia throughout the years – from Barnet Diggers Colony of 1650s, an offshoot of the George Hill one (see above) to Letchworth Garden City (see even further above). The county was also the birthplace of a number of utopian ideas, some of which had naturally turned dystopian in the end (I am talking about the post-WWII 'New Towns', the first of which was Stevenage, or 'St Evenage', as it is often sarcastically referred to by the locals).

Let me stress again that, unlike, say, *Utopia Britannica* by Chris Coates, this book is not a directory, but rather a travelogue, and its aim is not to cover as many utopian and dystopian settlements, communities and ideas as possible, but only those with which I had a chance to familiarise myself with properly; those which mean something to me and evoke my 'negative nostalgia' for the now-defunct country of my birth – the USSR. It is in a way a search for the British fragments of the world's largest Utopia turned dystopia where I had spent 37 years of my life. I was born in 1954, precisely 37 years after the Bolshevik coup d'etat of 1917 which laid the foundations of the Soviet Union (officially formed in 1922) and precisely 37 years before its final collapse in 1991.

It looks like I might have been destined for a fractured life...

One of my favourite Utopias coming from Hertfordshire is a literary one. The author of *The Coming Race*, Edward Bulwer-Lytton is another (after George Orwell) former 'neighbour' of mine. Edward Bulwer-Lytton (1804–1873), the 19th century's most prolific and famous writer – yes, even more famous (at that time) and more prolific than his friend Charles Dickens – lived in Knebworth, about 10 miles to the south of Letchworth. He was notorious for his tempestuous family life, his adoration of his formidable mother, Elizabeth, and for, reportedly, the worst ever *in media res* opening sentence of a novel – 'It was a dark and stormy night' – which, incidentally, is not that bad if you ask me, albeit inferior to my favourites: 'He sings on the toilet of a morning' from Yuri Olesha's *Envy*, and the anonymous 'When he woke up, the dinosaur was no longer there.'

Another unintended invention of Bulwer-Lytton was Bovril, a popular (if only in Britain) thick and salty meat extract, used widely by sportsmen and explorers to keep their spirits up. To be more precise, it was not the extract itself that Bulwer-Lytton had invented but its name, stemming from 'Vril' – a fictitious energy from *The Coming Race*, his most successful novel and, to my mind, the best literary Utopia to have come out of Britain.[5]

The book, which Bulwer-Lytton, a successful politician and an MP, referred to as a 'satirical Utopia', and some critics as 'evolutionary fantasy', is written in a disarmingly simple and surprisingly modern language and is all but unputdownable. It reminded me of the classic adventure story *The Lost World* by Arthur Conan-Doyle, which came out in 1912 long after *The Coming Race* and was obviously influenced by it. In *The Coming Race* two explorers accidentally discover an underground utopian land populated by a superior winged race propelled by 'Vril', the magic energy that feeds their 'vril'ya', the wings, and makes them fly.

The utopian Province of Hertfordshire

First published in 1871, it draws upon ideas of Darwinism to describe the future world, dominated by women and characterised by vast technological progress. And if the former distinctive feature could have been prompted by his own dominating mother and the difficulties of his marriage, the latter was almost certainly inspired by the writer's visit to New Lanark – Robert Owen's utopian industrial community in Southern Scotland (see Chapter 12). But whereas Owen saw technology as the main tool of human liberation, Bulwer-Lytton believed in the power of the collective character and the leading role of human qualities in social transformation, with technology being secondary –an opinion with which I agree completely, for, as I have already stated, the problem with all Utopias is not their insufficient technological prowess but their failure to create what the Soviet Communist Manifesto termed 'a new human being', an ideal creature with supreme intelligence and high morals.

Here's a typical description of 'some great factory' in the utopian underground world:

> There was a huge engine in the wall which was in full play, with wheels and cylinders resembling our own steam-engines, except that it was richly ornamented with precious stones and metals, and appeared to emanate a pale phosphorescent atmosphere of shifting light.

While reading *The Coming Race*, I made a discovery – a small, yet significant, detail, which none of the Bulwer-Lytton biographers seemed to spot – a discovery that shows Bulwer-Lytton's interest in Russia and Russian philosophy, particularly in the works of Helena Blavatsky (1831–1891), herself a utopian author as well as one of the founders and the leading theoretician of theosophy, a kind of a religion, based mostly on Blavatsky's own works: a mixture of Eastern beliefs with Western occultism. And although there are no official records of Blavatsky ever visiting Knebworth, I have little doubt that she did. Having spent most of her life in London, she could not have avoided knowing Bulwer-Lytton, whom she calls 'one of our own' in a letter, and she shared his life-long interest in black magic and occultism.

He didn't have to travel far to look for things bizarre and paranormal: Knebworh House itself was full of nooks and crannies, including a false door in the Regency-style bedroom of Edward's formidable mother. That door led nowhere and had given Edward the idea of the secret door inside the bookshop in his early novel *Zanoni*, opening up to a whole concealed new world – the idea that later became the foundation of his most famous book, *The Coming Race*.

Bulwer-Lytton must have had a hard time trying to find a name for that magic elixir of life which propelled his angelic winged creatures. When describing the plot to Blavatsky, he could have asked her: 'What's the Russian for "wings"?', to which she could have answered: 'Kril'ya!' He must have liked the sound of that word and derived the name of the magic energy from it, having changed the word's first letter 'K' to 'V' to make it less obviously Russian, Consequently, he calls the wings of the subterranean advanced beings 'Vril'ya', a rhyming spoonerism-like analogue of the Slavonic word 'Kril'ya'.

My thorough search in dozens other languages showed that the word 'wings' sounds similar to 'kril'ya' only in Russian, Ukrainian ('krila'), Czech and Slovak ('kridla') and several other Slavonic languages, of which Russian was by far the best known and the most accessible (via Blavatsky) to Bulwer-Lytton.

So popular was *The Coming Race* that the word 'vril' later evolved into the trademark 'Bovril' – an allegedly energising, beef extract used for food flavouring. My late friend Sir Peter Ustinov once told me that although he was conceived in St Petersburg, he was born in Britain, which made us both 'fellow defectors' from Russia – me escaping on board a train, and he in his mother's womb! He liked to recall how during his first train rides around Britain at the age of five or six in the mid-1920s, when he had just learned to read, he used to be genuinely puzzled by the fact that most train stations were called 'Bovril'!

In March 1891, a special event was held at the Royal Albert Hall in London to celebrate *The Coming Race*. The three-day extravaganza, organised by Herbert Tibbits, was called The Vril-Ya Bazaar and Fete. Although its main aim was raising funds for the West End Hospital and the London School of Massage and Electricity, it went down in history as the world's first science fiction conference. The entertainments at the event included magic shows and a fortune-telling dog, as well as 'scientific' discussions of the magical powers of Vril and Vril'ya. It was probably for the best that attempts to recreate Bulwer-Lytton's Utopia in reality were limited to the Vril'ya Bazaar and hadn't spilled out into the streets of Britain's cities and towns, as was the case with the much inferior in the literary sense and badly researched writings of Marx, Engels and Lenin in Petrograd and Moscow in 1917.

The peculiar world of Utopias is full of strange connections and bizarre coincidences. As we have seen already, not only Britain's most important literary Utopia since Thomas More's (and I do have reasons to regard *The Coming Race* as such) was influenced – even if adversely – by the teachings of Robert Owen, it also carried traces of theosophy, eastern religions (Buddhism, Hinduism and Taoism), a touch of occultism mixed with the Swedenborgian 'Heaven and Hell' theory, and a sprinkle of 'Russian-ness', or Russian Cosmism.

There's even a bizarre architectural connection to Letchworth Garden City. I can see the superficial similarities between one of Letchworth's most iconic buildings, Annie Jay Lawrence's the Cloisters, with its asymmetric turrets, trompe l'oeil windows and the trailblazing 'sleeping towers' (see Chapter 2) and the Gothic and madly eclectic Knebworth House, Edward Bulwer-Lytton's patrimony. Architects would perhaps laugh off that casual observation, but, as I said, I do not aim at serious scholarly or artistic discoveries, but simply want to share the personal observations and feelings of someone who lived most of his life in the world's largest and longest-lived Utopia-cum-dystopia and has survived to tell the tale.

'Ignore the people's moral qualities at your peril!' Such was the warning that *The Coming Race* – the mother of all post-Thomas-More British Literary Utopias and Britain's first ever science-fiction novel – prophetically, even if unconsciously, gave to the impending Soviet dystopia, the warning which, as shown again by Russia's fratricidal war against Ukraine, has fallen on deaf ears.

No more than 10 miles from Knebworth lies a small and leafy Hertfordshire village, Ayot St Lawrence, which for many years had been home to George Bernard Shaw (1856–1950) – the Irish writer, playwright and wit, who lived there in the mansion called Shaw's Corner from 1906 to his death in 1950.

Among Shaw's Corner's numerous utopian features is Shaw's own writing shed – a tiny (5.9 sq m) revolving hut on a steel-pole frame with circular track, so that it could be rotated (with a special steering wheel) to follow the sun during the day. The writer referred to the hut as 'London', and his wife would routinely turn away unwanted visitors and callers by saying that Mr Shaw was 'away in London'.

A brilliant playwright, a person with irrepressible wit and modesty, who once noted that the biggest service he had rendered to his native Ireland was leaving it as soon as he could, a democrat, who abhorred racism and, particularly, anti-Semitism in all its forms, Shaw underwent an incredible character change from a liberal Western intellectual to the Soviet's Union's ardent and unquestioning supporter. His transformation started in 1917 – the year of the Bolshevik coup d'etat in Russia – and culminated in his ignominious 1931 visit to Moscow ('I can't die without having seen the USSR,' he stated infamously) on the invitation of Stalin himself, when Shaw was driven around the Soviet capital in a specially allocated chauffeured car and was bombarded day and night with Stalinist propaganda. In fact, he didn't need to be brainwashed, for – unlike some other Western literary celebrities of the 1930s, whom Stalin had failed to woo with primitive, yet tested, concoctions of bribery and lies, such as Water Durante, Andre Zide et al – by the time of his visit, Shaw had already been converted to supporting the Kremlin and hadn't even tried to hide his admiration for the openly totalitarian Soviet state in his numerous post-1917 articles and essays.

Why and how could it happen to one of Europe's best writers and thinkers? Literary and other scholars have been trying to understand that transformation, but until now have been unable to crack the enigma – the puzzle which I seemed (false modesty – if not a bit of irony – aside) to solve after my very first visit to Shaw's Corner.

I could not believe my eyes when both on the mantelpiece in the lounge of that typically 'bourgeois' country mansion and in on the writing desk in Shaw's own 'in-house' (as opposed to the rotating 'London') study, I spotted the portraits not just of Marx, Engels and Lenin, but also of dictators, murderers and international criminals like Stalin, Trotsky and – to my particular astonishment – of Felix Dzerzhinsky an odious Polish-born sadist and executioner who liked watching his victims being tortured, the founder of GULAG and the VCHK, which later, like a hardened criminal kept changing its abbreviated name from VCHK to NKVD, GPU, KGB, FSB etc.). It was the first (and so far the last, thank God) time that I saw Dzerzhinsky's mug, which used to grin from the walls of all KGB offices, particularly those of their staff interrogators

The utopian Province of Hertfordshire

and torturers (it did grin at me, too, on a couple of occasions) on display anywhere in the West.

Staring at the haggard goatee-bearded face of 'Iron Felix', as Lenin had nicknamed his favourite executioner, I was frantically trying to comprehend how such a massive 180 degrees turnaround could occur. Unexpectedly, I found an answer right there in the mansion's kitchen, or rather in an old dog-eared log book put on display there. In it, Shaw's Corner's faithful servants had been encouraged by the writer himself to leave their notes and observations.

Many of the entries, made between 1917 (when Shaw turned 61) to the day of his death in 1950, described the ageing writer's small (and not- so-small) 'eccentricities': his difficulty in remembering the servants' names; his peculiar and rather strange little habits, growing in frequency as time went by. I remember one of such entries almost word-for word:' Mr Shaw is a very, very nice man, very kind, but with some strange habits: he wears a warm felt hat in summer and a light straw Panama in winter.'

Having not quite recovered from looking after my own mother – a wonderful, intelligent and very literary lady, who had gone through six long years of debilitating Alzheimer's disease, confusion over seasons being one of the symptoms, I realised that Shaw must have been suffering from a fairly early progressive dementia, starting in his 60s. They say that no two cases of dementia are identical, but there may be certain 'overlaps' – like an inability to distinguish between children and parents, friends and foes, virtue and evil, and so on...

Although the many Shaw scholars of the world are likely to pooh-pooh my (never aimed at being medically solid) 'diagnosis', which implies that only someone who is mentally ill could seriously believe in communism, by pointing out that Shaw had been a leftie and a Fabian since the days of his youth, I will stick to my tongue-in-cheek guns. It is one thing to be a young Fabian and support 'democratic socialism', and a totally different one to openly worship history's worst and bloodiest cannibals, like Stalin and Dzerzhinsky, as well as to publicly (and repeatedly) profess one's firm belief in the verdicts of the hastily arranged 'Troika trials', when many thousands of Stalin's opponents and many of his supporters – otherwise totally innocent, if somewhat naive (not unlike Shaw himself) and mostly decent people – were rounded up on trumped-up charges, imprisoned and sentenced to death.

Trucks in the Garden of Eden

Again, if he wanted, Shaw could have gleaned the truth of what was really going on in the 'glorious' USSR from Western newspapers and other sources. But he, obviously, was not mentally up to it, and just like Prince Potemkin in the face of Catherine the Great a couple of centuries earlier, chose to swallow the Soviet 'truth-less news' and to embrace the primitive propaganda without questioning it. In short, the great writer had (somewhat prematurely) grown first fuddy-duddy and then ga-ga, thus undermining the Utopia he had created for himself in his reclusive and luxurious hideout, where he ended his life 'shaw-cornered' by his own dangerous delusions.

One thing that doesn't stop surprising me since moving to Hertfordshire is the fact that two great British Dystopian/utopian writers, Shaw and Orwell, never met each other, despite residing for a number of years within 15 miles of each other and going to shop for basic commodities (Shaw from Ayot St Lawrence, Orwell from Wallington) in the same town, Hitchin. It was probably for the best, for their encounter could have easily led to a vociferous row, or even to a fistfight! It would have been hard to find two authors so different in both their views and lifestyles. They would have had to agree to disagree on food (Shaw a vegetarian, Orwell a lover of traditional English fare); drink (Shaw a teetotaller, Orwell a connoisseur of beer and wine); the war in Spain (Shaw a pacifist who had opposed the Great War in 1914, Orwell a volunteer in Spain, where he became deeply disillusioned by socialist ideas as they were presented and pursued by the so-called 'Interbrigades'); and the Communist Party and Stalin (Shaw an apologist and supporter, Orwell vehemently critical).

The conclusion is that some highly desirable, yet unlikely and potentially explosive (read utopian), literary encounters are best avoided.

At a first glance, Hoddesdon strikes an accidental visitor as unremarkable and hectic (the result of several touches of the failed 1960s New Town Movement experiment) a town in Hertfordshire's Borough of Broxbourne and constituting part of Greater London, Yet even a casual stroller in the town centre cannot fail to spot a couple of unexpected features: a disproportionate number of genuine-looking Italian restaurants,

The utopian Province of Hertfordshire

an Italian Consul's office; job vacancy ads in shop windows not in English, but in Italian, and the mansion-like house of the famous Italian chef Gino da Campo.

And if the same visitor wanders into the characteristic Nonna's Kitchen restaurant off the High Street, they are bound to be overwhelmed with delicious Italian smells, generous displays of dozens of multi-coloured pastas in the in-house Delicatessen; a lordly maitre d' in a tuxedo, and Italian families – babies, toddlers, youngsters and oldies – sitting at long tables sagging under Italian food to celebrate their Nonna's or Nonno's birthdays.

Almost all Hoddeston Italians originate from two Sicilian villages – Cianciana and Mussomeli. Small farmers, gardeners, nursery owners and cucumber growers, they came to England from post-Mussolini Italy after WWII to start a new life. Their descendants now claim to own over 70 per cent of all Lee Valley nurseries and produce 75 per cent of all UK-grown cucumbers. A small Italian Utopia in the middle of England.

Yet, my several visits to Hoddesdon were not aimed at writing about the Italian community, interesting and peculiar as it was. My aim was to locate the building of the former Clarion Socialist Youth Hostel, established in 1933 by the London Labour League of Youth as a branch of the nationwide Clarion Cycling Club.

The Hostel was mentioned in passing by the lonely receptionist of Hoddesdon's local history museum, to where I popped in rather out of habit (when in an unknown town for the first time, I always try to visit four places: a coffee shop, a bookshop or a library, a local museum and a railway station, if any, in that particular order). The nice little museum was still trying to cope with the recent near-utopian bonanza when several allegedly 'important' 16th-century wall paintings were accidentally uncovered during renovations at a Hugh Street pub, right above the bar (where else?). Postcards of the paintings were already on sale in the museum shop.

'Was that amazing find reported in the national media?' I asked the receptionist, who, for some reason, looked offended by my question.

'No. Just in our *Hertfordshire Mercury*,' she shrugged.

Her eyes suddenly briefly lit up, as if from some pleasant recollection.

'But we have a photo of our Clarion Youth Hostel on display in the Science Museum in London!' she declared proudly.

Trucks in the Garden of Eden

'What's so special about that hostel?' I asked.

'It is no more. But in the 1930s, it had thousands if people staying inside and camping on its grounds. Camping and cycling. "Cycling for socialism", as they said. It was also called a Labour playground!'

You won't believe it, but I somehow knew that I was going to find a Utopia in Hoddesdon. There was something there, if not in the water, then definitely in the town's dusty streets, where through the continuous din and roar of passing trucks one could overhear the muffled yet still melodious Italian greetings: 'Buon Giorno, Gino!' (Gino Da Campo himself could be on the receiving end of that one) and 'Buona Notte, Signora!'

No matter how hard I tried, I failed to find any traces of the 'Labour playground' in or around Hoddesdon. But I could sense the spirit of it in the polluted air above the town centre as I walked back from the museum towards the local library where the well-stocked local history section was located in a damp, badly lit basement, as if it was hiding there with the aim of making research into the town's 'socialist' past as difficult and unpleasant as possible.

The Clarion Socialist Youth Hostel was established in 1933 by the London Labour League of Youth. In 1934, over 13,000 members of the Clarion Club camped on the hostel's grounds. The original Club itself was formed in 1895 at Broadley Common, near Nazeing in Essex, when six young men decided to 'combine the pleasures of cycling with the propaganda of socialism'. In the following year, the name was changed to the Clarion Cycling Club after the *Clarion* socialist newspaper, which ceased in 1934.

From a handful of random newspaper clippings, I gleaned that apart from 'cycling for socialism', the tenants of the Hoddesdon Hostel indulged in boating, tennis, dancing etc. They listened to the talks by visiting and, no doubt, committed 'socialist' speakers with titles like 'Socialism and Art' and ... wait for it ... 'Breeding out of the unfit'. (Was the latter prompted by the growing popularity of their German socialist, if somewhat 'nationalist' comrades, I was wondering?) In the words of one of the hostellers, 'We had a great deal of fun in those days, as well as serious politicking.' No wonder: 'breeding out the unfit' must have been a very 'serious' political matter.

In an abnormally thin, as if undernourished or suffering from anorexia, archive folder I found a faded photo, taken by George

Woodbine, on 22 July 1934 during the hostel's heyday. In it, a large group of cyclists ('socialists', no doubt) is pictured reclining on a grassy knoll, next to an ancient jalopy of a clearly 'socialist' truck on the foreground.

A truck in the Garden of Eden?

Next to the truck stands Herbert Morrison (1888–1965), Lord Morrison of Lambeth, one-time Labour MP and Minister for Transport, in a wide-brimmed straw hat of the type George Bernard Shaw preferred to wear in winter (see above).

Looking at his bespectacled face of a typical deputy schoolmaster (somehow, it did not appear authoritative enough and did not carry enough hidden menace to pass for that of the headmaster himself), I couldn't help thinking that he reminded me of someone. The mystery was solved by a quick peep into Wikipedia: Herbert Morrison was the grandfather of a modern Labour politician, Peter Mandelson, Baron Mendelson PC, who, unlike his granddad, was not a cyclist.

The tenants of the Socialist Youth Hostel kept happily 'cycling for socialism' right until the end of the Second World War when the building and the surrounding cycling tracks – like socialist ideas themselves – went into terminal disrepair and were eventually abandoned.

Yet, the coda of that protracted utopian saga happened as recently as in 2021, when the Clarion Cycling Club, which had outlived the hostel, made national headlines (including a *Guardian* newspaper editorial) by publicly abandoning its historical association with socialism. Its members went so far as to vote for the removal of the word 'socialism' from the Club's constitution, thus abandoning the initial attractive principles of 'Clarion Socialism': 'promotion of democracy and opposition to all forms of inequality and exploitation' and replacing them with a more down-to-earth 'support for fairness, equality, inclusion and diversity'.

Well, what can I say? Better late than never. These days, the National Clarion Cycling Club continues to exist and to thrive under a much less utopian logo, 'Fellowship is Life', borrowed from William Morris and at times tweaked to read 'Fellowship through Cycling'. The Club's London branch sees its main aim as proving that cycling in the capital does not have to be expensive, thus echoing the old pedalling-for-socialism Utopia, as, from what I know, these days there's nothing in London that could qualify as inexpensive. Except perhaps for 'Boris Bikes', but with Boris's ultra-Conservative credentials in mind, the latter can hardly be classified as a socialist achievement.

Sharp right!' the normally suave and velvety voice of my faithful Satnav was suddenly brusque and peremptory, as it irritated by such an unexpected turn of the road. And of the story too...

It was a true 'bear's corner', to use a good Russian expression. Just yards away from the permanently busy St Albans Ring Road, there was an unpaved one-line track, so densely lined with trees and shrubs that it looked more like a dark tunnel than a B-class road, along which I was cautiously steering Alphie, my Toyota Alphard campervan, until we came to a stop at an ornate yet sturdy steel gate with the sign 'Spielplatz' across it. For some reason, it brought back to memory the famous Zen koan of a gateless gate.

I pressed the intercom button to introduce myself: the visit had been planned well in advance. Slowly, as if reluctantly, the gate came apart to reveal an empty parking lot strewn with pebbles. We waited for a couple of minutes in total solitude, surrounded only by the Bricket Forest trees rustling soothingly above our heads.

Our host Tom suddenly emerged from behind the green hedge, like a marionette from behind a puppet theatre curtain. He was tall, slender and sun-tanned. He was wearing – I cannot recall who said that until the writer describes their characters' clothes, the reader is bound to perceive them as naked. Well, here we go. Tom was wearing socks and sneakers. That was it! Yet, contrary to the above-mentioned statement, those 'clothes' made him look more naked than he actually was! In my puritanical, fully clothed eyes that is. Yes, in a stark contrast to the leafy trees and bushes behind him, Tom was not wearing anything above the level of his roots, read ankles.

'I've been doing some maintenance work on the house,' he said pointing at his trainers, as if apologising for not being naked enough.

'Welcome to Spielplatz – UK's largest naturist community,' he then declared with a slight American accent as we shook hands. To me, his palm felt much barer than mine. Tom led the way along the narrow path to the camp, looking back from time to time, as if to make sure that I was listening to his running commentary carefully enough.

The utopian Province of Hertfordshire

Spielplatz was founded in 1929 by Charles Macaskie and his wife Dorothy, who purchased a patch of virgin land not far from St Albans. Their tent was the first dwelling on the compound which they monikered a Play Place, or *Spieplatz* in German. They were soon joined by other proponents of naturism, i.e. a way of life in harmony with nature, of which nudity was just one aspect.

These days Spielplatz occupies 12 acres of land, with 65 mostly wooden houses for its residents as well as several communal structures: club, swimming pool, tennis courts etc. – all hardly visible behind trees, bushes, flower beds and other lush vegetation – a true Garden of Eden of sorts, with a small crowd of Adams and Eves in their birthday suits.

As we walked around the compound, which resembled a middle-range sylvan resort or a sanatorium, I couldn't help craning my neck to stare at a jolly, small group of stark naked tennis players – males and females, their flesh bouncing as they jumped.

There were other nude people around: working in their gardens, mowing the lawns, or doing other little jobs in the compound. Like Tom, many of them were wearing shoes, which paradoxically and from my fully clothed viewpoint made them look more nude than those who were indeed stark naked.

Having grown up in the falsely puritanical USSR, where any depiction of naked bodies counted as porn and such pictures could only be acquired from some dodgy illegit sellers pretending to be deaf-and-mute and operating mostly on shuttle trains, I was thoroughly unused to other people's nudity and kept feeling awkward about it even after 30-odd years in the West.

I remember how shocked I was to stumble onto a nudist beach in Brighton while recording a Radio 4 Breakaway slot there in the mid-1990s. The sight of a handful of elderly nudists, shivering with cold and wearing only goose pimples (it was late autumn) was embarrassing and made me want to put on another jacket on top of the one I was already wearing. It made me appreciate the irony (or so I thought) of the 'Nudity Required' slogan I had once spotted in the offices of the *Sunday Sport* tabloid (I would stop short of calling it a newspaper) while filming my first BBC documentary, 'My Friend Little Ben'. The most unpleasant nudity-related episode, however, happened on an assignment in Germany when, having ventured into a unisex sauna in my swimming trunks, I was shouted at by the stark-naked patrons. Insulted and shamed. I had to retreat back to the cloakroom and feeling morally (and almost physically) unable to fully undress

Trucks in the Garden of Eden

in front of a bunch of aggressive strangers, left the premises un-steamed.

No one wanted to shout at me in Spielplatz, where, as Tom hurried to explain, nudity had never been enforced, and it was entirely up to you whether to wear any clothes or not. As we walked around the resort (that was what Tom called it), I was paying less and less attention to its naked residents, whose attire, or rather lack of it, was appearing more and more natural to me, whereas my own jeans and T-shirt were looking more and more superficial, unnecessary and out of place.

Old Einstein was right: everything in the world is relative.

Naturism as a cultural movement has never focused on nakedness alone. If fact, nudity has always been second to its several main principles – worship of nature, a means to be as close to our natural environment as possible, not just in one's mind, but also in the body. The naturists' nudity therefore was thoroughly non-sexual and nothing to be concealed or ashamed of. Just another bare (in the true sense of the word) necessity of life.

Prior to visiting Spielplatz, I browsed through several nudists' websites. One claim that was repeated on all of them by a number of long-standing members of the naturist communities was that in all their years of nakedness among the naked they had never got sexually aroused. Not once! What can I say? Adam and Eve could have certainly learned some prudence from them. Yet, on the other hand, had they (Adam and Eve) stuck to non-sexual nudism, humankind would have never existed and this book would have never been written.

Tom invited me to have tea in his garden. We were joined by his wife Victoria, also naked (of course), though I could hardly register that by then.

Naked or not, Victoria was a charming lady. With Tom, she came to live in Spielplatz 4 years earlier and never looked back. A chronic health condition she had been suffering from had all but disappeared since then, due to the constant exposure to fresh air she herself suggested. Like most of the Spielplatz residents, both she and Tom had part-time jobs outside the compound. Before leaving the resort to go to work, they all had to – reluctantly – put their clothes back on to correspond to our distorted (as I was beginning to think) notions of 'decency', even Tom – who worked as a nude life model posing for artists and sculptors! I was greatly impressed by such pure devotion to one's beliefs.

'It is all about the choices you make,' said Victoria. 'There is no compulsion to be naked at all times. When we do gardening, cook our meals, or simply feel cold, we can wear any clothes we want. That gives us the feeling of complete freedom.'

As Tom was escorting me back to the car park, I felt like shedding my clothes, too, but thought better of it. Even if by then I felt morally ready to get naked, I still wasn't prepared to do so; for purely aesthetic reasons.

But I did carry out of Spielplatz a strong feeling of having come closer to a true Utopia than ever before.

Chapter 4

Tavi and Chucho

The last thing we really need is more utopian visions.
    Immanuel Wallerstein, American sociologist, 1930-2019

Right on the north-western edge of Letchworth Garden City, less than a mile away from the Wilbury Cemetery, where lies modest grave of Ebenezer Howard, the Garden City founder, the county of Hertfordshire, with the official motto 'Trust and Fear Not', ends, and Bedfordshire (motto 'Constant Be') begins. The village of Fairfield is the first Bedfordshire settlement after the border, so I didn't have to travel far to acquaint myself with one of Britain's quirkiest Utopias of the past: the former Stotfold Three Counties Lunatic Asylum, now Fairfiel, one of Bedfordshire's newest towns, built on the hospital's grounds.

Designed by George Fowler Jones and unveiled in 1860, the main building of the hospital, now housing dozens of modern luxury flats with huge bay windows and high ceilings, is one of Britain's most impressive architectural structures, boasting, among other features, the UK's (and, allegedly, Europe's) longest in-house corridor stretching for a good half a mile. When I saw that enormous building for the first time, I could hardly believe my eyes, so incongruous and, yes, utopian it appeared amongst the cottagey and predominantly one-storied dwellings of the nearby villages of Hertfordshire and Bedfordshire.

The asylum in Fairfield initially had only twelve patients: six females and six males, all from Bedford, yet just one year after its opening their number increased to 460. Was it due to a sudden increase in the ranks of 'pauper lunatics' (as they used to be officially known) in the three counties, Bedfordshire,

Hertfordshire and now-defunct Huntingdonshire? Or could it be that some poorer residents of those counties, attracted by the truly amazing (utopian?) facilities of the hospital chose to simulate lunacy? History does not carry the answer, but the conditions and attitudes at Fairfield were outstanding even for Victorian times, when in the wake of the 1845 Lunacy Act, the approaches to treating mental disorders changed dramatically, new 'humane' treatment methods were introduced and new bespoke hospital buildings constructed for the mentally ill, who prior to the Act had been confined to prisons, workhouses and so-called 'retreats'. Victorian and post-Victorian society was obsessed with 'lunatic asylums' – an official term for psychiatric hospitals until 1930, when a special parliament act changed the word 'asylum' to' hospital' – to the point when they became tourist attractions of sorts, and a typical family day out in the country could include a visit to the 'lunatics' and their exquisite, near-palatial homes, their hospitals. Murray, Baedeker and other early guidebook writers would routinely list 'lunatic asylums' among the not-to-be-missed local attractions.

Fairfield Hospital, however, stood out even against that innovative background. It was one of the first in Britain to carry out so-called 'moral treatment' – a concept that was pioneered at the York Retreat in the early 19th century. 'Moral treatment' regarded the natural environment as the primary therapeutic tool. The hospital was to make sure that the patients were accommodated in safe and comfortable conditions, with lots of space and natural lighting. It aimed at providing them with fresh air, a good diet and daily chores which included work in a farmyard, where the patients could grow wheat and raise livestock, and an orchard, where they picked fruit and berries, pruned the trees and so on as part of what is now known as 'occupational therapy'. The patients were also encouraged to work in the laundry and to carry out all kinds of maintenance and repairs. They were paid with tokens, which they could use to buy things they needed or wanted within the asylum. Each working patient was entitled to half a pint of beer each day. The beer was brewed on site and was generally preferable to water, which was at times undrinkable.

If that was not a utopian scenario, than nothing is!

After the 1930 Act, the conditions had improved to the point when performers from London came regularly to Fairfield Hospital to entertain the patients, for whom New Year's Eve Balls were also held annually.

Trucks in the Garden of Eden

In their book *A Place in the Country. Three Counties Asylum 1860-1999*, Judith Pettigrew, Rory W. Reynolds and Sandra Rouse describe the week of celebrations staged by the hospital to mark the coronation of Queen Elizabeth II in June 1953:

> A large-screen Decca television was purchased for £185 and the chaplain arranged a programme of events. The patients were allowed to watch the ceremony in relays during the day and evening on the television which had been set up in the female hall. A patients' 'Coronation Dance' was held on Wednesday 3 June, a concert by the hospital orchestra on Thursday, and on Friday here was a large Coronation Ball for staff and guests.

All things considered, Fairfield was more a sanatorium than a hospital – a thoroughly utopian place where one could escape from all worldly stresses and worries.

That calm and quietness can still be felt in Fairfield these days. I often take my dog for walks in the village, now built up with rows of modern pseudo-Victorian houses and cottages that make me think of Disneyland and, particularly of Celebration, Florida, real-life (not fairy-tale) utopian town, designed by Walk Disney himself and built by Disney Corporation in the mid-1990s , which I visited briefly in 1999 when it was going through a severe crisis due to lack of working opportunities for its residents, tied to the place by severe property ownership contracts. No wonder it didn't occur to Disney, who himself had never had a proper job, that ordinary people had to work somewhere to survive. The crisis was eventually successfully resolved.

Yet, unlike modern Fairfield Park, even at its worst times Celebration, Florida, had shops and restaurants, even if empty of customers. Modern Fairfield, with a population of nearly 5000, has just one Tesco Express and no restaurants or pubs. It does have a gym and an 'Eden' hair salon, right next to Tesco. The gruesome public catering situation is not hugely helped by the vans selling pizzas, crepes and ice-cream which visit Fairfield occasionally and park in the town square, right opposite the mini supermarket – the true hub of the Fairfield community.

An ordinary day of a Fairfield dweller should therefore look approximately like this: a quick visit to the gym, or alternatively, a jog or a stroll along UK's longest corridor inside the former hospital building, in the morning; a haircut at the 'Eden'; a shopping spree in Tesco Express in the afternoon, and dinner of a takeaway pizza from the visiting van.

But please do not rush to the conclusion that – just like in the times of the asylum – you have to be mad to live in Fairfield now. What makes life in it not simply bearable, but actually quite pleasant, is nature, or rather the hospital's environmental heritage, so to speak. I mean a number of well-kept gardens and parks, with flowerbeds, sycamores and plane trees, to where happy 'lunatics' in grey hospital gowns used to come for their morning and evening strolls, and an enormous old orchard, working in which was part of the hospital's occupational therapy as well as of its trailblazing 'moral treatment'. In autumn, the orchard keeps shedding loads of large and ripe apples, which look sweet and yummy, but have a bitter taste from lack of cultivation and pruning. That abandoned Garden-of-Eden-cum-orchard neatly places Fairfield Park at the end of the normal utopian cycle, approaching an inevitable dystopia. In Adam's shoes (probably, similar to those worn by my new naturist friends from Spielplatz), I would have thought twice before taking a bite.

When in Fairfield, I am always reminded of Colin Thubron's *Cruel Madness* (1984), one of the best novels I have ever read. It starts with a description of a fictitious 'lunatic asylum … a Gothic fantasy [with] grey-red walls and 'pointed windows' resembling 'some desanctified cathedral'. And although by mentioning the mist that 'pours out of the Black Mountains', Thubron clearly identifies Wales as the location of his imaginary 'madhouse', I cannot help the feeling that he was – at least partially – 'inspired' by Fairfield. This feeling grows considerably in the gardens, which, in Thubron's words, 'flower into a sombre beauty' in summer. 'There are handsome, isolated trees; cedars, yews and willows,' exactly like Fairfield.

> Glass galleries circle the building's southern front, where the inmates sit as if ripening in the sun. A few pavilions scatter the lawns. From the highest wards you can glimpse a road beyond the outer walls, and a village in a dip of the hills. But that's all. The hospital is self-contained. It is like a factory devoted to nothing but its own upkeep; because hardly anybody ever comes out of it.

Yes, such was the seemingly comforting yet ultimately cruel reality of Britain's 'vintage' show-case psychiatric hospitals – be it Colin Thubron's fictional 'madhouse' in Wales, or the Three Counties

Asylum, in Bedfordshire. I see it as another clear indicator of the fact that the Garden of Eden, be it real or metaphorical, can only work for 'lunatics' and dreamers. And even for them, only temporarily.

❦

'When everything else fails, read notice boards' is one of my self-invented rules of journalistic research.

'Do you need financial help?' runs the one and only notice on the village notice board. 'Who doesn't?' I want to reply. But there's no one around I could address my rhetorical question to. It is an early afternoon on Saturday, but the village seems empty and abandoned, as if evacuated hastily in the wake of some impending environmental disaster – an earthquake or a volcano eruption. I turn around to make sure there are no volcanoes, or mountains, or even sizeable hillocks around – total flatness, with lots of Soviet-style 'public voids' (Owen's Hatherley's term for squares and other purposeless public spaces of a typical 'socialist' townscape), with handfuls of red-brick cottages here and there. And – towering above it all – four huge priapic chimneys, the tallest I've ever seen, like some giant sentries guarding all that pointless nothingness,

I am in the centre of Stewartby, a 'model village' about 20 miles to the West of Fairfield, in the very heart of Bedfordshire. I stopped in that living (albeit already moribund) model of a modern Utopia-turned-Dystopia on the way to Panacea Headquarters in Bedford (see below). 'Model village' is here in quotes because, just like a New Town, or a Garden City, it denotes a particular type of a self-contained 'utopian' community, in this case, a settlement built by land or factory owners specifically to accommodate their workers. Other, better-known examples of British model villages include Port Sunlight, Bourneville and Saltaire, all of which we are going to visit later. Although more obscure than these, Stewartby is supremely graphic and therefore is indeed a model (this time without quotes) for studying the nature of a post-utopian settlement.

North Bedfordshire has always been famous for its special Lower Oxford Clay, formed 150 million years ago. With its 20 per cent moisture and 5 per cent marine organics, it could be pressed into a mould and fired without drying – all due to a high carbon content that ignited itself and brought itself up to full burning temperature without the need for using coal, which made the bricks much cheaper to manufacture.

Started in 1926 to house the workers of the famous London Brick Company, the village was named Stewartby after the company owners, the Stewart family. By 1936, it became the world's biggest producer of bricks, home to the world's biggest kiln and no fewer than 167 giant chimneys, of which there were just four left during my first visit there, in 2020 (see above). The factory churned out an astounding 18 million bricks a year They could produce more, yet never any fewer, and its brick makers enjoyed exemplary working conditions: pension schemes, paid holidays, profit sharing etc., and the use of an indoor swimming pool – a truly utopian scenario for the 1920s-30s, all courtesy of Sir Malcolm Stewart, who succeeded his father as the company's chairman in 1924.

The village quickly evolved into a model settlement, with neat Scandinavian-style workers' cottages, sports grounds, offices, canteens and a memorial hall. It all but absorbed the nearby hamlets of Wooton Pillinge and Wooton Broadmead and transformed itself into a lively near-urban settlement of the type of Cadbury's Bournville (see Chapter 10).

None of the original 167 chimneys are left at the moment of writing (as I made sure during my latest –and, most likely, last, flying visit to the village in November 2022): the last four were demolished on 28 September 2021. The brickworks themselves closed down in 2008 unable to meet the UK limits for sulphur dioxide emissions. Thus, the village had lost not just its main – and pretty much only – distinctive feature, but its very raison d'etre.

I could sense a strong feeling of something important being amiss, probably because the chimney silhouettes were still featuring prominently on many Stewartby symbols: on the village's emblem opposite the village hall, depicting a red-brick house and a kiln on the background of the Stewart clan tartan; in the letterheads of the parish council official documents, displayed on the notice board and probably (I couldn't discern the small print under the opaque misted glass) offering more financial help to the residents; and in the sign above the barred windows of the permanently closed Kiln restaurant, where letter 'I' was cleverly executed by an anonymous sign painter in the shape of a smoking chimney and in the style of a legendary Georgian artist Niko Pirosmani, who used to draw pub signs in exchange for food and booze.

Ironically, they were then talking of restoring one of the chimneys either as a historic monument, or as a functioning state-of-the-art giant incinerator of the type of Vienna's Spittelau one, designed by the famous Austrian artist Hundertwasser. That struck as a typically dystopian and typically Soviet scenario: it was habitual in the USSR to be allocated lots of money and other resources, including the ever-so-uncomplaining workforce, to undo the recently completed jobs.

History had nearly made a full circle in Stewartby – the village that had come back to the declining farming settlement it was before the brickworks. In short, the model village had hit a brick wall....

Stewartby's village hall was empty. A defibrillator was positioned at the entrance, and next to it, on a windowsill there rested a thick 'Accident Register', with all its pages reassuringly blank. I popped into a solitary corner shop, when during my previous visit one year earlier I found the lonely salesman asleep on the counter. This time there was no one inside. In response to my diplomatic loud cough, the same somnambulic salesman, looking dishevelled, as if he hadn't quite woken up for the whole year that had elapsed since my previous visit, stumbled in from a side room looking angry at having been disturbed.

'Do you sell scratch cards?' I ask him, just for the sake of asking.

'No, we don't do lottery!' he grumbled, avoiding eye-contact.

He was right. Stewartby had nothing left to gamble upon. Like many formerly utopian places, it had lost in the lottery of life. Yes, the village was still alive, but only just.

Apart from the suggested one-chimney revival, there have been other attempts to breathe new life into Stewartby. The most unlikely of them was the plan to make the inland village the location for the would-be 'National Institute for Research into Aquatic Habitats', just another name for a freshwater public aquarium. The project, with an expected cost of £350 million, was bound to fail, for a 'public aquarium' was the last thing needed in an inland village struggling for survival. And so it did, with the proposed aquarium site of 100 hectares sold with a loss of £4 million in 2015.

To me, it was almost physically painful to see the formerly thriving utopian community in decline. I firmly believe that Stewartby, with all its amazing industrial history and its unique identity, must be saved. While staring ruefully at the now chimneyless and therefore empty Stewartby skyline, I suddenly had an idea. Instead of the aquarium, good only for drowning one's sorrows, why not transform the village into an open-air museum of Britain's industrial Utopias, with many potential exhibits already in place?

I would be keen to visit such a museum.

That sad brick-and-chimneys story had an unexpected happy ending. Or so it sounded in February 2024 when it was announced that the site of the former Stewartby brickworks had been bought by ... wait for it ... Hollywood, or by Universal Studios, to be more exact, with a view of turning it into a theme park! What can I say? As an old Russian proverb goes, a sacred place is never empty!

There's much more to the county town of Bedford than its unforgettable 01234 phone code. In its rich history, in its quirkiness, its Georgian town squares and its present-day highly cosmopolitan character, it reminds me of London. A mini-London of sorts.

When in Bedford, I walk past Italian churches, social clubs and even an Italian Vice-Consulate. I spot cars with UK number plates adorned with small Italian flags. I drink espresso in the town's coffee shops (not necessarily with Italian names) full of smartly dressed brown-eyed *ragazzi* chatting away in a distinct Sicilian dialect. Yes, just like Hoddesdon, Bedford has a large Italian population, mostly comprised of the descendants of migrant workers from Sicily and Sardinia, recruited by the local brick factories in the 1950s. Unlike Stewartby, however, it was then far from a Utopia: no swimming pools here. Bedford's Italian diaspora was largely driven by poverty and despair.

In the early 1950s, Bedford's Marston Valley Brick Company found itself short of qualified workmen for the post-war reconstruction effort which, understandably, required lots of bricks. Emissaries were sent to the South of Italy, with its traditional 'insufficient employment'. Naples was made the centre of recruitment, and soon 7,500 workers from Apulia, Campania, Sicily, Abruzzo and Calabria arrived in Bedford on lucrative four-year contracts, often to the chagrin of their wives and other family members put off by cold weather and terrible post-war rations, mostly consisting of potatoes. In many cases, rather than fleeing poverty, the recruited workers and engineers ended up in worse living conditions than in Italy. They found solace in hard work, which included, among other things, the engineering of the revolutionary and then unique Fletton bricks, the 'greenest' ever produced. Those were made from the local Lower Oxford Clay, with its very high inbuilt fuel content.

Somewhat encouraged by the example of the first contractors, other Italian workers started arriving with their families. It was not long before specialist Italian shops, La Bottega Italiani and Ferretti's, opened in Bedford. Differences in work attitudes, however, led to mounting friction with the locals. In the words of the 1960s Bedford Mayor, 'an Italian singing in the street as he goes to work at 6.30 am is perhaps not appreciated by the rather staid Englishman who wants another hour in bed!' That and the shortage of accommodation for the new arrivals soon – a little over ten years after it started – brought the recruitment of Italian workers and engineers to a stop.

By then, the foundations of Bedford's Italian community had been firmly laid, and the persisting Italian subculture: all those authentic restaurants and cafes churning out the uniquely delicious pasta and the arrestingly aromatic espresso and cappuccino now constitute one good reason for visiting the town. That and Bedford's clean, cosy and famously quiet family pubs, which only tend to get lively when England plays Italy at soccer or rugby.

It wasn't just Italians who felt drawn to Bedford. In 1904, a large group of people, mostly women, moved there from different parts of Britain, firmly convinced that the real Garden of Eden used to be located there, heaven knows why (which may be true in this case). They were led and motivated by a certain Mabel Barltrop, also known as Octavia Daughter of God.

In 1919, the group, calling themselves the Panacea (meaning a magical cure for all ailments, a Utopia in its own right) Society, bought a large Victorian mansion in what is now Newnham Road in Bedford's poshest and leafiest residential area, with a vast garden and a number of outbuildings. Thus, they laid foundations for what was probably the most properly utopian settlement in British history, a unique community which only ceased to exist in 2013.

The story of that highly peculiar religious sect is fascinating, like a well-crafted fairy tale. Panacea's beliefs were based on the teachings of Joanna Southcott (1750–1814), a self-proclaimed prophetess from Devon who had faith in the imminent arrival of a messiah called Shiloh to lead herself and her followers to a Heaven on Earth. Southcott's best-known claim to sainthood was getting, allegedly (and I stress – allegedly), pregnant with the baby Shiloh at the tender age of 64, having been a virgin until then. Better late than never, as they say.

As numerous eye-witnesses hurried to confirm, Joanna's belly had indeed started growing, at which point her faithful followers hurried to buy baby's toys and clothes for the imminent arrival of little messiah Shiloh, or Messy Shilly, as they might have monikered the would-be baby among themselves, having either forgotten or being unaware of an old superstition to the effect that buying baby's paraphernalia before it is actually born is a bad omen that may result in a tragedy.

And so it happened. Or rather it didn't. The baby had never materialised and the hapless Joanna died of an aggressive form of stomach cancer. What everyone had thought was a baby bump was a large and eventually lethal malignant tumour.

One thing Joanna Southcott did manage to accomplish before her tragic death was sealing all her 65 books of prophesies in a large wooden box, having stipulated that they should only be opened, read and made public after twenty conditions were fulfilled, the most important of them being that the contents of the box could only be revealed in the presence of twenty-four bishops of the Church of England.

To cut a long story short, the box, wherever it may be now, apparently remains unopened. In the Panacea headquarters in Bedford, they had the accommodation for all 24 bishops ready and waiting until the sect's final demise in 2013. You can see all those spotless beds and bedrooms together with a life-size copy of Joanna's Box of Prophecies in the excellent Panacea Museum in Bedford on the very Newnham Street compound where the sect had thrived for over a hundred years.

There is no consensus as to the state, contents and the present-day whereabouts of the original box. Some believe that it contains the exact timetable of the second coming, while others assert that it holds nothing more than Joanna's lacy nightcap and, possibly, her silk nightgown. There's also an opinion that the box was opened in 1927 and its seemingly non-important contents were housed in one of London's libraries, possibly even in the British Library, whereas the empty box itself, having lost its purpose, is being kept in a British Museum cellar. Many hold the pessimistic view that the box exists no longer, with the maximalists (or rather the minimalists) in their ranks thinking that it had never existed at all. Who of the esteemed 'boxologists' is right, only time will tell. All it takes is getting 24 Anglican Church bishops – out of 106 presently in existence – together in the same little room (in the Panacea former HQ, it is indeed a small room), but which, all their cumbersome Episcopal gear considered, looks like an impossible task.

But back to the life of that incredible sect. The beautifully preserved, or rather conserved, mansion in Newnham Road, Bedford, is full of convincing proofs of how structured and orderly the routine of the Panacea Society was. Mabel Barltrop (née Andrews) had a fairly conventional middle-class upbringing and was the widow of a Church of England curate, Arthur Barltrop. After moving to Bedford with her four children (all boys) in 1904, she made a living by reviewing theological books under the pseudonym Mark Procter. Prone to depression, she was placed in mental institutions twice. Her followers were mostly well-off ladies

Trucks in the Garden of Eden

from a Church of England background who felt marginalised by society and barred from any significant role in the church. Among them were several suffragettes. Looking for solace and redemption, they became convinced that Mabel was the reincarnation of Shiloh, the eighth modern prophet, and named her Octavia.

In the Society's heyday, it had some 66 resident members (local schoolkids used to call them 'Bedford Witches'), all living in and around Newnham and Albany Road mansion, strikingly middle-class in the furnishings and interior design of its apexes and outbuildings. The sect then had over 2,000 other members all over the world.

The entrepreneurial ladies soon found an easy way to earn their living and even to make themselves wealthy. They started selling, mostly by postal orders, small bottles of water and pieces of linen which Octavia had, supposedly, breathed upon, thus turning them into a panacea – the cure for all ills. Thousands of orders were coming in from all over the globe (one can still see piles of them in the museum), which meant that many people were finding the pieces of cloth and drops of Bedford tap water helpful – another proof of the healing powers of strong beliefs and firm convictions. The sect was soon able to buy expensive furniture, and to hire cooks, servants and gardeners. The women had acquired their own printing press and had it installed next to the 'wireless room', where they would gather to listen to the radio. To recruit new members, they frequently threw lavish parties and held amateur theatre performances in the grounds.

Octavia choreographed all those events to the last detail. In her book *Octavia, Daughter of God: The Story of a Female Messiah and her Followers*, historian Jane Shaw reproduces her hand-written note in preparation for a January 1928 buffet supper party:

> No cider cup. More sugar in claret cup. No plum cake. Another kind of sandwich. Learn waltzes. Must have sufficient chairs for all in blue room. Servants should dress better. More light in supper rooms. Get all the plates very hot & each set out before they come to table.

One can be forgiven for visualising Octavia as a cross between a banana republic dictator and a modern self-aggrandising celebrity chef.

Alongside worshipping Octavia as 'the daughter of God', the Panaceans' main belief was that they inhabited the true Garden of Eden, extending for a three-mile radius from their mansion and the

Tavi and Chucho

chapel in which they prayed, whereas the rest of the world was the realm of Satan. In the words of Jane Shaw, 'Octavia had a vision that when Jesus came again, they would be strolling around the Garden of Eden with him and chatting on a first-name basis (as the two children of the same God should be – VV), eating delicious foods.'

I've gathered enough temerity to take that super-utopian vision one step further by assuming that Jesus would address his 'sister in spirit' Octavia (aka Mabel) as 'Tavi', and she would call Him 'Chucho' – as it is common to address men called Jesus in Mexico and some other Latin American countries. Below I will try and reproduce their imaginary verbal exchange during their leisurely stroll in Bedford's own 'Garden of Eden'.

> Octavia: So, Chucho, how do you like this Garden of Eden of ours? It is the authentic one, isn't it?
>
> Jesus: It does look good, Tavi, but my Garden is much bigger than yours. And much quieter.
>
> Octavia: Of course, brother Chucho, but don't forget that our Eden incorporates not just the little garden where we now walk, but also all the streets within the three-mile radius from it. The whole area of Bedford, in fact.
>
> Jesus: In which case, Octavia, you should do something about the traffic in those nearby streets. I can hardly hear what you are saying because of the noise behind the fence. The only sound one should hear in paradise is the divine chirping of my heavenly birds and the ear-caressing singing of my angels, not the din of cars and lorries. There are no trucks in *my* Garden of Eden!

I'm not sure if Jesus would have approved of Octavia's brisk trade in tap water and pieces of linen, transformed and sanctified by her own breath.

As I promenaded in the lush and beautifully landscaped gardens of the former 'Panacea Estate', now a popular venue for al fresco office parties, I felt that, all things considered, Panacea remained one of the most colourful and unorthodox religious communities in the whole of British history, for its members had demonstrated very clearly the amazing (and rather disturbing) ability of the human mind to cure all kinds of illnesses and disorders by the sheer power of an unquestioning faith. The brisk trade in tap water and pieces of linen had allowed the Panacea members to live the life of Riley:

they spent their time partying, praying and not doing any work, apart from occasional gardening.

Thus, they have nearly succeeded in that ultimate utopian endeavour – trying to 'embrace the unembraceable'.

※ ※ ※

In contrast to Panacea's laughable claims to have created a paradise on earth in the traffic-blighted centre of Bedford, Grantchester Orchard in the outskirts of Cambridge constitutes the closest imaginable approximation to the mythical Garden of Eden.

Grantchester itself is an ancient suburban village, which had become hugely popular in the UK as the venue of the eponymous TV series *Grantchester*, featuring a local priest-turned-detective, played by James Norton. It is an extremely well-heeled and expensive place to live that claims the world's highest concentration of Nobel Prize winners, many of whom reside in the village's picture-postcard thatched cottages and enjoy wild swimming in the River Cam and dining in one of Grantchester's period taverns, now disembowelled, painted yellow and turned into pricey 'gastropubs'.

It was all very different in 1897, when a group of Cambridge University (or 'Varsity' as it is called in the peculiar Cambridge slang) students visited Grantchester Orchard, first planted in 1868, and asked its proprietor, Mrs Stevenson, if she would kindly serve them tea under the blossoming fruit trees, thus starting a great Cambridge tradition (still alive now) as well as one of the most successful, if relatively short-lasting, British Utopias.

The word about the beautiful rural garden where Varsity students could enjoy affordable tea in conjunction with meaningful conversation, followed by long walks in the surrounding meadows or swimming in the river, spread around the colleges. The Orchard gradually became a popular students' resort, yet it was only in 1909, when Rupert Brooke, a promising young poet and a recent Classics graduate of King's College, took up residence at the Orchard House as one of Mrs Stevenson's lodgers, that a new utopian community, known as the Grantchester Group, was founded.

The charismatic young poet, whom W. B. Yeats once described as the handsomest man in England, had a hectic social life. He drew to Grantchester a stream of his learned friends, many of whom stayed overnight and soon became part of the quickly growing literary and scholarly commune called the 'New Pagans' by Brooke's close friend, Virginia Wolf, herself a group member. In a scene reminiscent of Bulgakov's *Master and Margarita*, she and Brooke used to swim naked by moonlight in the so-called 'Byron Pool' – a small haven of quiet Cam water, where Lord Byron himself used to swim with the swans whilst a student. What an idyll! Or rather, what a Utopia!

This is how Brooke himself described his Grantchester days in a letter to his cousin Erica Cotterill in 1909:

> It is a lovely village on the river above Cambridge... I work at Shakespeare, read, write all day, and now and then wander in the woods or by the river. I bathe every morning, and sometimes by moonlight, have all my meals (chiefly fruit) brought to me out of doors, and am as happy as the day's long.

Apart from swimming, Brooke and his mates liked to walk barefoot – Leo Tolstoy style – in the meadows, to canoe in the river, to pick up fruit and to consume enormous amounts of milk and honey – that old utopian, if not to say heavenly, diet. No wonder that in his poems Brooke repeatedly referred to Granchester Orchard as a heaven on earth:[6]

> But Grantchester! Ah, Grantchester!
> There's peace and holy quiet there,
> Great clouds along pacific skies,
> And men and women with straight eyes...

So, who are those 'people with straight eyes' that surrounded Brooke in Grantchester? There were the *crème de la crème* of the Cambridge academic and literary world: E.M. Foster, Bertrand Russell, Augustus John, Maynard Keynes, Ludwig Wittgenstein, to name but a few. And Rupert Brooke with Virginia Wolf were in the centre of the group. Can you imagine the level of scholarly discussions and friendly conversations of a gathering like that? I would give a lot for a chance to eavesdrop on them.

> In Grantchester their skins are white;
> They bathe by day, they bathe by night;
> The women here do all they ought;
> The men observe the Rules of Thought.
> They love the Good; they worship Truth;
> They laugh uproariously in youth;
> (And when they get to feeling old,

Trucks in the Garden of Eden

They up and shoot themselves, I am told)...

The last two lines of that slightly naïve but playful, youthful poem turned out to be almost self-prophetic for Brooke. He didn't shoot himself, but, having joined the military at the outbreak of the First World War he died of food poisoning on board a troop ship bound for Gallipoli in April 1915. He wasn't 'feeling old' either: not at 27.

> Deep meadows yet, for to forget
> The lies and truths, and pain? ... oh! Yet
> Stands the Church clock at ten to three?
> And is there honey still for tea?

The death of Ruper Brooke and the start of a global war after years of relative peace and quiet in the world ended the Grantchester Utopia. But not quite the Grantchester Group per se, which continued well into 1950s, its final years associated with Ted Hughes and Sylvia Plath, who lived near Grantchester Meadows and often visited the Orchard. In a letter to her mother, Sylvia Plath wrote:

> Remember Rupert Brooke's poem? Well we had tea by the roaring fire at the Orchard (where they serve tea under flowering trees at ten to three spring) and the 'clock was set at ten to three' and there was the most delectable dark clover honey and scones.

It was not quite the same though. The utopian atmosphere, created and maintained by the devotion and romanticism of Brooke and his talented acquaintances, had been lost forever.

The Orchard as such is still a popular place for visitors from all over the world, most of whom have no idea of its utopian past. Probably even too popular. Too many tourists turn it into a tourist dystopia during holiday season. The queues to the original wooden tea pavilion stretch into the village streets. People are prepared to queue for hours for a chance to have a cup of tepid tea, or a plate of lukewarm soup while sitting under a fruit tree in a squeaky and fragile log chair. One such chair collapsed and fell apart the moment I tried to sit in it one fine day. I ended up on the grass which was not as soft as I had expected it to be from Brooke's poems. The Grantchester Utopia had given me a kick in the butt!

The sure sign of the Orchard's forthcoming transformation (or shall I say degradation) was an eight-foot billboard, erected by

Tavi and Chucho

the proprietor and placed at the Orchard's entrance in the 1960s. It urged the 'customers' to return their cups and saucers to the tray-rack in 35 languages! Enough for solitude-prone Rupert Brooke to turn in his grave!

I still love walking on Granchester Meadows in late autumn and early spring, when they are free from tourist crowds and the only living creatures around are birds, grazing cows and a few cold-resistant Cambridge academics, swimming in pairs down the River Cam on their backs and discussing some obscure scientific issues as they float. Could it be that Alan Turing, another frequent visitor to the post-Brooke Orchard, had first conceived the idea of artificial intelligence while floating down the Cam?

After a good walk on the Meadows, I lie on the grass and, looking at the vast satin skies, silently recite Rupert Brooke's beautiful lines:

In Grantchester, In Grantchester! –
Some, it may be, can get in touch
With Nature there, or Earth, or such.
And clever modern men have seen
A Faun a-peeping through the green,
And felt the Classics were not dead
To glimpse a Naiad's reedy head,
Or hear the Goat-foot piping low...
But these are things I do not know.
I only know that you may lie
Day-long and watch the Cambridge Sky...

At which point, time as such disappears and I can see in the distance Rupert's lanky translucent figure, walking slowly towards the burning sunset.

Less than 30 miles to the north of Grantchester lies an unremarkable patch of farmland, once occupied by the Manea Fen Colony, a highly peculiar and by now all but forgotten utopian community that existed in Cambridgeshire between 1838 and 1841.

As it often happens, I first came across it accidentally – while gathering material on Octavia Hill – a Victorian reformer and founder of the National Trust. Her former house (now a museum) in Wisbech contained a scale model of the Manea Fen Community, about which I hadn't heard a thing until then.

Trucks in the Garden of Eden

My curiosity was sparked. From the substantive and hard-to-obtain volume *Utopia Britannica* compiled by Chris Coates, I learned the following:

Manea Fen (1838-41) – Founder/Leader William Hobson. 'Unofficial' Owenite community on 200-acre fenland estate. Built cottages, school, pavilion and their own windmill. Was the most radical and notorious of the Owenite communities in the UK. Issued its own newspaper 'The Working Bee' and had a uniform of Lincoln Green suits which gave the men the appearance of being part of Robin Hood's merry men. Failed to find markets for its goods and collapsed.

That was all. Not hoping to find many traces of the long-gone 'Owenite' (i.e. following the utopian socialist philosophy of the 19th-century Welsh social reformer Robert Owen) community, I drove through the unremarkable Manea Village of today, where the only reminder of the Colony was a solitary, as if accidentally dropped off the cart and left behind in haste, toponym, 'Colony Farm' – a chunk of ordinary farmland, with cattle grazing on it.

I was able to find out more at the Cambridgeshire Collection – a section of the Cambridge City Library sitting right on top a busy shopping centre. There I sat for several days, leafing through the faded issues of the *Working Bee* newspaper and trying to teleport myself 184 years back in time, the muffled din of the jolly pre-Christmas shopping mall reaching me from below.

Robert Owen (1771–1858) sincerely believed that a brave new world could be built on two pillars: the end of poverty due to the advances of technology, plus rational thought. From the early 1820s, he encouraged the creation of new small communities all over Britain, the number of which was soon well over a hundred.

One of Owen's most devoted followers was Fenland farmer William Hodson, who publicly vowed to build an exemplary Owenite community – ' a union of working classes' – on 200 acres of his own land in the Cambridgeshire Fens. In that community, he promised, there would be no social distinctions, no classes and no private property. Everything would be shared equally among the colonists. There were also rather vague promises of 'freer sexual unions' and joint childcare – a new moral order of sorts. Hodson, just like Owen himself, was a convinced technocrat and a firm believer in the transforming power of new technologies. In his declaration 'I will Endeavour', published in the *Working Bee*, he wrote:

> The food will be cooked by a scientific apparatus thus saving an immense labour to the females... Machinery, which has hitherto been for the benefit of the rich, will be adopted in the colony for lessening labour. A steam engine will be erected for thrashing and grinding corn, as well as steaming food for cattle and many other purposes.

Invited by Hodson, the first colonists started trickling in in 1838, and the initial progress was encouraging. Working days at Manea were much shorter than anywhere else, yet the villagers from outside the community complained that the colonists did not observe Sabbath (they carried on working on Sundays) and were therefore often branded 'infidels'.

The drainage work at Manea, which many colonists were supposed to do, was made particularly difficult by the presence of a buried pit band, or 'rodham' in the Fens dialect, formed from the Old Bedford River silt deposits, right underneath the village.

In line with Hodson's promises, money was abolished at Manea Fen, if only for a short while. In full accordance with the thoroughly utopian 'Builders of Communism Manifesto', adopted in the USSR in the early 1960s, its main principle being 'from everyone according to their abilities; to everyone according to their needs', later condemned as premature and 'voluntarist', the 'Communionists' (that was how the colonists sometimes referred to themselves, and the word might have eventually evolved into 'communists') shared duties according to their skills, ate the same food and abstained from alcohol (again, only initially). They were paid with so-called 'labour notes', which could be exchanged for supplies in the colony stores. A public library, a school and a kindergarten were opened – a unique scenario for early-Victorian villages. Women's dress, just like men's, was also that of Robin Hood foresters: tunic, hats and trousers to be worn under the skirts. A letter in the *Working Bee* describes the colonists' diet: 'We have pork, mutton and beef, cabbages, beans and peas ... we shall have plenty of excellent potatoes. We bake our own bread and biscuits, as we keep a baker ... we have four meals a day.'

Hodson's new technology ideas had also been implemented, little by little. All colonists' homes were well-heated and ventilated. An 'observatory', which doubled as a dining room with a view for forty people and a Union Jack on the roof was erected, and so was an impressive windmill, used by the 'hodsonians' not just for making flour but also, rather ingeniously, for cleaning the sticky fenland mud from their boots with rotating brushes.

It all went well for over a year, and in summer 1840 Hodson announced in the Working Bee his intention to produce agricultural machinery, 'those implements which are made by the better order of mechanics, such as thrashing machines, drills, etc.'

And then there came the anti-climax! There was no one to operate Hodson's sophisticated contraptions. The new settlers were not vetted for their work experience and qualifications, and half of them were illiterate (Samuel Rowbotham, the community's Secretary, one of the top positions in the Colony, was ignorant to the point of believing that the Earth was flat – a fact that he tried to prove using as an example the Old Bedford River which flanked the village). The other half were hedonistic or plain lazy. They were enjoying the good life and were less and less inclined to work, spending their days in drunken orgies.

In short, 'working bees' mutated into sad sacks, and the Colony became a neighbour from hell for the nearby towns and villages, whose disapproving citizens were no longer eager to buy Manea's agricultural and other products. Wild rumours (both true and false) about the colony were spreading all over England and had reached Owen himself, who was furious to see his principles distorted by ignorance and dissipation. Soon, Hodson's considerable personal resources petered out, and the local bank that used to deal with the Colony refused to support him.

Thus, Manea's Utopia came to an end, ruined, as it often happens, by its own main asset – the people – who, as it turned out, were simply not up to the task spiritually, educationally and morally.

If to the convinced reformers and socialists, like Hodson, the Manea experiment was an opportunity to put their idealistic theories into practice, the majority of the colonists saw it as a chance of an easier life, having undermined the old Biblical principle 'He who does not work, he shall not eat,' which Hodson made the Colony's main motto. As Soviet Union's proletarian poet Vladimir Mayakovsky once wrote (for a totally different reason): 'The boat of love has crashed against the rock of reality.'

Very little had been written on the Manea Colony since its collapse in 1841 until a couple of years ago when a *Cambridge News* website published an article with the attention-grabbing headline 'Archaeologists uncover Cambridgeshire's long-lost wife-swapping colony'.

I thought it was unfortunate that the supposed wife-swapping (I was unable to find any convincing proofs of it in the *Working Bee* pages), and not the Colony's unquestionable technological and social achievements were chosen as its most distinctive feature, With the excavations still in progress, I hope that in time, Cambridge archaeologists will be able to dig up some more utopian relics at Manea.

Chapter 5

St Evenage, aka Silkingrad

If your final destination is a bland, concrete ' New Town'...
there's always going to be a part of you dragging its feet.

Ian Moore, *A la Mod*

Among the best opening sentences of all time (like Joseph Heller's *Now and Then*: 'The Gold ring on the carousels was made of brass' and E.B. White's *Charlotte's Web*: 'Where's Papa going with that ax?'), I would include Bill Bryson's 'I come from Des Moines. Somebody has to.' That was how Bill started *The Lost Continent*, a book about his native country, the US. To echo Bill Bryson, whom I first met and befriended over 30 years ago in Australia, and to help you (and me) plunge into this important chapter, I want to make the following confession: 'I worked in Stevenage. Someone has to.'

This sentence – apart from being entirely truthful – can be interpreted in two ways: 1. that there are not too many people in Stevenage who actually do any kind of work and 2. that working in Stevenage is best avoided.

Here we are dealing with that rare example of double entendre when both implications mean the same thing: that Stevenage is a dump. By that I mean not the so-called Old Town, which basically consists of just one long High Street, with nice-looking Victorian and Edwardian houses, but the areas of a more recent development (albeit 'decline' would be a more honest word to describe it), officially designated New Town.

In fact, Stevenage was Britain's first 'New Town', announced in 1946 by the then Minister of Town and Country Planning Lewis Silkin. It was later mockingly monickered 'Silkingrad' by the project's opponents.

St Evenage, aka Silkingrad

New Town Stevenage was soon to be followed by Crawley, Harlow, Hemel Hempstead, Newton Aycliffe, Hatfield, Welwyn, Basildon, Bracknell and, of course, Corby – 'Home of Britain's Finest Trouser Press' (the tag is mine).

Out of sheer laziness, I might have omitted a couple of other hard-to spell places, including Peterlee, Glenrothes and, particularly, the Welsh town of Cwmbran, which is not only difficult to spell but also impossible to pronounce. Yes, you are right: all those 'new' towns, started with the best utopian intentions, have now become, if not the universal, then definitely national, symbols of ugliness and decay, with Silkingrad as the true flagship of history's biggest town-planning monstrosities – first purely architectural and then –inevitably (remember Churchill's 'first we shape our buildings and afterwards our buildings shape us') – social, or rather anti-social. Who or what were they able to 'shape' and are still shaping? Criminals? Drunks? Drug addicts? Social pariahs and parasites? Ignoramuses? Serial rapists, like David Garrick, the recently apprehended Stevenage-based ex-policeman?

I am being too harsh. Stevenage, after all, has also produced some excellent sportsmen (and women), including Lewis Hamilton; some good journalists, like Gary Younge; as well as the players of the eponymous – once non-league and now League Two – football club, who some time ago scored a spectacular FA Cup 3-1 win over Newcastle.

I worked in Stevenage for nearly 15 years and did not turn anti-social probably only because my workplace was located not in the town as such, but in the so-called 'Leisure Park' (an obvious misnomer for any kind of a workplace) in one of the suburbs, which can itself be described as a classic example of the concept of 'a suburb without an urb', once used (by Alan Coren, I believe) to describe Canberra.

To get to the town centre, the heart of the UK's first ever New Town, I had to cross a railway bridge and a couple of acres of wasteland occupied by endless semi-deserted car parks, where one could only park at the peril of being immediately towed away and therefore populated only with flocks of aggressive giant (and clearly anti-social) ravens and crows, who once brutally attacked a bald colleague of mine, attracted, or possibly irritated, by his gleaming dome. Initially, the town centre itself, dominated by the super-ugly and utterly (and Hatherley) dysfunctional Westgate shopping centre, had some nostalgic attraction, for it reminded me – much more so than Letchworth – of the similarly deprived and purposeless squares in the outskirts of Moscow.[7] Yet with time, going there daily during office breaks to do essential shopping had become disheartening and oppressive. I started avoiding those lunch-time pilgrimages, with each non-visit to Stevenage making me feel a better person.

I wasn't the only one to experience an aversion to New Town Stevenage. Here's how Clare Chambers, my fellow Royal Literary Fund Fellow and a talented novelist, described the place as seen by the protagonist of her novel *Editor's Wife* from the train window:

> A grey sky was made even greyer by the film of filth on the train windows, which gave onto a grim dystopia of identical biscuit-coloured houses, with patio doors like gaping mouths, and tiny shrubless gardens in which aluminium whirligigs of laundry bloomed in place of trees. On either side, the embankments of blackened brambles were strewn with discarded beer cans, broken bottles, car tyres, wooden pallets and whatever other trash the local residents could heave over their back fences. The sense of loathing for mankind that this scene provoked was out of all proportion...

My first-hand experience shows that the above description of an 'aversion' to (or a disgust for) Stevenage, so emotionally summarised by the protagonist of *Editor's Wife* as 'a downward pressure on my ribcage', could be applied to most of Britain's New Towns, with the possible exception of Milton Keyes, better known as 'model town'.

The British as a nation have a strong masochistic streak. They (you, we) love being ridiculed and laughed at by outsiders, but not half as much as making fun of themselves. The proof is the popularity of such self-denigrating books as *Crap Towns*, *Dull Men of Great Britain*, *Britain's Worst Walks* (which I was once asked to endorse and was very happy to oblige) and *Boring Postcards*. A second-hand copy of the latter, released by Phaidon and acquired by me for £2.99 at the Oxfam bookshop in Hertford, is now on the desk in front of me. Its title page, with no visible title, carries a handwritten dedication: 'Happy 50th Mike. With best wishes Keith and Diane'. I can only guess how low was the regard that mysterious Keith and Diane held poor Mike in, if the only present they thought he was worthy of on his 50th was *Boring Postcards* – and yet paradoxically, in a very British way, how high their esteem. It's the thought that counts.

St Evenage, aka Silkingrad

Leafing through this book for a tad over five minutes made me want to first climb walls and then to choke on my computer mouse – anything not to see those horrific postcards, which struck me as not just boring, but soul-destroying, in the aggressive drabness of the city- and townscapes they depicted alongside bridges, factories, shopping malls and motorway service areas. Significantly, the so-called 'New Towns' featured on most of the postcards, with Basildon and Stevenage as undisputed 'star models'– Naomi Campbells and Gigi Hadids of urban ugliness.

So, how did it all begin? Like all failed Utopias, Stevenage and other New Town projects started with generally good intentions, embedded in the post-WWII Abecrombie Greater London plan, which proposed eight new satellite towns 'to serve Greater London', with another six in other parts of Britain. Stevenage was to be the first victim of that deeply 'socialist' urban planning, sacrificing quality in favour of quantity and beauty in favour of immediate ostensible practicality. It was not surprising therefore that the 37-year-old Liverpool-born architect Gordon Stevenson, who had studied at the Institute of Urbanism in Paris and was heavily influenced by the iconic modernist planner Le Corbusier (he was the first ever Briton to work in his atelier), was appointed the head of the Town and Country Planning Ministry's planning team.

A much more surprising choice was the appointment of the architect Clough William-Ellis, the legendary creator of the fanciful Welsh town of Portmeirion (see Chapter 9), whose famous motto was 'Cherish the past, adorn the present, construct for the future', the Chair of the hastily created Stevenage New Town Development Corporation. The past was certainly not 'cherished', nor the present 'adorned' (it was rather disfigured) in the New Towns project.

Speaking at a public meeting in Stevenage on 6 May 1946, Lewis Silkin stated:

> During the war years we in this country stood together and suffered together, whilst fighting for an ideal, for democracy in which we all believed. I am sure that this spirit is not dead in Stevenage, and if you are satisfied that this project is worthwhile, and for the benefit of your fellow human beings, you will be prepared to play your part to make it a success.

To me, Silkin's rhetoric sounds painfully familiar. Whenever Soviet leaders introduced yet another totalitarian law or regulation, they would always invoke collective suffering, democracy and fighting for ideals. Silkin's words were like a quote from one of the speeches of Stalin or Brezhnev. But post-war Britain was not quite like the Stalinist USSR, and Silkin's words about the quiet farming town's massive expansion through the construction of hundreds of new apartment blocks, industrial estates, car parks and shopping malls in the middle of the pristine Hertfordshire countryside did not go down that well with the 350 people crammed into the Stevenage Town Hall and the 3000 more who had gathered outside and were listening to the speech via the loudspeakers. The crowd was unenthusiastic about the suggested increase of Stevenage's population from 6000 to 60000.

According to a *Manchester Guardian* report, the people, worried for their livelihoods, were voicing concerns that Stevenage was bearing the brunt of some crazy national experiment, that the whole of the town's history had been uprooted and that it had been done in a dictatorial fashion. Silkin's speech was frequently interrupted by jeering, to which he at some point reacted with: 'It's no use jibbing, it's going to be done!' The remark was countered with cries of 'Gestapo!' and 'Hark, hark the dictator!'

Towards the end if his speech, Silkin stated that 'the project with go forward because it must go forward' (reminding me of the gibberish Soviet slogan 'The teachings of Marx are powerful because they are correct!'). He also assured listeners that soon 'People from all over the world will come to Stevenage to see how we here in this country are building for the new way of life.'

He left the hall to find that a tyre of his official car had been deflated and sugar in the petrol tank.

In December 1946, shortly after Stevenage New Town was formally designated despite all the protests, local activists replaced the Stevenage railway station nameboards on the platforms and at the station entrance with 'Silkingrad', which, in the words of a witness, 'consciously evoked Soviet totalitarianism'. The boards were removed after a day, but the story soon spread around the world (you can still see a photo featuring that sign in the permanently deserted Stevenage Museum, right across the busy road from the brutalist – and, possibly, the world's ugliest – church, St Andrew and St George, another unfortunate creation of the New Town project). The challenge against Silkin's decision was then lodged in the High Court, which eventually ruled in support of the project.

The construction of a new urban Utopia got under way. Unsurprisingly (this time), the first human casualty of the endeavour

St Evenage, aka Silkingrad

was Clough William-Ellis, who resigned from his post of Development Corporation Chair in 1947. For anyone familiar with the uncanny beauty, historical accuracy and impressive functionality of Portmeirion (see Chapter 9), it is not hard to guess why.

What was so objectionable, you may ask, in that nice-sounding plan, which, according to the 1946 New Town Act, aimed to liberate the working people from the smog and cramped living conditions of London and other big cities and move them into new, neat and close-knit urban settlements? What was it that prevented the realisation of the utopian dream, so clearly expressed by Lord Beveridge MP, who was also the Chair of the Newton Aycliffle development corporation: 'We have set out to try to make a perfect town, a town in which every man, and above all, every housewife, will want to live – a town of beauty and happiness and community spirit.'?

Well, I've already shared with you some of my first-hand impressions of present-day Stevenage and will share some more later. For reasons of impartiality, however, I refer you to a November 2016 online BBC feature with an evocative headline: 'Stevenage: the town that aimed for Utopia'. Who could be more impartial than the viewer- and listener-supported national public broadcaster with a strict remit to maintain balance in its reporting? Here's how it starts:

> Viewed on a grey November day, Stevenage town centre is perhaps not seen in its best light. The wind whips loose leaves round a large public square dominated by a Mondrian-inspired clock tower and fountain. Faded, tired concrete is visible as far as the eye can see. It is a bit bleak. Many of the buildings look in dire need of a bit of TLC and no-one seems keen on hanging around to people-watch or admire the view. Grey and somewhat uninspiring it may be, but Stevenage's political architect Lewis Silkin originally envisaged it as a 'gay and bright' place.

I liked the 'political architect bit! It reminded me of my times as an interpreter for the Soviet Ministry of Culture in Moscow in the late 1970s. I enjoyed interpreting at official receptions and banquets. At one such banquet, the USSR Deputy Minister of Culture Ivanov asked a high-ranking foreign visitor what parts of the Soviet Union he would particularly like to see. The foreign guest decided to respond with a joke: 'Just don't send me to Gorky, where you have exiled your Academician Sakharov.'[8] I diligently interpreted his remark, and that very second was tugged on the sleeve by a woman

Trucks in the Garden of Eden

from the Soviet Ministry of Culture sitting beside me. 'Change the subject quickly!' she hissed. After the banquet, she approached me and said: 'Vitali, you've committed a gross political mistake. You shouldn't have translated that sentence about Sakharov.'

'But as an interpreter I surely must convey all remarks adequately,' I objected.

'A Soviet interpreter must be more than just an interpreter,' she declared gravely. 'He must be a political interpreter!'

The BBC feature goes on to say that 'Silkin presented a utopian vision' whereby the rich would mix with the poor ... a new type of citizen, a healthy, self-respecting, dignified person with a sense of beauty, culture and civic pride' would be created.

Was it from Silkin's inane pronouncements that the anonymous Soviet writers copied their 'Builders of Communism Moral Code', released in 1961, right after the 21st Congress of the CPSU? At which Khrushchev opportunistically (as it was claimed later) proclaimed that the 'current generation of Soviet people will live under Communism!' The main point of that utopian Manifesto, the one on which the totalitarian state had failed to deliver so spectacularly was precisely that, the 'creation of the new type of a perfect human being'.

To be fair, it was not just St Evenage that kept receiving such negative coverage from independent media and other sources. 'The village green community is being replaced by elongated terraces in rows upon rows of barracks, with no privacy, no refinement and very little green to break them up.' And more succinctly: 'A concrete jungle... Just loads of roundabouts... A dump.' These quotes refer to other New Towns (Newton Aycliffe, Harlow, Milton Keynes, etc.) but they can be readily applied to Stevenage, too.

In the Stevenage Museum, I picked up a glossy brochure published by the Museum itself and featuring the 'early memories of Stevenage New Town', mostly euphoric, but also mildly critical, like this one by a Mrs Rees:

> One of the big problems we had in town was earwigs. The town was swarming with earwigs, thousands of earwigs, they said it was because of the chalk and under the stones [sic]. And McDougal was General Manager [of Stevenage Development Corporation] at the time and I wrote him a letter in which I said that: 'Old McDougal had a town, earwig, earwig, go, with an earwig here, an earwig there, an earwig nearly everywhere, Old McDougal had a town, earwig, earwig go.

St Evenage, aka Silkingrad

The anonymous authors of the brochure had committed a significant error in its title – 'Brave New World', which they had borrowed from Aldous Huxley's eponymous dystopian novel. They obviously did not bother to read the novel and had missed the not-too-subtle irony of the Shakespearean title Huxley had chosen for his famous literary dystopia, in which he satirises the very idea of scientific progress and – to quote my own 'Utopia Primer' (see Appendix 2) – describes' a scientifically engineered technocratic hell ... awash with recreational drugs, test-tube babies, "feelie" cinemas and Neo-Pavlovian conditioning of humans'.

With the possible exception of test-tube babies and 'feelies', this sounds like a passable description of modern Stevenage, with its conspicuous 'sex drugs and sausage rolls' attitude to life.

'First, we shape the buildings.'

Yes, Stevenage's notorious multi-storied beehives, together with its 'elongated' and graceless terraced houses, have shaped a vigorous culture of drugs and crime. In 2023, the crime rate in Stevenage was 17 per cent higher than the overall East of England figure and 8 per cent higher than the UK figure (excluding Scotland), according to www.crimerate.co.uk. The headlines of an issue of North Hertfordshire's local newspaper, the *Comet*, speak for themselves: 'Woman sexually assaulted'; 'Class A drugs and weapons seized in raid'; 'Chances missed to stop serial rapist'; In response to damage in Fairlands Valley Park, the paper quotes a spokesperson for Stevenage Borough Council as saying: 'Unfortunately, the newly-planted woodland has been subject to mindless vandalism.'[9]

Unfortunately? I would rather say, logically! Mindless architecture and mindless town planning inevitably lead to mindless vandalism.

That sad conclusion comes from nearly 15 years of working in Stevenage. Looking back at that St Evenage period in my life, I recall several seemingly disconnected episodes, which – taken together – should give an adequate impression of *my* perception of Britain's first, and, sadly, not last, New Town.

Episode One. Stolen rolls.

The first episode comprises not my own impressions, but those of a couple of my dear friends from Kent who once came to spend a day with me in Letchworth but chose to spend the night in a Stevenage hotel, right in the middle of the 'new' town centre. It was their first ever visit to Silkingrad, and that's why they found themselves thoroughly unprepared for the scene they witnessed in the morning, while having a buffet breakfast at the hotel's ground-floor restaurant. The hotel's breakfast buffet would not have won three Michelin stars. In all honesty, it wouldn't have won one tenth of one star. In an unfinished book of mine, I suggested grading bad hotels and restaurants not with stars, but with spiders. Had my suggestion been taken onboard, that breakfast buffet, consisting of a plateful of tired wrinkled sausages, cold goo-like scrambled eggs (which looked as if they had been expurgated from the previous breakfasters' stomachs), brownish and suspiciously foamy 'orange juice' in a tall glass tank with a tap, and such like.

My life-loving friends did not dare to touch (let alone to eat) anything from that potentially deadly buffet and were about to leave the restaurant when the chef, or some other kitchen worker in striped pants and an almost white jacket brought in a large tray with freshly baked and still slightly steaming bread rolls on it. The rolls were round and temptingly puffy, like faces of well-nourished babies who have just woken up after a good night's sleep and keep smiling happily at the world around them. They were silently inviting the accidental tenants of that bedraggled Stevenage hotel and customers of the toxic novichok-like breakfast buffet to gobble them up.

My friends turned around and, with their hands longingly outstretched towards the rolls hurried back to the buffet. But before they could reach the coveted tray, a drunk woman burst into the restaurant through the door, open to the grim and littered New Town streets. In fact, she almost fell into the room – being so drunk (at 8am) that she could hardly maintain her balance as she stumbled towards the buffet, grabbed the tray with both hands and staggered back into the street.

For moment, both the customers and the restaurant staff, including the striped chef, shocked by such blatant day-time robbery, froze. Then they all rushed out into the street hoping to apprehend the thief. But the adroit (even if squiffy) roll-stealer was nowhere to be seen. The street was deserted except for a couple of blanket-wrapped rough-sleepers in doorways and piles of yesterday's litter, stirred and moved along the pavement lazily by a gentle morning breeze.

So deeply shocked were my friends by that near-surreal episode of Stevenage life that they could hardly talk about anything else for several days. They solemnly vowed not to set foot in Stevenage for as long as they lived...

St Evenage, aka Silkingrad

Episode 2. St Andrew, St George and St Evenage.

The massive brutalist Church of St Andrew and St George – the largest Parish church built in the UK since the Second World War – is rightly considered one of Stevenage's main tourist attractions. I would even call it the one and only proper tourist attraction of the New Town, for the only other touristy site, designated by the brown road signs, is the 'Leisure Park', that vast US-style shopping mall-like area where I had the misfortune to work for a number of years. I was always puzzled by that 'Tourist Attraction' sign, for the only new experience a tourist arriving by accident could glean from the Leisure Park, adjoining the railway station, would be getting his car clamped by the merciless security agency zealously patrolling the Park's only square as if it were their own backyard, or being attacked by either an unkindness of ravens or a murder of aggressive crows (see above).

If it were up to me, I would add to the scanty list of Stevenage's tourist attractions the local police station – a giant multi-storied glass-and-concrete near-skyscraper on the way from the Leisure Park to the New Town centre. It used to strike me as possibly the largest police station in the world, a Police Mahal, to draw an analogy with the enormous Tesco store in the neighbouring town of Baldock, which I dubbed Tesco Mahal for its ornate facade, gables and Corinthian columns. A police station of such size would not be out of place in the roughest areas of Detroit, Johannesburg, Port-au-Prince or Mexico City, but seems a tad over the top for a town of 89,000 people. The policemen must be having a lot of work in Stevenage. And they certainly do, as I myself discovered on the day when with my partner Christine we decided to take some photos of the famously brutalist Stevenage Parish Church which I would have been tempted to brand Church Mahal for its enormous size, were it not for its extreme ugliness.

We parked our car in one of the windswept and permanently empty car parks, built as part of the same New Town project. Leaving our Toyota there on its own that Sunday afternoon did not feel either safe or right. Our only hope was that the jalopy was too old and unattractive to temp any possible carjackers. We then had to walk past a row of three- or four-storied prefab apartment blocks, built by the New Town Development Corporation in the 1950s, now looking drab, battered and in desperate need of repairs.[7] Judging by the rags drying on each balcony and the frequent drunken shouting reaching us from behind the windows, those good intentions – as it often happens – led to something directly opposite to happiness: poverty and despair.

Trucks in the Garden of Eden

We then had to walk through a dark and smelly underground subway, so scary and uninviting that even graffiti artists must have been discouraged by its damp, crumbling walls. In the middle of the passage, we were suddenly overtaken by a cyclist on a rusty squeaky bike sagging under his semi-exposed ample buttocks, spilling out of his soiled tracksuit pants. From one of the bike's handles, a heavy plastic carrier bag was swinging. The biker himself, stout and middle-aged, was pressing the pedals with an effort. His whole appearance and demeanour seemed incompatible with cycling as a sport, or even a healthy pastime.

The moment we emerged from the subway, the Church of St Andrew and St George, founded in 1956 and consecrated in 1960, all but fell on top of us, with all its precast concrete columns, its vast interfacing arches and its 106-feet-high campanile, with a huge concrete cross on top.

While Christine was busy taking photos, I kept squinting past the Church into a dark leafy alley of a small park, no more than 150 yards from where I stood, where a group of males congregated. I could even hear their muffled agitated voices, as if they were arguing. They were all taking part in a succession of transactions, with small white packets of something passed around and sniffed. For some reason, the scene brought to memory a Russian expression to describe a commotion: 'Lots of noise but no fighting!'

The fat subway cyclist was there too, still astride his bike, now stationary. He suddenly looked back straight at me, said something to his cronies and pedalled on further away from them and from me. He was probably a 'shuttle', a courier who delivers stuff to street sellers.

Having watched my share of gangster movies, I told Christine to pack up her camera pronto. 'One moment!' she said. As a devoted tyro photographer, she was clearly mesmerised with the heavy gracelessness of the Church.

I looked back at the non-religious congregation in the park and realised it was too late to retreat: the small crowd had dispersed and one of them, a lanky lad, with his right hand in his trouser pocket, was pacing towards me decisively, if somewhat unsteadily. He stopped a couple of metres in front of me, squinting suspiciously at Christine, who was hurriedly packing up her tele-lens.

'Tourists?' he barked out. 'Taking pictures?' Those sounded like statements rather than questions.

He had a young, yet already chronically puffed-up face, that of a teenage alcoholic, with the blank glassy eyes of the long-time drug addict and a red nose resembling a sloppily printed map of London

St Evenage, aka Silkingrad

Underground. As he spoke, he kept his right hand in his pocket, which contained something heavy and bulky.

I looked around: the whole surrounding area was deserted and I suddenly realised that our lives could depend on my answer.

I remembered how a colleague from *The European* newspaper where I worked as a staff columnist in the 1990s kept telling me: 'Vitali, please never lose your lovely accent!' He also advised me to always speak Russian to the notoriously fraudulent and bullish Prague taxi drivers of the 1990s, who were afraid of only one thing, the Russian mafia, as the best guarantee against being fleeced by them.

'*Da, mi turisti iz Moskvi!*' ('Yes, we are tourists from Moscow!'), I answered in Russian and repeated in a deliberately broken English, with an exaggerated Russian accent: 'Us are turisti of Moscow!'

The lad's shapeless face got further distorted by a grimace, probably intended as a smile. 'I thought you were f***ing cops!' he mumbled through his clenched brown teeth and added more amicably: 'Nice church, innit?'

Having said that, he turned away, spat on the ground and waddled off.

Two weeks later I read in a local newspaper about a police raid on the small park near the Church of St Andrew and St George, where drugs and small arms were routinely changing hands.

Episode 3. 8XL Dan.

Here's an extract (paragraph 2.25, with the orthography and punctuation of the original kept intact), from 'Stevenage District Plan. Alterations', released by Stevenage Borough Council in March 1986. I accidentally came across that sloppily printed and carelessly stapled brochure at the very bottom of the cardboard box, full of local ephemera and paraphernalia inside 'Junk & Disorderly' antiques barn in Letchworth:

> Although the layout and the design of the town centre is considered to be of historic importance the concept of an open-air pedestrian shopping centre is becoming increasingly dated. It is essential that the Town Centre shopping area is commercially attractive as possible. Careful consideration must be given to any proposals to cover the malls to avoid a claustrophobic design. Partial covering at the intersections may avoid some of this problem.

And covered it was (or shall I say 'covered up'?). The next, TC17 paragraph of this amazingly sincere, if not too literate, document, which I am tempted to call a confession of the town's ugliness, says (all in capital letters – to add authority to the statement, no doubt): 'THE BOROUGH COUNCIL WILL FAVOURABLY CONSIDER PROPOSALS FOR COVERING THE MAIN SHOPPING MALLS WHERE APPROPRIATE.'

That was probably the first and only attempt to avoid claustrophobia by covering an open-air space (unless, of course the District Plan authors were not quite sure what the word 'claustrophobia' meant).

Little did St Evenage town fathers know that by covering up some of the town centre's spectacular ugliness (of which, to be honest, quite a lot still remained undisguised) they were following in the footsteps of Prince Potemkin of Russia (See Chapter 1), who once famously misled Empress Catherine the Great by installing huge canvasses, with idyllic prosperous villages painted on them, along the banks of the Dnieper River, down which the notoriously short-signed Empress sailed to inspect her dominions.

Well, actually, I am wrong here: that comparison does not quite suit the stealthily concealed Stevenage street market, for even when covered it looked ugly and all but blended into the surrounding brutalist house facades.

A much better metaphor would be that of the brown wrapping paper– cheap and rough – in which they used to wrap anything untoward and embarrassing in the USSR; for example, special food parcels for the elite. I watched repeatedly how the entitled bureaucrats and apparatchiks were carrying such bashfully wrapped brown parcels out of a 'closed shop' (another Soviet oxymoron) in Granovskogo Street, a stone's throw from the Kremlin. And once, my Moscow landlady, a General's widow, who was entitled to special food supplies courtesy of her dead husband, asked me to pick up her food parcel from there. On leaving the 'closed' shop, the lucky clients were looking around like troubled birds, as if ashamed of their privileged status (which they certainly were not). While doing so, they pressed their plain-looking parcels close to their chests, as if protecting them from being snatched by passing pedestrians – members of the *naseleniye*, the 'population', as they used to refer to the ordinary Soviet citizens. And rightly so, for under the unpretentious cover, some utopian delicacies, unseen and often unheard of by that very 'population', could be found:

St Evenage, aka Silkingrad

from hard-to-obtain oranges and quality sausages to impossible-to-obtain sturgeon caviar and smoked salmon.

It is important to understand that the wrapping paper, used in 'ordinary' shops for the 'population' to wrap up semi-rotten potatoes or stale loafs was exactly the same: cheap, rough and greyish brown. They used it in 'closed shops' to disguise the elitist food parcels – the complete opposite to the Potemkin Villages, yet no less shameful and disgusting a gimmick. As Karl Shlogel, a German writer and historian, noted in his remarkably comprehensive book, *The Soviet Century*, it was that 'coarse grey-brown' Soviet wrapping paper that 'really had been representative of an entire [Soviet] period'.

The wrapping paper, not the state window-dressing of space exploration, ballet and nuclear physics, represented the Soviet regime's true nature. Such typically 'socialist' types of camouflage could be summarised by the English expression 'out of sight – out of mind'; or by another one that I have just invented: 'If you have a problem, cover it up and pretend it never existed!'

Both of the above expressions could be used to describe the way Stevenage Street Market was dealt with. With the covering up completed, it was of course renamed Stevenage Indoor Market.

During my countless, almost daily, lunchtime walks around the shopping area in the town centre, I was for some time unable to spot the Street Market, so well it was covered. But when I finally did find it and popped in, I was disappointed. The newly covered area was nearly free of customers. A handful of sleepy stall holders were calling out to each other across the aisles – just to keep each other awake, most likely. The goods on sale – clothes, shoes, VHS cassettes and vinyl discs – all appeared second-hand. The food stuffs, lollies, cheeses, fruit and breads, looked as if they had already been eaten by someone. Wandering around the coyly covered market was like journeying back in time, into 1950s England as I imagined it from books and movies.

But there was one notable big exception. I would say even an XXXXXXXX Large exception – 'BIG DAN'S CLOTHING STALL – 2XL UP TO 8XL'. You must forgive me for using the capitals here again, but this time it wasn't under the influence of paragraph TC17 of the above-quoted District Plan. I simply could not make myself use small letters on this occasion, for everything about Dan's Clothing Stall was huge. Including Dan himself – a giant of a man with an unexpectedly pleasant and polite tone of voice.

Here I have to confess that, not being so slimline myself, I had a secret mission: to find a large, possibly even an extra-large, jacket for myself. But Dan promptly dashed my hopes: 'Sorry, mate, but we do not do the 40s or 50s sizes – too small for us!'

It turned out that the smallest jacket they had on offer was a XXXX. In contrast to other stalls inside the market, Dan's clothes were smart and good-quality (with prices to match), but they were all super-super-size. I thought that a stall like that would not be out of place in a Sumo wrestlers' training camp. But Dan assured me that business was good. 'We are very busy here in Stevenage!' he said as I was leaving, and he invited me to come back. I was relieved that he didn't add 'when you put on five stone'.

Back at home, having checked online the ever-changing obesity scale of Britain, I realised that Dan had a point: several New Towns, including Stevenage and Milton Keynes, were in the top ten highest obesity rate areas. That added a new meaning to the famous expression by Winston Churchill, no sylph himself, that we first shaped buildings and then they started shaping (or misshaping) us.

Here I have to repeat that the last thing I wanted to do was thoughtlessly to malign Stevenage, the town where I had worked and where I still have many friends. And although it is not one of my pleasantest memories, I will never forget the three weeks I spent in Stevenage's Lister Hospital, where I ended up with severe infection after open-heart surgery in 2017. Several times I was close to dying, but I was saved by the wonderful doctors and nurses of the hospital's cardiological unit. As well as by two intravenous drips, which I christened Debby and Dea, my only company for up to 20 hours a day.

Stevenage's deplorable state – both architectural and social – is the cause of my concern, and my criticism of the town as it is now has only one purpose, to make it better, which is also the aim of the latest town regeneration plan, striving, according to the *Hertfordshire Mercury* newspaper, 'to bring the UK's first New Town back to life' – a rare acknowledgement of the existing moribund state of St Evenage, which the paper describes as 'a grey, depressing, ugly, negative place'.

The latest 1-billion-pound town centre regeneration plan includes over 7,300 new properties by 2028, new shops, bars and restaurants, an expanded railway station and so on. When I first saw it, it appeared scary. I have always been of the opinion that to radically change a place, you have first to erase and create something different in the vacated space. It looks like in Stevenage they are thinking of preserving the New Town's architectural monstrosities and adding new structures to them. The very thought of 7,300 new houses, no matter how modern and practical, in the same long-suffering town that – prior to the New Town 'revolution' – used to be home to just over 6000 people, gives me the creeps.

That ambitious (perhaps overambitious) Stevenage redevelopment plan is not the first. The previous one fell apart in 2008 after the financial crisis, and then all new construction sites were shut down by the coronavirus pandemic. At the time of writing, reconstruction has resumed on most of the projects, including in the long-suffering Town Square. My only hope is that it will focus not on expanding the 'depressing, ugly' Stevenage metropolis even further but will focus on underused spaces and forgotten parts of the town.

In its entirety, the regeneration plan sounds like a good idea which, I hope, will work and will play the role of my life-saving Lister Hospital drips: Debby and Dea – for neither Silkingrad, nor St Evenage, but just for Stevenage, the town that desperately needs an intake of fresh blood to avoid terminal heart failure.

I could have gone on and on about the New Towns disaster. The history and the present-day state of most of those hapless places are similar to those of Stevenage. Apart perhaps from Milton Keynes, which is sometimes called a token successful New Town. Yes, to be honest, it does stand out, while being also a 'model town', with its un-English grid-style layout, lots of green spaces and lakes inside the urban area, and its multiple post-Soviet-city-style 'public voids'. Those are the features I like about Milton Keynes. On the other hand, I actively detest its street numbers instead of street names – a poor imitation of Manhattan, its endless and faceless semi-underground shopping malls, and its 150-odd roundabouts, more even than in Stevenage! But all things considered, Milton Keynes is not such a bad place to live in after all.

To recapitulate, let's ask ourselves what lay at the base of the spectacular fiasco of the New Town Utopia? To me, the answer is obvious: it was a blatant disregard for basic human needs and values for the sake of the dictatorial (or electoral, for that matter) bureaucratic ambitions – the same as it was in the USSR and other totalitarian states. A different but allied reason can be found in John Boughton's heartfelt book *Municipal Dreams. The Rise and Fall of Council Housing*, according to which it was 'a gulf ... between aspiration and economic reality'.

My long-time exposure to the tragic decline of Stevenage and other Britain's 'New Towns' made me think that, alongside the trials for crimes against humanity, it would be good to set up an international tribunal for the misdeeds against towns and cities to name and punish those responsible for destroying their faces and souls!

I hate to bring you (and myself) back to St Evenage, but as I was in the middle of writing this book there came the news of yet another, the umpteenth, grand plan to galvanise the town. 'Stevenage new town is set for a revamp with almost 1,900 extra homes and new shopping areas,' the indispensable *Comet* newspaper reported triumphantly on 15 June 2023. The latest plan engenders a strong feeling of déjà vu: more shopping malls and car parks, with a couple of new 'public voids' and happy workers' fountains, euphemistically, or rather 'PC-mystically referred to in the plan as 'enhanced natural landscaping for town centre living'.

There is, however, one new and rather prominent, in more than one sense, feature to this plan: a cluster of high-rise blocks, including a 19-storey 'landmark building', the Vista Tower, to to further enhance the already 'enhanced natural landscape'. If this plan comes to fruition, then the vista from the top of the new Vista Tower could be reminiscent of a huge sack of potatoes that had burst at the seams and had been carelessly dropped onto the ground by a tired stevedore. 'When everything else fails, build skyscrapers!' seems to be the favourite slogan of the architects trying to 'regenerate' the decaying British towns these days.

And here's the first local feedback to this plan that hasn't been started yet, and, hopefully, never will be:

> The plan will turn Stevenage, already not a pretty part of the country [classic English understatement] into a commuter sleeping town in which no one will take care of the local environment... This [Vista Tower] is atrocious. Look at the sheer size of the building!

Nothing can deter the dogged Stevenage town planners, however. They have solemnly declared the plan is nothing but 'a catalyst for future phases which will deliver new homes, in addition to retail and commercial floorspace'. (Don't you think that their clumsy way of expressing themselves is similar to the architectural mess they have created?) This is how Utopias end!

So for St Evenage it's 'plus ca change!' and 'deja vu', which, in plain English, add up to one rhetorical question: 'will we ever learn?'[10]

Chapter 6

Motopia, or 'Let's Kill the Car'!

The real nightmare begins when some idiot tries to turn a Utopia into reality.

> Dmitri Bikov, a Russian dissident
> writer living in the US

Before we embark on a long and dangerous South-North car journey from the village of Wraysbury off the M25 (in this chapter) all the way to the UK's Foula and Fair Islands in search of Britain's Utopias, let us take a short and only partially motorised detour.

We begin with a protracted, yet highly relevant, quote:

Pedestrians should be loved.

Pedestrians make up the greater part of mankind. Not only that, the finer part. Pedestrians created the world. It was they who built towns, put up skyscrapers, installed drainage and plumbing, paved the streets and lit them with electric lights. It was they who ... invented printing, thought up gunpowder, built bridges across rivers, deciphered the Egyptian hieroglyphs, introduced the safety razor, abolished slavery and discovered that a hundred and fourteen tasty, wholesome dishes could be made from beans.

And then, when everything was ready, when our planet had acquired a comparatively well-planned appearance, the motorists appeared.

It should be noted that the motor car was also invented by pedestrians. But for some reason the motorists soon forgot about that. They began to run over the meek and mild, clever pedestrians. The streets, built by the pedestrians, passed into the hands of the motorists. The roads were doubled in width and the sidewalks were narrowed down to the size of a tobacco wrapper...

In a large city, pedestrians lead the life of martyrs, just as though they were in a traffic-run ghetto. They are allowed to cross the street only at crossings – that is to say, at points where the traffic is heaviest and where the thread by which a pedestrian's life usually hangs may most easily snap... The ordinary motor car, which the pedestrians intended to be used for peaceful purposes, has taken on the menacing aspect of a fratricidal missile.[11]

This passionate (if somewhat tongue-in-cheek) anti-car diatribe comes from *The Golden Calf*, a satirical novel by Soviet writers Ilya Ilf and Evgeny Petrov, first published in 1931. As you see, even then, 93 years ago, when the overall number of cars in the world was no more than 23 million (now it is approaching 1.5 billion) and those were mostly in the US, the problem of separating those mechanical monsters from the cheerful crowds of peaceful pedestrians was very acute.

Since then, despite all those (largely futile) attempts by engineers, architects and town planners to resolve this ever-mounting problem with the help of autobahns, spaghetti junctions, electronic traffic lights and multi-storied car parks, the confrontation between cars and pedestrians keeps growing. In the overall number of casualties, it has come to resemble a major military conflict – a perpetual and bloody World War III that had never been officially declared.

Not that there hadn't been any promising utopian projects to radically change the situation. As early as in 1929, for example, Clarence Stein (1882–1975), an American urban planner, designed a 'masterplan' of a 'garden city for the motor age', his main goal being to create 'a safe place to raise children in the age of the automobile'. He tried to achieve it in Radburn, a small town in Bergen County, New Jersey (present-day population 25,000), by separating the traffic from pedestrians and reducing the contact between the two.

Stein created a pedestrian circulation system that allowed people to walk to the local centre, park and the school without the need to cross a road. He designed a row of 300m by 600m housing blocks with a series of cul-de-sacs pointing into the centre of each block. These cul-de-sacs provided car access to

Motopia, or 'Let's Kill the Car'!

the front of each home while a separate pedestrian network was linked to the back gardens via which residents could walk to local facilities.

Only a small section was completed before the Great Depression stalled development amidst complaints that the cul-de-sac-based layout made the Radburn estates difficult to navigate and hard to police. The town gradually returned to a more traditional street layout, and with the skyrocketing car ownership numbers in the US, the remaining cul-de-sacs, packed with parked vehicles, had become nearly impossible to negotiate, as I found when visiting the town some 20 years ago.

The same system was tried in Letchworth Garden City, in the rundown Jackman's Estate, connected with the neatly laid-out arts-and-crafts areas of the town with a winding lane called Radburn Way. Just like in Radburn, the eponymous 'Way' is a long cul-de-sac that leads nowhere, or, to be more exact, to one of the most crime-ridden, dysfunctional and ugliest council estates in Britain. It is next to impossible to find the way out from the cobweb of its treeless litter-ridden blind alleys, crammed with haphazardly parked cars and motorbikes.

It took me forever to find the estate's only pharmacy, to where I was once referred by my GP for a Covid booster jab. I lost count of how many times I had to face dead ends and turn back, while the sought-after pharmacy was literally several metres away, in a parallel cul-de-sac, getting to which would take another long detour. Facing an umpteenth dead end I nearly gave up my search and started thinking that I'd much rather be laid up with a mild form of Covid than stay exposed to that utopian-turned-dystopian town-planning disaster for another five minutes. The pharmacy was of course just round the corner, up a couple flights of concrete steps from where I had eventually parked my car.

Instead of restricting the movement of vehicles on the ground, the famous French architect Le Corbusier (1887–1965) tried to resort to a more radical solution – lifting pedestrians high above the road level. Several years ago, I had a chance to take a close look at that amazing 1950s urban Utopia, which hasn't quite become a dystopia yet (although, it looks as if it is approaching it – slowly but surely). Here is the story of that 'vertical garden city', as that amazing project is sometimes called.

'Shock! Horror!' These words sum up my first impression of architect Le Corbusier's famous Radiant City (Ville Radieuse) in the outskirts of Marseille.

Trucks in the Garden of Eden

Exhausted after a prolonged train journey (I was on an assignment to test the newly opened Eurostar direct speedy route from London to Marseille, which turned out to be neither direct, I had to change trains twice, nor speedy, the train was five hours late). I arrived on a scorching July afternoon. The moment I stepped out of the cab, the enormous 56-metre-high fortress-like building fell on top of me. Well, it actually didn't, but it felt as if I was about to be squashed by its oppressive raw-concrete brutalism.

I walked through the rows of *piloti*, concrete columns that prop up the structure like stilts, and entered the semi-dark lobby. I was inundated with memories of similar high-rise concrete dwellings in the Soviet Union. The only thing missing was the all-permeating cabbage-soup stench that used to dominate the doorways, the stairs and other communal spaces of Moscow apartment blocks in the 1960s and 70s.

Unlike in the latter, however, the lifts in the Radiant City were all in good order and appeared not to be used as public toilets. I got out on the 3rd floor and checked into my room, one of Le Corbusier's renowned cellules ('cells'), modelled on a monastic cell of Galluzo, a Carthusian monastery in Tuscany visited by the architect in 1907. To reach my cell, I had to walk along a long, dimly lit corridor, lined on both sides with flats and occasional offices. The cell was tiny and ascetic: a bunk, with a capacious storage compartment underneath, a bedside table that doubled as a cupboard, a small balcony and a minuscule walk-in shower cabin of the type you find on board overnight ferry boats. The outside toilet was to be shared with the dwellers of neighbouring units – again, a familiar feature of a Soviet communal apartment, where multiple wooden toilet seats, one for each of the sharing families, used to hang in the corridors like oversized and totally luckless horseshoes.

Notwithstanding the shared toilet, the room was surprisingly cosy, pleasantly cool and perfectly functional. Having shoved my few luggage items into the abundant wall closets and storage boxes ('as little furniture as possible' was one of the main principles of Charlotte Perriand, Le Corbusier's interior designer), I installed myself in one of the iconic LC04 steel chairs to look through my notes on Le Corbusier, the most famous and controversial 20th-century architect, and his equally famous and controversial creation – the Radiant City.

Motopia, or 'Let's Kill the Car'!

The design of the Ville Radieuse was largely inspired by the shared utilities inside the Constructivist Narkomfin building, which Le Corbusier spotted in Moscow while working on a blueprint for the House of the Soviets in the 1920s (his project was eventually rejected by Stalin). As mentioned earlier, the young architect was at the time hugely influenced by Ebenezer Howard, the founder of Letchworth Garden City, and his book *Garden Cities of To-morrow* (see Chapter 2).

Le Corbusier hated the very concept of a conventional urban dwelling ('Let's kill the street!' was one of his favourite mottoes, which could also be interpreted as 'Let's kill the car!'). He aspired to build 'a garden city in the sky' to provide affordable accommodation for those who had lost their homes in the First World War. His dream was to create 'a calm and powerful architecture', which, in his view, necessitated (among other things) the use of reinforced concrete. His vertical city was supposed to be a truly 'brutalist' structure (nothing to do with 'brutality', but from the French 'betonbrut', meaning 'raw concrete') – unappealing and even shocking (as it was initially for me) from the outside, Brutalist architecture cared little about appearances, but was practical and comfortable for the residents. The building's dimensions were to be calculated using Le Corbusier's own 'Modulor' system, based on the proportions of a human body.

The Marseille Project, commissioned by Raoul Dautry, then France's Minister of City Planning, took many years to mature and over five years to complete. It was initially pooh-poohed by the locals, who christened it 'La Maison du Fada' ('the nutter's house' in the Provencal dialect). When the building finally took shape in 1952, it was astounding: a 50,000-tonne tower block sitting on 34 pillars of bare reinforced concrete. The structure had 337 apartments of 15 different kinds, yet each of them, irrespective of the style, had a large balcony and a bay window.

Most of the Radiant City's public spaces, high above the ground, were situated in fully functioning but traffic-free 'mid-air streets' on every third floor, including the main 'high street' on floor 3, with shops (a bakery, a café, a supermarket – now closed and turned into a disco) and later a hotel. In the long and straight 'streets' (corridors) on other levels, one could find a primary school, a kindergarten, doctors' surgeries and small workshops.

The main communal area, with its Narkomfin-style shared utilities, was on the vast roof terrace. It consisted of a running track, a playground, a paddling pool and a gym. In Le Corbusier's eyes, the roof, with its 180-degree sea views, was supposed to represent the upper deck of an ocean liner, moored in the Marseille cityscape.

Not very popular in the beginning, the Radiant City eventually became one of the most desired residential properties in Marseille. Its Corbusian duplexes (two-level apartments) now attract affluent upper-middle-class professionals.

After a much-needed nap, I went for an evening Radiant City walk inside the single-building 'Machine for Living' – Le Corbusier's vision for urban dwellings.

Having left my room on the fourth floor, I walked past Dr Herve Aubin's surgery, then descended to the 3rd floor 'high street' from where muffled sounds of music could be heard. The bakery, the café and the bookshop were closed, but in a small public square near the lifts a party was in full swing: several dozen youngsters were dancing to music played by a DJ.

I took the lift to the top floor and the spacious roof terrace. Large and bright southern stars mingled with the distant lights of the Frioul Islands.

Despite the late hour, the roof was full of people. As in many southern cities, where siesta is more or less observed during the hottest hours of the day, the residents were out for a stroll. Families paced the perimeter of the roof leisurely. Occasionally, they were overtaken by joggers running around the circular racing track. Children splashed in a paddling pool, lit up with blue lights, while their mothers practised Pilates nearby. Older residents, with coffee cups in their hands, sat on benches between a funnel-shaped ventilation shaft and a windbreak protecting the now-empty outdoor theatre stage. They sipped coffee and looked up at the stars.

I was pleased to see that despite the off-putting Brutalist exterior, the community inside the Radiant City was thriving. The 'Machine for Living' was very much alive.

I also came to realise why the building appeared so painfully familiar to me. Le Corbusier's far-reaching plans were picked up by urban developers all over the world but were never implemented in their entirety. And whereas the Corbusian concepts of high-rise, high-density buildings were put into practice almost everywhere, the architect's 'quality of space' principle (both inside and outside the tower blocks) was mostly forgotten. Hence all those drab residential 'estates' of Sheffield, Glasgow, East Berlin and East London, the 'new development suburbs' of Moscow and other Soviet cities: all poor imitations of Le Corbusier's radical, yet fully functional (as shown by the Radiant City) projects.

In the morning, the corridors of the Radiant City swarmed with dog-walkers returning to their flats with their pets.

I had breakfast in a superb in-house restaurant, Le Ventre de l'Architecte ('The Architect's Belly'), on the terrace overlooking the sea. The restaurant, just like the hotel, the bookshop and the estate agency specialising in 'unusual living spaces', were not part of Le Corbusier's original plan. In fact, he would have probably been unnerved by the fact that a hotel named after him was now part of the Radiant City, intended for permanent dwellers, not tourists. But tourists these days are a daily reality of the Ville Radieuse.

'Inside the building, there used to be lots of unused and abandoned spaces,' Alban Gerardin, who bought the would-be hotel in 2003, told me. 'We were passionate about architecture and tried to restore the rooms, corridors and terraces to the original Le Corbusier design. We scoured antique shops and flea markets in search of Charlotte Perriand's furniture pieces and placed them in the hotel rooms. The idea was to reproduce the soul of the place without too much glitz.'

I had a chance to look at a number of other cells and duplexes where Le Corbusier's *esprit nouveau* was lovingly preserved, including the legendary apartment number 50, which used to belong to Lillete Ripert, the Radiant City's in-house nursery schoolteacher and Le Corbusier's friend. Yet perhaps the most convincing example of how well vintage Corbusian spaces could be adapted for modern use was, again, on the building's multi-purpose roof. In 2010, Marseille-based artist Ora Ito discovered that the old 1960s gym was up for sale. With the support of the Le Corbusier Foundation, he bought the space, restored it to its original design and, in line with the Radiant City philosophy of a 'place for all to share', opened MAMO Gallery, an arts centre to which all residents of the building have free access. When I was there, it hosted an exhibition of Dan Graham's breathtaking large-scale steel-and-glass pavilions. They fitted beautifully in the uncomplaining roof terrace, next to the children's playground.

Trucks in the Garden of Eden

So, what was (and still is) the Radiant City? A radical architectural statement? A masterpiece of modern design and construction engineering? A village in the sky? It is all those and more. If Schelling described architecture as 'frozen music', I would rather call the Ville Radieuse Le Corbusier's 'frozen dream' – his concrete, in both senses, vision of what modern public housing was supposed to be like. Though to be honest, my acrophobia made promenading on the building's roof a bit of a torture.

Yes, the Vertical City (another nickname of the building), is still there in all its crude brutalist beauty (or ugliness, depending on your perception of brutalism), yet the present-day residents of that 'garden city in the sky' still have to come back down to earth frequently (for work, proper shopping and other daily needs), to the traffic-ridden streets of Marseilles, thus further exacerbating the city's chronically unresolved cars-versus-pedestrians problem – a convincing proof that Le Corbusier's anti-car Utopia has not quite worked out.

Now, back to the UK.

In 1944, Sir Patrick Abercrombie (1879–1957) came up with his much-debated County of London Plan (or Greater London Plan, as it is also known), aimed at reducing the traffic congestion in the capital. It proposed a series of ring roads, labelled from A to E, to remove traffic from central London, due to undergo a substantial 'pedestrianisation', to which most of the London-based small business were naturally opposed. It was partly because of that, and partly (as I assume) due to the sheer impossibility of pronouncing the tongue-breaking neologism 'pedestrianisation' without stuttering, that the plan had not been carried out in full.

And then, in 1959, Motopia came into the picture. Its creator, Geoffrey Jellicoe (1900–1996) – an architect, a town planner and a dreamer – was a fan of Le Corbusier's Vertical City, but instead of lifting pedestrians above the ground, he brazenly suggested the opposite – to relocate the traffic onto the rooftops!

'No person will walk where automobiles move, and no car can encroach upon the area, sacred to the pedestrian,' he wrote in his manifesto of a book *Motopia: A Study in the Evolution of Urban Landscape*. This 1961 book is now a rarity. I managed to get a dodgy publisher's reprint, with the characters so tiny that it can only be read with a magnifying glass, which makes the very process of reading it feel like a discovery in its own right.

I first heard of Motopia from Bill Bryson, who visited its intended location on Staines Moor near Wraysbury Village

Motopia, or 'Let's Kill the Car'!

close to Heathrow airport and (rather ironically) squeezed between Britain's busiest M25 and M4 motorways. In his book *The Road to Little Dribbling*, Bill sums up Motopia as 'a proposed model community, based on the uniquely unexpected idea of banishing cars', intended 'to provide housing, shopping, offices, theatres, libraries, cinemas and schools for a population of 30,000'.

All those 'motopians' (my neo-toponym) were supposed to live in a grid-pattern of buildings modelled by Jellicoe on London's Bedford Square, with an expanse of rooftop motorways in the sky. In actual fact, it was to be just one giant edifice – a superblock of the type of Le Corbusier's 'Living Machine', with residential quarters and elevated streets, linked together by moving walkways, where there was no danger of being hit by a car. 'In this town, we will separate the biological elements from the mechanical,' Jellicoe wrote.

As it becomes clear from his book, Jellicoe himself did not fully believe in the practicality of his utopian plan of a 'pedestrian paradise', which he himself considered to be mostly of a 'diagrammatic value'. There is also a strong element of irony and even satire in *Motopia*. The author includes an imaginary interview with a future Motopia traffic warden, who thinks that bicycles should be banned from the town as 'an anachronism in the modern world'.

And yet, so beguiling and so topical were Jellicoe's ideas that the government did designate a provisional site for building Motopia, that town of 30,000 people with rooftop motorways, 17 miles West of London, at an estimated cost of $170 million. It was a decision that surprised Jellicoe himself, who remarked in his book: 'The site chosen in the Green Belt round London is ... an exercise only.'

Those plans were duly shelved and the construction of Motopia never got under way. But the clearly designated site of the one of the boldest utopian projects ever remains. I visited it to see if I could visualise Motopia on the exact spot where it was meant to be. As we have already learned, every Utopia sooner or later becomes its opposite. Few things can illustrate that sad conclusion better than the present-date state of the intended Motopia site.

The village of Wraysbury in the Royal Borough of Windsor and Maidenhead next to Heathrow, unexpectedly charming, leafy and old-fashioned, is one of the UK's most unfortunate places to live in.

Trucks in the Garden of Eden

Its residents never look up at the sky where planes fly so low above their heads while landing or taking off that one seems to be able to touch them with an outstretched hand. Every 30 or 40 seconds, all through the day, with a short 4-hour break at night-time, a deafening roar, similar to that of a volcano eruption, assails the villager's uncomplaining ear drums. And then there is the never-ending din of the M25 and M40 motorways, which can only be heard during the brief intervals between the ear-splitting thunder of the planes. In comparison to the latter, it sounds like a lullaby.

Paradoxically, it was the proximity of the world's busiest airport that had made Wraysbury one of the few places in the country that benefited from the Covid pandemic, when the number of flights to and from Heathrow was drastically reduced.

'It was great here during Covid!' a local woman walking her dog in the lush village green told me. 'So quiet that...' Her last words were drowned in the uproar from the sky.

A failed motor-car Utopia turned into a thriving aircraft dystopia. History must have had a laugh in placing planes, instead of cars as Jellicoe had suggested, in the Wraysbury skies.

The same woman assured me that the villagers had learned to shut out the noise – something I had reason to doubt, for why then had they been so active in campaigning against Heathrow's extension? I could hear the echoes of that campaign in the name of one of the village's pubs – the Perseverance, which turned out to be welcoming and cosy, and served excellent food. Opposite it was a garage, nostalgically called 'Dr Clutch' – the name straight from a 1950s Utopia.

Yes, despite its unfortunate situation, Wraysbury is not devoid of some utopian traits. I saw them in the solid ivy-covered houses, richly– almost excessively, like in the US – decorated for Halloween, albeit I found it hard to imagine what the ever-so-resilient 'wraysburnians' can be scared of. I was pleasantly surprised to discover that the villagers enjoy scuba-diving in the nearby Staines Reservoir, which is also considered UK's best spot for carp fishing (fishing must be popular here as a source of much needed calm and peace of mind).

I have to confess that after the brief visit to Wraysbury, I fell in love with that unfortunate, down-to-earth and at the same time beautiful and vivacious village, situated in a notorious 'alienation zone' (an expression coined by Ilf and Petrov) right under the Western approach path of Heathrow airport.

Motopia, or 'Let's Kill the Car'!

Next time, moments after taking off from Heathrow, do look down through your porthole and give a thought to the village below that has absorbed some of the stress of your flight.

I want to finish this chapter with one reassuring statistic: there are 1.446 billion cars presently listed in the world, but there are 'only' 25,578 registered aircraft!

Chapter 7

Utopias in the Time of Pandemic

Can we, should we, try and excavate utopia?
  Owen Hatherley, *Militant Modernism*

The following several chapters will cover a number of separate journeys in search of Britain's Utopias, undertaken between 2020 and 2022. Those were relatively short, maximum 10-day-long, trips, which (with the exception of the expedition to the remote Scottish Islands on board HMV *Greg Mortimer* – see Chapter 13) were made in the specially purchased second-hand Toyota Alphard campervan, nicknamed Alphie, in the company of my wife Christine and our dog Tashi. The trips had to be both short and at times sporadic largely due to the raging Covid 19 pandemic, which had succeeded in generating a global dystopia of previously unseen proportions and eventually all but paralyzed most of the habitual human routines and activities, including travel.

Looking through the notes and photos made during those forays, I decided that for reasons of continuity, rather than presenting the reader with a discontinued and frequently interrupted narrative, I would merge all those trips into two extended travelogues: from South no North (from Letchworth to New Lanark), and from Edinburgh to the Western Isles, Inner and Outer Hebrides, and on to Orkneys and Shetland.

Let me start with introducing my crew and its most important member – Alphie the campervan, which used to represent (and still does) a real Utopia on wheels. A couple of months prior to the intended Utopia-searching trip, I rather spontaneously acquired a second-hand 'grey-import' Toyota Alphard, converted into a campervan in the UK. My 'Alphie' (as I named the new

Utopias in the Time of Pandemic

acquisition) came straight from Japan, where for over 15 years it (he?) had been in the possession of a Mr Jamamoto (or perhaps a Mr Miyazawa – only guessing), who took excellent care of him to the point that he looked, smelled and drove like new. My only reservations prior to the purchase were: a) the dealership where I spotted Alphie was off a Thieves Lane in a Hertfordshire town suburb; and b) both the embedded Satnav and the car manual were in Japanese.

Those were promptly sorted by the dealer, who agreed to lower the price, which allowed me to say to my friends that, as the lane name suggested, the van was indeed a 'steal'. As for the language of the Satnav and the manual, the dealer promptly replaced both with their English versions – not that the latter was always helpful, for up to now I keep struggling with the sentences like: 'After the TRC operation is stopped with the TRC OFF switch, if the ignition is turned to ACC or LOCK, the TRC will become operational automatically' – which make me want to change the manual back to its Japanese original.

Due to the long pandemic-induced queues at the DVLA in Swansea, it took nearly two months to get Alfie a UK registration. Finally, I back-squeezed it – with only a couple of scratches – through the narrow gates into my yard, thus turning my age-long house-on-wheels utopian dream into a sweet OAP reality, for this OAP still prefers trainers and parkas to slippers and cardigans!

Yes, owning a mobile home had been my 'crazy dream' ever since my Soviet childhood. It was largely triggered by a piece of doggerel, 'The House Has Moved', written by the famous (there and then) children's poet Agniya Barto, In it, a typical Soviet block of flats is put on wheels as it 'goes off to Leningrad to take part in a parade'. We had to learn it by heart in the kindergarten, and I still remember a drawing from the book featuring a little boy peeping out of a fifth-floor window of a drab Soviet-style block of flats, rolling merrily along a country road. I often imagined myself as that boy, experiencing the world from the inside of his habitual communal-flat interior.

And there it was – the utopian dream coming true and being parked right in my backyard!

Initially, it was enough for me just to stare at the stationary Alphie – at its graceful, aerodynamically perfect shapes, its wooden dashboard, its compact Le Corbusier-style (see the previous chapter) salon-cum-lounge-cum-kitchen-cum-bedroom, with lots of hidden (at times, very well hidden) storage spaces, switches, vents and other appliances. It even had a DVD player (for passengers, not for the driver, as I had reckoned), which, luckily, did not work, for who would want to be watching some silly movies while Alphie made its way through beautiful British landscapes?

Satisfying as mere looking at it was, sooner or later I had to start driving Alphie in my quest for Britain's Utopias. And if the driving bit was easy and familiar, the camping part of campervan ownership was not. With my previous camping experience limited to reading about the hilarious adventures of the protagonists of Jerome K Jerome's classic *Three Men in a Boat* ('To Say Nothing of the Dog'), it was a constant, and not always a pleasant, revelation.

The reasons – in order of importance – were as follows: 1. Difficulties with moving, turning, opening and closing things inside the van; 2. Inability to set up a tent before or after dark; 3. Forgetting to bring such essentials as plates, cups, cutlery, hooks for setting up tent, mallets for hammering the above-mentioned forgotten hooks into the ground; and – most importantly – salt and pepper.

The lowest point came one morning at the very start of the journey, when the van's battery went flat and we were unable to start the engine, let alone boil the kettle. We were saved by a lovely lady, camping on the spot next to ours, who happened to carry a heavy-duty jump starter in the boot of her car. She was an aircraft engineer from Leicester.

It was not all failure of course. Among the main achievements were delicious (even if without salt or pepper) omelettes, cooked by my wife on one of the two hobs in the van's minuscule kitchen.

Our dog Tashi fell in love with Alphie to the point that he would staunchly refuse to get out of the van. At home, he would sit next to Alphie's doors all day long, waiting to be taken on yet another adventure.

Well, what can I say? Travelling in a campervan can indeed be exciting and liberating in equal measure. As long as there's a kindly aircraft engineer camping next to you...

One lesson I learned after several weeks on the road was that you cannot have it all at once. And if you decided to use your bespoke 'toilet tent' for storage, instead of having a portaloo (in our case, a miniature Thetford 'porta potti/campa potti', complete with flush-water and waste-holding tanks and a 'hold-down kit' – all perfectly suitable for any of the Seven Dwarfs, yet not quite up

Utopias in the Time of Pandemic

to the size of an average adult – installed in it, as we did, you'll have to rely on the 'facilities' when on site and on public toilets when on the road.

Before we embark on our Utopia-finding journey, I have another important point to make: most of the trip took place at the time of the Covid 19 pandemic. That couldn't but reflect on the nature of the research, with certain stretches of the trip curtailed or scrapped altogether, and the number of in situ contacts, as well as the duration of conversations with them, significantly reduced.

Surely, not everything was grim in the pandemic-ridden Britain of the early 2020s. Despite the nagging apocalyptic feel and the terrifying casualty figures, numerous positive signs were everywhere; one only needed to be optimistic enough to keep noticing them on the road: the unusual proliferation of birds, including the ever-so-hardworking woodpeckers and ever-so-tireless blackbirds, whose morning and evening chorus above the empty villages and towns was louder and more life-inspiring than ever; the foolhardy hedgehogs rolling across the deserted roads and getting flattened occasionally by the rare passing cars (don't they ever get their tyres punctured by such encounters?); and the muntjac deer, those illegal migrants of the animal world, that kept appearing regularly and fearlessly in gardens and on doorsteps – all of which made it so easy to forget about the omnipresence of the crafty and invisible killer that Covid 19 was.

Britain at the times of the pandemic was like a perverted version of paradise, devised by the devil, a hell's heaven of sorts ('a hell's heaven', incidentally, would be a nice definition of dystopia!).

Was Nature trying to demonstrate to the world that it did not need us humans at all and would do much better without us being around (the only kind of scenario which would have made Utopia a real possibility)?

But who would then tell the world how beautiful it actually was?

It was not by chance that we started the longest leg of our search for Utopias with a detour to the modest and semi-forgotten grave of the creator of history's best literary dystopia, *Nineteen Eighty-Four*, Eric Blair, aka George Orwell.

To me it was a revelation that the great writer's final abode was neither in London which he had loved and where he died, nor in

Wallington, where he had enjoyed his happiest times, nor even in the Orkneys where he had spent his last couple of years, terminally ill, but in the non-descript Oxfordshire (formerly Berkshire) village of Sutton Courtenay, in the graveyard of the local parish church of All Saints, where he now rests next to his long-time friend David Astor, who passed away long after Orwell and – in accordance with the latter's will – helped to secure the churchyard plot for both of them. Orwell, despite being an atheist, often expressed the wish to be buried in a village church graveyard. Was it a subconscious continuation of his life-long, well-concealed quest for a rural English Utopia, even if posthumous? Securing that patch was not easy due to the general shortages of burial places in the country in 1950.

Orwell died of pulmonary tuberculosis, the bane of most of his life, made far worse by the wound he had brought back from Spain. He died in University College Hospital London on 21 January 1950. His body was then transported to Sutton Courtney. Only David Astor and Orwell's wife Sonya were present when the coffin was lowered into the clay and chalk-ridden soil under a strikingly ordinary headstone, with just his name, Eric Arthur Blair and the dates 1903–1950.

We wandered in silence around the permanently (or so it seemed!) deserted, windswept graveyard. Old trashy bunches of withered flowers could be seen on many a grave, yet not on Orwell's. The only 'decorations' on the grave of one of history's greatest writers were two empty jugs and a rusty 50-pence coin on top of the gravestone. There could be no better illustration of the old Latin dictum *sic transit gloria mundi*. Like all other Utopias, Orwell's posthumous country churchyard idyll (if he had ever cherished any) proved unworkable.

Standing there, next to Orwell's tombstone, I was reminded of another posthumous Utopia, which we were briefly exposed to on the way to Sutton Courtney, in the Buckinghamshire hamlet of Jordans, the centre of Britain's Quakerism and the burial place of William Penn, founder of Pennsylvania. The village's Friends Meeting House, built in 1688, is famous not so much for its history and architecture as for its two 'in-house' cemeteries, from which all headstones were removed in the 18th century in an unparalleled gesture of utopian egalitarianism, whereby all men and women were equal before God in life and even after their deaths.

And, as if that was not enough, in 1937 the Quaker architect Hubert Lidbetter arranged the graves in a circle to reflect a typical

Utopias in the Time of Pandemic

Quaker gathering of worship, which was supposed to carry on for eternity. History's longest meeting lasting forever: the compilers of *The Guinness Book of Records* should be alerted to that highly unusual post-mortem Utopia.

We left a bunch of field flowers on Orwell's abandoned grave. Tashi was lying on the ground next to it, his legs outstretched, like a pile of black-and-white fluff, as if trying to embrace and, possibly, even to warm up, the whole of planet Earth...

Armed with Orwell's (imaginary) blessings, we hit the A415 motorway and soon entered the Cotswolds, once described by writer Stuart Maconie as an area 'playing up to an image of itself confected by painters, writers, composers and, latterly, telemarketers'. We were heading to the small Cotswolds village of Kelmscott, with its world-famous Kelmscott Manor, which in the 1870s became the country retreat of William Morris, writer, designer, craftsman and one of Britain's most prominent utopians, who had referred to both the manor house, with its lush gardens, and the village itself as 'heaven on earth'. Surely, we could not miss a place like that.

The village was well-hidden. Having left the motorway, we found ourselves in a seemingly endless winding country road, barely wide enough for Alphie. Repeatedly, I had to back down to give way to posh-looking horse-riders (to be fair, all horse-riders appear posh to me). Behind the intercom-equipped ornate gates of the few secluded houses, many a gleaming 4-by-4 could be spotted.

My several previous attempts to visit Kelmscott Manor had been unsuccessful. The house, now a Grade 1 listed building, seemed to have some elusive, I would even say, schizophrenic and largely unpredictable opening times: it was only open to visitors on three (changeable) days a week and only between April and October. The unbeatable Murphy's Law of my existence made sure that I had always arrived there on the days when the massive wooden gates leading to the house and the gardens were firmly shut.

This time, however, we were in luck. Or were we? The impression I've taken away from the visit is controversial. Like Morris's life and work, I hasten to add.

I find it mildly ironic, that, according to the anonymous introduction to the Kindle edition of his best-known book, *News from Nowhere* – a fantasy novel that had, reportedly, inspired Ebenezer Howard to create the world's first Garden City (see Chapter 2), Morris is 'perhaps best known as a designer of wallpaper and patterned fabrics'.

Having looked at the quirky (and rather messy, to my taste) arts-and-crafts interior of Kelmscott Manor, I was wondering if the Morris-designed Willow Bough wallpaper in it was of the type that prompted the famous 'One of us has to go' remark of Oscar Wilde addressed to the peeling wallpaper in the cheap Paris hotel room, where he lay dying.

Born in Essex in 1834, William – like most caviar and champagne socialists – enjoyed a carefree, privileged lifestyle in a large country house near Epping Forest. His father, a rich self-made businessman, died when William was just 13, having made sure that his son studied at the prestigious Marlborough College in Wiltshire, where, as Morris himself later claimed, he had 'learned next to nothing'.

Having learned nothing, he nevertheless developed an interest in the works of John Ruskin which he had carried all through his life. Morris experimented with painting (drawing mostly some mediaeval women in period clothes), poetry, embroidery, architecture, which he regarded as 'the foundation of all the arts' (is it really?) and tapestry – a classic Jack of All Trades, who tried to do several different things at a time, most of them successfully, it has to be said, and yet failing to find one true passion. 'If a chap can't compose an epic poem while he is weaving tapestry he had better shut up,' he once stated in his habitual spoilt-brat manner. As for Morris's poetry, his own best friend, artist Edward Burne-Jones, once remarked: 'You cannot find short quotations in him; he must be taken in great gulps.'

That, in turn, adds a different meaning to another of Burne Jones's pronouncements in which he described Kelmscott Manor as 'more a poem than a house'. Did he mean one of Morris's poems? Alas, we'll never know the answer.

My own view of Morris's writing style is not too positive either, I'm afraid. utopian and revolutionary ideas aside, I found his novel *News from Nowhere* extremely hard-going. Here's a typical sentence describing the protagonist on a train: 'As he sat in that vapour-bath of hurried and discontented humanity, a carriage of the underground railway, he, like others, stewed discontentedly, while in self-reproachful mood he turned over the many excellent and conclusive arguments, which though they lay at his fingers' ends, he had forgotten in the just past discussion.'

Well, if one of my students at the University of Cambridge, where I teach Writing, came up with something as grammatically and stylistically inaccurate: full of tautologies and questionable metaphors and lacking coherence (let alone cadence), I wouldn't hesitate to call this sentence gobbledygook and would insist on having it changed.

It is highly ironic that a person with such a background was to become Britain's leading social thinker, the proponent of peaceful and not-so-peaceful revolutions and socialist utopias. Or perhaps it was a kind of a character trait of many famous 'revolutionaries' (Marx, Lenin, Stalin, Ceaucescu, to name just a few), who, having failed to achieve true distinction artistically or academically, found solace in upending the existing order of things – in theory and in practice.

Please note that my intention here is not so much to judge Morris's artistic and literary merits and drawbacks as to understand what it was that had made him – a wealthy person with a privileged background – a utopian and a revolutionary. And on a larger scale, what it is that shapes a utopian in general. Apart from the obvious failure to become the true polymath he so wanted to be, there could be another reason for Morris's on-paper rebellion...

Morris's life and career changed significantly after he met and befriended the poet and painter of Italian origins Dante Gabriel Rossetti (the latter's father, an Italian political refugee, had been an authority on the 13th-century poet Dante Alighieri, hence the name). They rented Kelmscott Manor. From there, Morris would often travel to his beloved Iceland or elsewhere, having left his children and his wife Jane in the company of his friend, who did not try to hide his long-time affection for Jane, whom he described as a 'stunner'. During one such absence, Jane and Rossetti became lovers.

Mrs Morris herself later admitted that she had never loved her husband, of which he must have been aware, for even after her affair became known to Morris he insisted on Rossetti's continuing presence in Kelmscott Manor, thus creating another famous historical love triangle. My favourite one (little known to British readers) was of the Soviet Union's 'great proletarian poet' Vladimir Mayakovsky (1893–1930), Lilya Brik, an unlikely 1920s Moscow 'socialite', and her husband, poet Osip Brik. The trio happily resided together in a 'communal' flat (sharing kitchen, bathroom and, possibly, as it happened, wives too, with several other tenants) until Mayakovsky committed suicide by shooting himself in the head in 1930. I cannot refrain here from quoting some of his propaganda verses, which became painfully topical from 24 February 2022, when Russia invaded my native Ukraine. On a number of YouTube videos one could see formations of kindergarten 4- and 5-year-olds in military fatigues marching with their teachers to the accompaniment of some Soviet bravura music.

'Let's Take Up New Guns, Children! Let's take up new guns, stick red flags to their barrels, and with cheerful songs, let's all join snipers' ranks!'

I first saw that jingoistic doggerel in the *Jolly Pictures* magazine for Soviet children of 6 and under, to which I had a subscription as a child. The illustration to the 'poem' featured a number of not-too-jolly pictures of guns, with red flags attached to their bayonets, as well as Soviet warships and missiles.

Back to the Kelmscott Manor. Quietly watching his beloved wife 'Janey' falling in love with Rossetti must have been painful for Morris and was likely to generate some kind of rebellion – first internal, and then, possibly, external, too. Significantly, if prior to moving to Kelmscott, Morris seemed to be a firm proponent of a peaceful social transformation via arts and architecture, then, as asserted by American scholar Michael H. Lang in his book *Designing Utopia*, by 1883, after several years of the Kelmscott Manor love triangle, 'Morris clearly believed that the only way to affect the change in society was by revolution.'

Lang then goes on to brand Morris's altered views as 'Marxian' (sic). Wasn't that sudden trend towards aggression (for revolutions are almost always violent) Morris's subconscious attempt to take revenge on the world for his own suffering and humiliation? Jealousy can make anyone into a rebel. Or else lead to suicide, as in the case of Mayakovsky.

I may be wrong of course, but as you may have noticed already, I always try to avoid being 100 per cent serious in my descriptions, let alone conclusions, which I strive to avoid in the firm belief that the writer's mission is not to provide answers, but to show (not to tell!), and let the readers make their own judgement and come up with more questions.

Our first day on the road proved tiring and we decided by democratic vote (with two in favour and Tashi abstaining) to forsake the camping for the night and to stay instead in the famous Thames Head Inn near Cirencester, not far from the spot where the River Thames begins its slow 184-mile journey to the Thames Barrier in London. The source of the Thames was just a short walk away, but we were too tired to leave our warm and cosy room in a converted barn – our last little Utopia of the day.

At breakfast, we realised how wise we were not to walk to the great river's source the night before. A helpful member of the Thames Head staff assured us that there was absolutely nothing to see on the spot, except a crumbling old stone with an illegible inscription. The little spring at the source was at the moment dry and would only fill up with water after a heavy rain. 'For most of the year no water is visible, just a dry and shallow riverbed,' he said, adding that at its source and further – all the way to Dorchester – the Thames is called the Isis. It only becomes the Thames when joined by the Thame in the middle of Oxfordshire. You live and learn.

As we were driving past the town of Cirencester, I spotted a road sign with a seemingly mysterious abbreviation, RAU. To me, there was no mystery about it, however: the sign designated the campus of the Royal Agricultural University and the temporary location of the annual Buddhist Summer School run by the London Buddhist Society, of which I've been a member for several years. The place was also an unlikely reminder of my 2017 open-heart surgery. Here is the story.

My Dad died of a heart attack at the age of 56, just like his own father, so my cardio history was never too promising. I knew I'd have to do the valve replacement soon but thought I should first fix my dental problems; one of the main preconditions for open-heart surgery, according to the British Heart Foundation, is having healthy teeth and gums.

A victim of merciless Soviet dentistry, with tooth extraction as its main and often only method of treatment, I had not one, but 13 dental problems – equal to the number of my remaining teeth. I was told they all had to go to make space for implants, and when I asked if I could keep at least one as a souvenir of all the beautiful food I had consumed, they said that I could indeed, but I would have to carry it in my pocket. My dental Dignitas experience was to take place in the Smile Savers Clinic, the best in Budapest. Why Budapest? Because the Hungarian capital has been Europe's dental tourism Mecca for nearly a hundred years and dental treatment there was not only better quality but also much cheaper than at home.

To cut a long story short, this, the first of my three medical procedures, was a success. I was subjected (under general anaesthetic) to '13 teeth extraction and the placement of 10 SGS implants by Alpha-Bio', carried out by Europe's leading implantologist Dr Attila Kaman. It was done within a couple of days and was all but painless, if we don't count the initial discomfort of coming to grips with my new, unusually crowded, mouth cavity.

Yet before I had time to start stuffing my face with previously inedible steaks, apples and stiff Hungarian dumplings, there came a phone call from my London cardiologist, who, having examined the results of my latest angiogram, concluded that I had to undergo a coronary artery bypass grafting and aortic valve replacement pronto.

Ten days after returning to the UK, I found myself in the operating theatre of Harefield Hospital. In that theatre I was not an actor, not even a stagehand, but rather a prop, the undisputed star of the show being the surgeon. I was certainly physically unaware of all the technological intricacies of the procedure, whereby my chest was carved open, my heart stopped and I was put on a heart-lung machine – a circuit outside the body containing a mechanical blood pump and the oxygenator (an artificial lung). My malfunctioning valve was then removed and replaced with a bovine-tissue one. No more beef for me, thanks.

I vaguely recall waking up in intensive care with cables, tubes and wires sticking out of my hands, chest and neck, making me look and feel like an Ood from *Doctor Who*. I also remember bizarre hallucinations caused by the drugs I was pumped with, the scariest of which was being laminated alive by some smart Asian students.

Feeling (and looking) like I had been chewed up and spat out, I was transferred to a recovery ward equipped, among other things, with an old-fashioned telephone carrying the rather discouraging sticker 'Cardiac Arrest 2222'.

It was not the end of my ordeal. My systolic blood pressure suddenly dropped to below 50, while my heartbeat jumped up to 140, as if I was running constantly on an invisible treadmill. I was experiencing post-surgery atrial fibrillation, and the team of worried nurses and doctors, all muttering 'We are losing him!' (or maybe, having watched too many Hollywood thrillers, I just imagined that through the haze of my fading consciousness), rolled me to a high-dependency ward, and from there back to the already familiar operating theatre on the following day.

For the third time in three weeks, and with my mutilated heart jumping sporadically in my chest like a monkey in a cage, I was put to sleep and subjected to an electrical cardioversion procedure – a powerful electric shock sent through the heart to stun it in the hope that it 'forgets' about the fibrillation and reverts to its normal sinus rhythm.

It worked, at least for the time being, and several days later I was discharged. When my wife came to pick me up, I realised with awe the sheer inability of walking unassisted 100 metres from the hospital to the parked car and was ready to cry with helplessness and despair...

Recovering from that procedure was like starting my life anew (I experienced a couple of major setbacks and ended up in Stevenage's Lister Hospital, where I nearly died – twice – due to a chest infection, see Chapter Five). My eventual recovery was nothing short of a miracle – a Utopia that had become reality. Unsurprisingly, I felt an acute need for some kind of faith that could give me hope.

Having spent the first 35 years of my life in the rampantly atheistic USSR, where any kind of faith or religion was banished to be replaced with a blunt communist dogma, where all my childish hopes and beliefs had been first ridiculed and then mercilessly crushed, I was finding it hard to find anything to believe in when in the West. The choices were multiple, but at times, as I had concluded during my first post-defection years in Australia, too much choice was as hard to take as no choice at all. In the end, I opted for Buddhism, which struck me as being thoroughly undogmatic: more a philosophy than a faith. The Buddha had always encouraged his followers *not* to take his preachings as commandments, but always to check and see if they worked for themselves. I loved his beautifully metaphorical pronouncement to the effect that if we saw him pointing his finger at the Moon, we should look at the Moon, and not at his finger. 'Buddhism does not have beliefs, it only has teachings,' as Yashadaka, my first Buddhist teacher, kept telling me.

I spent a lot of time in meditation and became a frequent visitor (not a pilgrim, mind you) to the Amaravati Buddhist Monastery near Hemel Hempstead, one of the unfortunate New Towns, the ugliness of which was in stark contrast to the neat, cosy and welcoming

Trucks in the Garden of Eden

monastery grounds, with the dashing modernistic Temple, where mediation happened effortlessly and almost naturally. I befriended the monastery's Abbot, the brilliant Ajahn Amaro, formerly Jeremy Horner, a Kentish lad prone (in his own words) to 'sex, drugs and rock'n'roll', who was salvaged by Buddhism and became a monastic.

I enjoyed reading Buddhist literature and therefore eagerly signed up for the last pre-pandemic one-week-long Buddhist Society's Summer School of 2020 on the Royal Agricultural University grounds. It was a truly utopian experience.

Because of summer holidays, the huge leafy campus was empty of students, not counting those who worked in the canteen where we ate. The proverbial Buddhist austerity was nowhere to be seen: the dishes were all delicious, using the freshest farm produce, and the portions more than generous. All day we could listen to talks and lectures by the leading Buddhist scholars, and group mediations were held in the RAU's Chapel four times a day. I had a pleasant en-suite room for myself in one of the on-campus residential halls, next to the University's well-equipped gym, which we were encouraged to use.

In short, I had an amazing week, spiritual and teetotal (if not quite dietary) and returned home feeling healthier, calmer and more Buddhist than ever.

My expectations of one of Britain's oldest and most peculiar utopian communities, Whiteway Colony near Stroud, were based on scanty information gained mostly from the Internet (the reclusive Colony was not mentioned in the existing guidebooks, not even in the otherwise detailed and in-depth Bradt Slow Travel Guide to the Cotswolds) and a couple of out-of-print monographs, were vague. Perhaps I would find a mixture of the 1930s Letchworth, populated (according to George Orwell et al – see Chapter 2) with sandal-wearing Esperanto-speaking vegetarians, and Nikolaevsk in Alaska, the time-frozen Jurassic Park-like village of Russian Old Believers; probably the most amazing (and thoroughly utopian) settlement I've ever visited?

Driving (without taking my eyes off the road, or, God forbid, falling asleep behind the wheel) along the winding Cotswolds roads, past some detached cottages built of yellow limestone and crowned with disproportionately huge chimneys, almost the size of the cottages themselves, towards Britain's oldest remaining secular utopian community, I was carried away (while still wide awake, no doubt!) by the Whiteway-relevant (or so I was hoping) reveries.

It is not common knowledge that Alaska is home to the world's most obscure community of Russian outcasts, confined to a cluster of small villages (Nikolaevsk, Voznesenka, Razdolna, Kachemak-Selo, Port Graham and Nanwalek – no more than two or three thousand people altogether) in the south-west of the Kenai Peninsula. Visitors are not welcome there, and the villagers' contacts with the outside world are kept to the minimum. (This obscure Old Believers' community has nothing to do with the thousands of Russians who stayed in Alaska after it was purchased by America from the Russian Empire for a meagre $7.2 million – the USA's ever-best bargain. Even so, the sale was debated in the US Senate for over six months!)

The origins of the Old Believers' movement go back to the so-called 'Great Schism' of 1650s, when Nikon, a strong-minded Russian Orthodox Patriarch and a strict disciplinarian, decided to correct the Church-Slavonic holy texts and the method of worship practised by the Russian masses. His reforms were opposed by a section of the Orthodox church, who accused Nikon of heresy and vowed to stick to the old ways. Nikon's reforms were far from iconoclastic and concerned such seemingly insignificant issues as how many fingers (two or three) would be used to make the sign of the cross; whether 'Alleluia' should be sung two or three times; whether the priests should walk around the altar with or against the passage of the sun, and so on. But in the eyes of the more conservative believers, this constituted a huge change in their rituals.

Organically opposed to any reform, the Old Believers (as they came to be known) suffered severe persecution under Peter the Great, whom they saw as the Antichrist. As a result, many had to flee to the outskirts of the vast Russian Empire. After the Communist coup d'etat of 1917, a considerable number escaped over the border to China, where they stayed until the Chinese revolution of 1949 forced them even farther away from home, to South America and Australia. The majority of Nikolaevsk residents came to Alaska (in 1968) from Brazil, via Oregon, where they survived by growing wheat and corn.

Each Old Believer family has 10-15 offspring (it is not unusual for a girl to get married at 14 or 15). The girls always wear their traditional long dresses ('talichkas') and coloured kerchiefs, which they later change for more sophisticated headwear, the 'shashmura', a cap covered with a scarf, after getting married and becoming 'khoziaiki' ('house-hostesses'), preoccupied mainly with cooking and childbearing. Marriages in Nikolaevsk have still to be approved and blessed by the 'Batiushka'.

The community is the proud owner of a small fleet of ultra-modern fishing vessels with the latest electronic equipment. Fishing and selling smoked fish constitute the villagers' main source of sustenance and income.

Nikolaevsk has an excellent secondary school, one of the best in Alaska, where all the subjects, except for Russian, are taught in English. No wonder the village teenagers prefer communicating in English, although most of them retain a reasonably good command of their melodious old-fashioned Russian language. As for smaller kids, they hardly speak any Russian at all.

The adults' Russian speech, however, is the language of Tolstoy and Turgenev, free of foreign borrowings and clumsy modern abbreviations. Like their lifestyle and customs, the Old Believers' mother-tongue was frozen in the time warp of 1917-1920, when their grandparents, with bag and baggage and under cover of darkness, crossed the Russian-Chinese border into Manchuria, only to find themselves in Alaska four decades later.

One evening while in NIkolaevsk, I was invited to watch fish-canning in the courtyard of Feopent Ivanovich Reutov, a thick-set elderly man who was born in Russia ('My parents didn't tell me where') and grew up in Brazil. The canning was done in an antediluvian way: tins of pink salmon were placed into a capacious iron barrel with water and boiled for 4 hours on a powerful bonfire, 'to kill all the microbes'. Two youngsters, Iona and Flegon, both bearded (the Old Believers' men are not allowed to cut their facial hair) and wearing baseball caps, came to help.

A neighbour, Father Deacon Josip, popped in, allegedly to borrow a scythe, and stayed.

I felt at ease in the company of my fellow outcasts, who seemed to accept my 'Western' attire, my 'modernised' Russian language, my shaven face, even my camera (the Old Believers are notoriously camera-shy). There was only one thing about me that they could not come to grips with: smoking. 'In Voznesenka, they would attack you with an axe, if they saw you with a cigarette in your mouth,' Iona told me with a grimace of disapproval on his face. I made a mental note never to come close to the village of Voznesenka, which had a reputation of being even more reclusive and more conservative than Nikolaevsk. They told me off, when I inadvertently dropped a cigarette end on the grass: 'Pick it up and hide it somewhere. If the Batiushka finds it, you are in trouble.'

'Don't you realise that smoking is a sin?' Josip, the Deacon, insisted. I mumbled something to the effect that we were all sinners in one way or another. 'This is true,' Josip said pensively, and the subject of smoking was dropped for the rest of the night, although the word 'sin' came up again, when Flegon mentioned his girlfriend, an American divorcee with a child.

'We must ask the Batiushka to marry you and to take you out of sin as soon as possible, in the name of Jesus Christ, our saviour,' Iona, who himself was properly married to an Old Beliver Russian girl, commented. 'He must be joking,' I thought, but Iona's face was dead serious, and his dark-brown eyes were full of sad reproach.

A warm and velvety summer night fell upon Nikolaevsk fast, as if the small village was suddenly covered with an oversized black and fluffy ushanka (a traditional Russian fur-hat with ear-flaps) from Nina's gift-shop. The fire was burning brightly in Feopent Ivanovich's courtyard, tearing the darkness into shreds, dagger-like. Iona produced a bottle of raspberry-flavoured (we were in America, after all!) Smirnoff. All the men, except for me, crossed themselves before every drink.

Deacon Josip was telling us about his childhood in Brazil. And although he had never been to Russia, his Russian speech was amazing: elegant and form an earlier age. Merciless and insatiable Alaskan mosquitoes were buzzing above our heads, and some big dark shadows were moving in the bushes, behind the lawn. Could they be moose? I felt as though I was watching a perfectly directed (by Andrei Tarkovsky?) Russian movie set in in the middle of the last century. Only this 'movie' was for real, and I myself was among the cast. It was already past midnight, when Josip and Iona burst into a heart-rending Russian folk-song which I had never heard before. They sang about long farewells, dusty roads and a hard life in a foreign land, which in Russian is called 'chuzhbina' – a word that doesn't have a direct equivalent in English. Contained in it are willows rustling soothingly above the winding creek, the wind whistling through a birch grove, and an endless snow-covered Russian steppe glistening like marble under the moon.

Trucks in the Garden of Eden

I suddenly understood why, after centuries of wanderings, these people chose to settle in Alaska, which looks so deceptively similar to their cruel, yet dear, homeland – the country that most of them have never been to and will never see. Like Russia, Alaska has willows above creeks, snow-covered plains, and birch-groves. It used to be a part of Russia and, in a sense, it still is, for the genuine Russian spirit destroyed by the Bolsheviks and no longer found in Russia itself, now waging an unprovoked fratricidal war against my native Ukraine, had been smuggled out and kept intact there by the Old Believers...

Chapter 8

Arcadia and the Real Estate

> For thinkers such as Isaiah Berlin and Karl Popper, utopianism was the highroad to totalitarianism.
> Ben Wilson, *Literary Review*, July 2023

Whiteway Colony was founded in 1898 by a group of anarchists, who broke away from another utopian community in Essex. the Purleigh Colony. Inspired by Leo Tolstoy's 'back to land' principle, it was founded in 1896 and by 1900 broke down and fell apart due to the endless internal squabbles.

Just like their Essex predecessors, the Whiteway 'separatists' rejected money, government, schools and private property and were preaching equality and non-violence – the utopian socialist ideas, inspired by Leo Tolstoy's early short story *Walk in the Light While There is Light*, of which Tolstoy himself was reportedly ashamed at a later stage of his life, and by his 1901 article 'How Shall We Escape' about the unfairness of land ownership.

Having bought the land, the new colonists symbolically burned the title deeds on the end of a pitchfork to underline the fact that everything in Whiteway (so named after the road that went through the plot) was common property from then on. It is important to note that the unique concept of the undocumented collective ownership in Whiteway was challenged at a Land Tribunal in 1955 but was upheld, with the regular general meetings of the colonists declared the licensor and the individual colonists the licensees of the land plots in question.

Entirely self-sufficient and refusing to handle money, or to buy anything (including building materials), they constructed their houses from the wooden parts of the disused railway carriages and sleepers. Some of those solidly built dwellings are still there and can be sold and bought for market prices of around half a million pounds, on condition that the buyers get approved by the general meeting of the Colony's residents – Whiteway's last clearly utopian trait, unless we include the preserved communal facilities: the Colony Hall, the open-air swimming pool and the common playing field.

If some of the first Whiteway colonists were openly eccentric and ostentatious – they spoke Esperanto and dressed like ancient Greeks – their present-day successors (about 150 people altogether) are much more 'normal'. Some of them work in Stroud and in the adjoining village of Miserden, and do not recoil from money any longer (no wonder – being the owners of expensive Cotswold properties!), yet, allegedly, still shun the banks and deal with cash alone. Just try and imagine a huge pile of banknotes worth half-a million pounds a potential buyer has to cough up to the house owner!

Another peculiar trait of modern-day colonists is their reclusiveness (or is it shyness?) – an impression we have carried away after a brief visit to the Colony during our campervan tour of utopian Britain.

'Whiteway Colony. Private Roads' read a billboard at the village's edge. The narrow unpaved path behind the sign, one of the 'private roads', or so we thought, was not particularly inviting, especially for Alphie, slightly wider than a normal Toyota. But there was no choice, and I carefully inserted Alphie into the track like a dagger into a sheath.

The path was lined on both sides with solid wooden structures of uncertain architectural styles that made me keep guessing what parts of discarded railway carriages they had been built from. The setting was similar to the village near Moscow, with the idiotic name Zaveti Ilyicha ('Lenin's Bequests'), the site of my tiny dacha – a ramshackle wooden shed, allocated to me courtesy of *Krokodil* magazine, where I worked in the 1980s. Only the 'sheds' here, in Whiteway, were much-much bigger.

Occasionally, we would spot a human carrying out some gardening or other chores in their smallish front yards. Initially I tried to wave to the colonists, who would invariably turn away from us, as if we were not actually there.

Their behaviour reminded me of a peculiar form of passive protest practised by residents of Estonia and other Baltic states

Arcadia and the Real Estate

during the Soviet occupation. Addressed by Russian speakers, asking for directions or inquiring about the price of this or that item in a shop, they would look right through them, as if they were an empty spot and did not exist. That was much better, however, than when having acknowledged your presence they would swear at you in Russian, or, worse, direct you politely to the part of the town opposite to the one you were looking for. As a Russian-speaking teenage boy frequently taken to the Baltics for holidays by my grandparents, I often used to find myself at the receiving end of such passive protests, but being sympathetic to the locals' plight (it was hard not to be), tried to take them calmly.

We soon reached the point where the path was solidly blocked by a giant tractor, with no sign of a driver behind the wheel, or under the wheels (in case he was repairing something there). After shouting Hello! into emptiness a couple of times, I decided we had to turn back which – considering the narrowness of the path – was easier said than done. After about a hundred three-point turns and as many unintended gentle contacts between the campervan and the tractor, I managed to turn Alphie around and was about to start steering him back down the track, when a woman materialised from a nearby wooden shack. She introduced herself as Sally and volunteered to escort us around the colony, or rather, as I suspected, to show us the quickest way out of it.

She climbed into Alphie and was providing a running commentary as we crawled on. Being an insider, she was nevertheless very cautious in sharing any information about the Colony on top of what I knew already. She even refused to reveal her last name. When I asked her what Tolstoyan principles, if any, the colonists were still adhering to, she mumbled something about general meetings at which garden plots were allocated to the colonists according to their needs. Slowly but resolutely, she led us out of the residential zone towards the colonial-style Colony Hall. With its cloister-like timber-front verandah and sloping roof, it was a grade II listed building.

'This Hall was originally part of the tuberculosis sanatorium in which George Orwell stayed before they transferred him to a London hospital where he died,' said Sally. 'We also had Mahatma Gandhi here in 1909.'

I couldn't help the impression that she was trying her best to distract us from looking deeper into the Colony's daily routine.

Trucks in the Garden of Eden

As for Gandhi's visit to the Cotswolds in 1909, I did read about it somewhere. The fact that for some reason got stuck in my memory was that he had, allegedly, bought his iconic rimless glasses, which he had worn all his life, at a pharmacy in Gloucester...

The Hall itself was closed indefinitely due to the pandemic. I peeped in through its dusty windows but could see nothing but bookshelves and a couple of empty cupboards. Following my old and tested dictum 'When everything else fails, read noticeboards', I shifted my attention to the building's exterior to study the following lengthy notice above the door:

WHITEWAY COLONY – DOGS

Colony meeting has received a number of complaints regarding dogs on Colony land. We have received complaints about dog litter on the sports field, around the children's play area and on Colony path and roads. Remember that the Colony sports field is not an off-lead exercise area...

There are 43 dogs in the Colony and most people are aware of the dangers of infection and how unpleasant in can be to step in some dog poo...

Please keep your dog on a lead on Colony land and clear up the inevitable deposits.

Please respect everyone else and do as you would be done by...

And so on.

What struck me most about that notice was how relatively well-written it was – in good English, without all those horrible bureaucratic and pseudo-PC clichés and such meaningless 'weedy' words as 'experience, 'solutions', 'in terms of', 'for the purposes of', with which most public notices in the UK are littered these days ('Toilet is closed for the purposes of cleaning' is a typical example). Could it be due to some mysterious blast-from-the-past Tolstoyan influence, I mused? It is amazing how much one can learn from a simple poop scoop sign. From the above notice, a curious visitor could deduce that:

1. The Colony still conducted its general meetings at which local issues were resolved by majority vote.
2. The initial 'utopian' facilities, like a common children's play area and the sports field were still in place.

Arcadia and the Real Estate

3. With 43 listed Colony canines and assuming that there was one dog for an average family of four, the number of modern-day human colonists would be around 150-160 people (which was the right number).
4. The Tolstoyan (or utopian, if you wish) community spirit of the initial colonists was still alive in Whiteway, if only just...

My last conclusion found support in the property pages of a local newspaper I browsed through in The Carpenter's Arms in the nearby village of Miserden. This confirmed that, as previously mentioned, modern-day colonists were happily offering for sale plots of land with their purpose-built environmentally friendly and once tax-free dwellings, constructed largely from freely available materials, for up to half-a-million quid each! 'The Colony is made up of a wide variety of properties with no deeds (remember, they were burned by the first colonists) so therefore (they) can only be sold to a cash purchaser...' the paper explained.

I particularly liked the following ad (the first colonists used to give nice utopian names, like Freedom, Meadow, The Cloisters etc. to their makeshift 'properties') 'Freedom, Whiteway, Stroud 3-bed detached house. Freedom is a spacious and bright detached single storey dwelling set in an idyllic rural location within the famous Whiteway Colony...'

'Freedom' was now available for cash! There could be no bigger clash with Tolstoy's guiding principles, on which the Colony had been founded:

'Every man that is born has the same right to support himself from the land as he has the right to air or the sunlight; and that therefore no man has the right to regard any land he does not cultivate as his own,' Tolstoy wrote in his article 'How Shall We Escape', which used be holy writ for the Colonists.

As I was happily sipping my Diet Coke in the Carpenters Arms, the final collapse of Whiteway's Utopia seemed both obvious and irreversible.

I was reminded of the words of Voland, the Devil reincarnate, from Mikhail Bulgakov's novel *The Master and Margarita*: 'They (the 1930s Muscovites) are like people anywhere ... they are ordinary people – only the housing issue has had a bad effect on them.'

Trucks in the Garden of Eden

After the Whiteway 'experience', we were in need of cheering up. That was why, having spotted a faded road sign 'Bourton-on-the-Water' off the A436, I decisively steered Alphie towards that village (or was it a town?), which, I knew, had the reputation of being the Cotwolds' quirkiest. Not that I expected to find any kind of Utopia there (well, maybe subconsciously I was), but the 'tillage' (let's call it that – a merger of 'town' and 'village'), popularly known as 'The Venice of the Cotwolds', simply could not be missed, not by a long-time fan of the real Venice, of which I even had the temerity to write in my book *Little is the Light* some years ago:

> After my many visits to this amazing city, I came to regard it as an ageing, yet still graceful, woman suffering from insomnia and dragging restlessly around the house in her worn-out, loose-fitting slippers in the night. Soft splashes of water against the ancient Venetian stones are like shuffling of slippers across the floor...
>
> At sunset, when the opaque, mica-like water in the canals begins gleaming suddenly with a magical translucent glow of its own, as if slowly, almost reluctantly, discharging the sunlight it has accumulated during the day; when blinds fall like thick black eye-lids of an Italian beauty on the gaping eye-sockets of tired old houses; when gentle tolling of distant church bells mingles with the soft sucking chorus of lovers' kisses – there suddenly comes a whiff of fresh sea breeze, a reminder of the days when Venice signified ships, exotic ports and new trade routes to be explored.'

By visiting Bourton-on-the-Water, I was also hoping to further extend my ever-growing collection of clichéd toponymical sobriquets, which already featured the following 'Venices' (in no particular order): Venice of the Orient (Suzhou, China); Venice of Ireland (Cork); Venice of Japan (Osaka); Venice of Mali (Mopti); Venice of Brazil (Recife); Venice of the East (Bangkok); Venice of the South (Tarpon Springs, Florida), as well as such multiple clichés as the 'Venices of the North': Amsterdam, Hamburg, Manchester, Ottawa, St. Petersburg, Stockholm, Birmingham (heaven knows why), and 'Venice of the West' (Glasgow, Nantes, San Antonio, Texas). Believe it or not, there even exists a 'Venice on Land' – a nickname for the Italian city of Vicenza, which has no canals, but a lot of palaces,

Arcadia and the Real Estate

just like Venice proper, which, due to the proliferation of its aspiring namesakes, will soon have to be renamed 'the Venice of all Venices'.

Each of those sobriquets can be regarded as a (failed) striving for a Utopia; or simply as toponymical laziness and lack of imagination. There is, however, one assumed 'Venice' in the world that, to my mind, fully deserves its sobriquet and its clearly utopian, in my eyes at least, status. Particularly since February 2022, when Russian troops invaded the country of my birth.

I am talking about the 'Venice of Ukraine', the town of Vilkovo in the Odessa region, one of the areas targeted by Putin's armoured fist. Situated in the Danube Delta where the river splits into three branches before entering the Black Sea, Vilkovo (population 8,000) is a unique – and thoroughly utopian – urban settlement. 'Ukraine's Venice' is built on 72 islands in the Danube Delta marshlands, with canals instead of streets and roads.

My main memory of Vilkovo is a botched fishing expedition, when at the age of 15 I was on holiday there with my Mum, who reluctantly allowed me to join a couple of local boys going fishing. In a boat, of course. And, as it turned out, in an old and leaky one, which duly overturned in the middle of a canal before we even had a chance to get our fishing rods ready.

Luckily, I was already a strong swimmer then (as for the Vilkovo boys, they all learn to swim before they walk), so we all had some fun splashing in the opaque, tepid water before stepping back onto the bank, like a bunch of young Neptunes in our soaked clothes. My mother, unsurprisingly, did not share our fun mood: I was banned from further fishing until the holiday's end, and therefore had plenty of time to admire the beauties of Vilkovo and to familiarise myself with the town's history, the knowledge that I had to fine-tune later.

Vilkovo was founded by the 'Old Believers' (see above), who fled Central Russia after the 'Great Schism' of 1650s and was declared a town in 1775. Boats were always the primary form of transport, and each home had (and still has) at least one moored at its doorstep. Most of them were built to resemble the distinctive Cossack 'seagull' boats, constructed centuries ago, although these days they are known as herring boats and are mostly used for catching same. Besides the Danube herring, sought after by restaurants throughout Europe, proper anglers, not prone to boating accidents, could (and still can) catch wild carp and catfish in Vilkovo's canals.

Trucks in the Garden of Eden

The houses in Vilkovo are all built on islets of the river sediment. They are high-maintenance homes, for each year a trench around the house has to be dug out to bring in new sediment, to allow boats access and to prevent flooding. Without that, they would sink back into the marsh. The sediment is fertile, and the gardens in Vilkovo are all lush and magnificent.

The islets are linked by a series of wooden walkways as well as some skilfully engineered bridges, making Vilkovo the ideal town for long walks, with fabulous views of the sea. In the past, the waterways, known as 'yeriks', were used for drinking water supplies, washing and cooking as well as transportation.

Vilkovo lies in a wetland that is home to over 950 plant species and almost 260 species of birds, including pelicans. I remember us taking a boat tour of the Danube Delta and admiring the landscape, with my Mum pointing out countless reed beds and lily-coated lakes. Human life in Vilkovo has always been defined by the natural rhythms of seasons, weather and water flows. The eternal life cycle will never be disturbed by the invaders' tanks...

It turned out that Bourton-on-the-Venice, sorry, on the Water, was well worth a detour. But not because of the town (village? 'tillage'?) itself, which proved as crowded, kitschy and unappealing as I had imagined. It did indeed, unlike the fully dry-land Vicenza, feature the narrow tributaries of the shallow Windrush River, straddled by a handful of miniature bridges, hard to discern behind the milling crowds of tourists and shops, with names like 'Past and Presents', 'Quirky', and 'So ScentiMentle': over a hundred of shops for a small 'tillage' of 3000 people, and – again, very much unlike in Vicenza –not a single bookshop among them!

No. That 'Bargain Venice', or else 'Lazy Man's Utopia' (new sobriquets of my own making) was well worth a visit due to one of its minuscule (in the true sense) attractions – 'The only grade II listed model village in the country', according to the flier I picked up in the Tourism Information Bureau.

Started in 1936 by a local publican to attract customers, the Model Village – a one-ninth scale exact replica of Bourton-on-the-Water – now contains around 100 little structures, built by specially commissioned local craftsmen from ashlars (slates) of Cotswold stone from a nearby Huntsman's Quarry.

Arcadia and the Real Estate

The most amazing (and dare I say utopian?) mini-structure of the model is the one-ninth scale replica of ... the Model Village itself, which, in turn, contains an even smaller (nine times smaller) copy of the first replica, which, in its turn, contains... and so forth, like in The House That Jack Built nursery rhyme, the only difference being that the latter does end with the 11th stanza about the farmer finally sowing his corn, whereas the number of the Model Village mini-replicas is infinite! At least theoretically it is, for the progressively tinier copies would soon become impossible to discern with a naked eye and would then require a hypothetical powerful microscope to be admired. This recursively (and, in theory, endlessly) appearing within itself of a picture or object is known as the Droste Effect, or *mise en abyme* (literally 'placement into abyss'). Named after a Dutch brand of cocoa, or rather a tin of such cocoa (of which I own a copy), designed by Jan Misset in 1904 and featuring a nun holding a tray with the same (yet, no doubt, much smaller) Cacao Droste tin, featuring a nun, holding a tray with the same tin, featuring... and so on until the famous blue-eye Dutch cows come home – and they never will.

I am not sure if the anonymous Model Village builders used that artistic device deliberately, or had even known of its existence, but the effect was striking. Standing there inside the Model Village, still located in a former pub garden, and looking at the Model's smaller replica inside the Model, and at even smaller ones inside even smaller Models, until the only thing I could discern was a paint-stained pea-size ball, I felt uncomfortable and dizzy, as if finding myself in between facing mirrors and staring into infinity.

The sensation was not helped by my self-appointed guide, a middle-aged lady from the Model Village's ticket office (I was the only visitor and she was following me around, probably to make sure that I didn't nick and pocket a minuscule model house or a church).

As I was staring at the model, she unexpectedly materialised from behind my back and suggested that we chanted a special Model Village visitors' mantra. 'Repeat after me!' she ordered, and started wailing in a surprisingly low, almost baritone-like, voice: 'And here's the village inside the village inside the village inside the village inside the village inside the village!'

I have to confess that I obeyed the pushy woman-guide (probably out of courtesy) and bleated: 'Inside the village' faintly a couple of times, but then stopped and – like a draft-dodger in hiding – tiptoed away quietly. Incredibly, the woman carried on chanting on her own, and I could hear her muffled 'inside the village' for a while as I was running along the street towards the spot where Alphie was parked.

Since that bizarre episode, I had been thinking about the reasons behind it. The most likely explanation I could think of initially was the Model Village ticket lady's eccentricity. That was until on a *Daily Mail* website, into which I wandered accidentally, I saw an article with the headline (or a 'teaser', as journalists say) so lengthy and self-explanatory that it made the article itself quite superfluous: 'Our beautiful home is NOT (capitals are not mine) a theme park! Life in the 'Venice of the Cotswolds' that's now so overrun with tourists locals yell "get out of the way" to selfie-loving hordes of day trippers'. Phew!

The article (or its rather the protracted 'teaser' in which, to my mind, the only excessive word was 'beautiful') made me think that perhaps the ticket lady's abrasive 'inside the village' shouting was but a modified (or, possibly, gentrified?) version of the same 'get out of the way' mantra the beleaguered residents of Bourton-on-the-Water are so used to chanting.

That brazen supposition of mine is supported by the objective and well-meaning *Bradt's Slow Travel Guide to the Cotswolds*:

> Unfortunately, Bourton is a victim of its own quaintness... It is not so idyllic when the coach parks fill up and the streets throng with tourists – and the grassy banks that border the river become a pleasure beach so cramped that the resident mallards' only respite is to stand on one leg on a protruding pebble in the river... The shops are aimed at the souvenir-seeking day-tripper while the plethora of olde worlde tea shoppes clatter to the merry ring of cash tills.

Not in the habit of quoting guide-books, I nevertheless decided to reproduce that, rather literary, description, which helped me understand why Bourton dwellers are so prone to unexpected shouting.

The detour to Bourton-on-the-Water therefore was not entirely wasted in my Utopia quest. It showed that any attempt to replicate, or to simulate, an old classical and, if you wish, utopian, beauty is bound to fail, just like it did in Bourton, where, instead of a mini-Venice, they have created a mini-Vegas. Why

Arcadia and the Real Estate

Las Vegas? Because to me it epitomises unadulterated kitsch, an ultimate dystopia – an inevitable result of thoughtless on-the-cheap replication, to which they seem to be prone in the US.

It was there in the US, to be more precise, in Alaska, that I once saw a price tag saying: 'This claw is an authentic replica from a grizzly bear,' spotted, in the gift shop of a museum in Kodiak. The 'authentic replica', what an oxymoron, a four-angled triangle so to speak, was naturally made of plastic.

A brilliant book, *Vinyl Leaves. Walt Disney World and America* by Stephen M. Fjellman, a leading American anthropologist, starts with the following description:

> There is a tree in Central Florida. It is maybe ninety feet high and huge around the base and has a crown that stretches across almost as many yards as the tree is tall. From the top of this tree, when the wind is still, you can see almost to the Caribbean. The trunk looks about as much like that of a live oak as one might wish. The bark is deeply grained and covered with that pea-soup green colored stuff you see on the trees in hot, wet places. It's a big nice tree, a good place for the treehouse that adorns it. But it's not made of wood. The trunk and the branches are formed out of pressed concrete wrapped around a steel-mesh frame. The bark and green stuff that cover much of it are painted on. The leaves, all 800,000 of them, are made of vinyl.

Stephen Fjellman explains that the tree, 'Disneyodendron eximus ('out-of-ordinary Disney tree')' is in the Adventureland part of Walt Disney's World Magic Kingdom. For him, it became a symbol of 'commodification', the modern American culture of replication, of which another (and much larger) specimen is Las Vegas.

I came to Las Vegas in the very end of my 6-month-long American journey. In a way, I liked the place for its boisterous and unadulterated kitsch (Las Vegas' 'culture', spelt with a capital 'K') and for its total lack of pretence, as if the city was constantly taking the mickey out of itself. 'Mechanic on duty. Free aspirin and tender sympathy', ran a sign on top of a city garage. One did need a lot of aspirin and even more 'tender sympathy' to cope with Las Vegas...

One evening I was walking along Las Vegas Boulevard, locally known as the Strip, on the way to 'New York-New York' Casino – not to gamble, but simply curious as to how Las Vegas city fathers could seriously claim to have 'recreated' the seemingly inimitable Big Apple inside it. 'We have saved you a lot of airfare,' I heard one of them saying earlier on local radio. I never made it to 'New York'. Blinded by the Strip's epileptic lights (anything without moving lights has no right to be there) and deafened by the din of traffic, I felt in desperate need of an aspirin, when my attention was distracted by a brightly lit and somewhat downsized Eiffel Tower in the middle of a sidewalk. Squeaky 'Victorian' lifts were taking tourists to the top and back down – straight to the entrance of the famous Paris opera house – 'Le Grand Opera'. I deduced it was the façade of the new 'Las Vegas-Paris' hotel-casino. After many months in the States, my nostalgia for Europe was such that I decided to pop in.

I dived underneath a duly replicated L'Arc De Triomphe and having passed through a huge and windowless gambling hall, found myself in an old Paris street. In fact, it was not just one street, but a whole Paris quarter, with cobbled narrow lanes, al fresco cafes, shops ('Le Tabac', 'Le Patisserie', 'Le Boulangerie'), plane trees and even Parisians themselves – sitting on benches, queuing for baguettes and kissing under the trees. A street busker, sporting a traditional French beret, stood on the corner with his accordion.

The power of illusion was so strong that it took me a while to realise that everything in that fake Paris quarter: the shops, the cobbles, the houses, the trees, the street signs ('Les Toilettes') and even the mannequins of the 'Parisians' – was made of plastic. The sultry blue sky above my head was but a vast painted canvas (or was it tarpaulin?), and the recorded plaintive sounds of the plastic busker's plastic accordion were mixing with the non-stop hungry bleating of the voracious fruit machines from a gambling hall behind the wall.

I popped into 'La Boulangerie', attracted by appetizing displays of freshly baked baguettes and croissants in its window: I hadn't had proper 'European' bread – as opposed to its cotton-wool-like American variety – for many weeks. Inside, they were selling nothing but muffins and waffles, and all the croissants and baguettes on display were purely 'decorative' and made of plastic.

Feeling claustrophobic, I could not wait to get out of this synthetic world of well-crafted make-believe. One sign you won't find easily in Las Vegas casinos, however, is 'Exit'. I didn't notice how I got lost in the cobweb of plastic streets. Exhausted and dizzy,

Arcadia and the Real Estate

I lowered myself on a plastic chair outside a 'Bistro' and ordered 'un café noir', which proved to be of a tepid and wishy-washy American type. Sipping the watery drink and making notes in my memo pad, I was suddenly blinded by a bright camera flash, then – another one, then – yet another.

I looked up. A flock of Japanese tourists on the opposite side of the plastic 'street' were aiming the gaping barrels of their Nikons at me. Ready to shoot. My first thought was that they had mistaken me for some obscure Hollywood star, but it didn't take me long to realise that they simply viewed me as part of the 'Paris' set: a writer scribbling away at a Paris café. Perhaps they even thought that – like all other mannequins in the quarter – I, too, was made of plastic...

'Stop it! I am not plastic! I am real!' I wanted to scream, but didn't, for a treacherous thought flashed through my aspirin-hungry brain: what if they were right and I – after six months in the United States – had become plastic?

I ducked, then jumped up from my seat and, having overturned the plastic table and the chair, took to my heels, not stopping until I was back in the Strip. Until now, I have no idea how I managed to find the exit.

The feverish lights of Las Vegas Boulevard kept blinking tirelessly, as if searching for something they were never meant to find...

Our last Utopia of the day was supposed to be Chipping Camden – the name that sounds a bit like an attempt at swearing, particularly if pronounced through clenched teeth (try it). In fact, according to Adrian Room, the guru of British place names and the compiler of numerous place name dictionaries, 'Chipping' represents the Old English 'ceping' (market place), from 'ceap', market, as in Cheapside. This word was added to an earlier name when a particular place gained a market... Chipping interesting (forgive my Old English) it all is!

We were out of chipping luck. At nearly 5 pm, the town was all but closed, partly due to the ongoing Covid pandemic, partly to the end of the working day at those few shops and offices that had not been indefinitely shut down. The Utopia was nowhere to be found, it seemed.

We managed, however, to talk (and, in Tashi's case, to bark) our way inside the Museum of Craft and Design in the old Court Barn, which was about to close its doors for the day. One of the Museum guides, charmed by all three of us, but, most of all, I suspect, by Tashi, kindly agreed to conduct us on a blitz ten-minute guided tour. Having done my homework (as I always try to), I already knew most of the things she was talking about.

In our guide's words, it was a 'romantic dream' of Charles Robert Ashbee, an English architect and jewellery designer, that made him (under the influence of William Morris's socialist ideas) relocate his London-based Guild and School of Handicraft of 50 craftsmen and their families, altogether about 170 people, to Chipping Campden. His aim was to establish a rural Utopia, satisfying work in a healthy environment. But why Chipping Campden, not somewhere else?

One reason was that in 1902 the town was in decline and had a number of cottages and industrial buildings standing empty and adaptable to the Guild's needs. The Old Silk Mill buildings, for example, could potentially house the printing presses on the ground floor, with metalwork and furniture workshops above.

Another reason for choosing Chipping Campden was Ashbee's innate romanticism. He inherited from his father interest in things strange and exotic, of which the town of 1500 people had plenty: from the slightly leaning Pisa-style Town Hall Clock Tower to its own Olympic Games, the so-called Cotswold Olimpicks, taking place annually from 1612 and incorporating events like coursing with hounds, tug of war and shin-kicking! Now you understand why Ashbee and his fellow craftsmen could be forgiven for regarding (initially at least) Chipping Campden as a sort of an Arcadia – a Utopia-like pastoral place of peace and beauty, populated with simple and innocent people.

Fiona MacCarthy, in the aptly-titled chapter 'Cockneys in Arcadia' from her informative and well-written book, *'The Simple Life, C. R. Ashbee in the Cotwolds'*, published in London in 1981, offers an interesting description of the early 20th-century town's quirkiness: Chipping Campden 'had more than its fair share of 'rum old orkard (Victorian slang for 'drunk) characters', one of the standard figures in all accounts of village life as it once was in England, 'when the village lunatic, the village quack and the village politician still existed'.

She then lists a couple of 'such notable eccentrics full of old orkard: Dolphin, the cottager who kept his small room full of potting earth and sometimes cleaned the front of his house with a pail of water and a toothbrush dressed in an ancient postman's hat

Arcadia and the Real Estate

and coat; and Malin, the saddler's boy, who got under his bench when anyone looked through the window; and Sykes, who started as a medical student and ended up driving cattle'.

'The life of the community was very self-contained,' MacCarthy concludes in what I would call a classic English understatement, which nevertheless poses the question: did that highly eccentric (if not to say haywire) 'self-contained' community need the sudden influx of the crowd of London artists and craftsmen, with their utopian aspirations and families in tow?

It was perhaps a bit short-sighted and even selfish on Ashbee's part to expect a warm welcome in Chipping Campden – a poor and 'self-contained' community that was happy in its own way. Why selfish? Because, as I think, the real underlying reason for the move was the fact that compared to London, Chipping Campden was incredibly cheap. The Cotswolds in general was then a deprived part of the country, not yet besieged by hordes of tourists. Food, property and everything else there was considerably less expensive than in London. The turn-of-the-century Chipping Camden, to where the already hard-up Guild relocated, could be renamed Cheap-ish Campden, or even Cheap-ish Camden (without the 'p', as in the London borough, the name, according to Adrian Room, stemming from 'Campden' – 'the valley enclosure').

The move was a mistake of course. The locals, who loved spending time in the village inns, which Ashbee and his followers hated as anathema to socialist progress, did not want the craftsmen in Chipping Camden. As MacCarthy observed, 'news of the incursion of 150 socialists from London was regarded by the locals with suspicion, if not out and out hostility.' That hostility resulted not just in occasional clashes (verbal and physical) in the Swan Inn, but in the locals refusing to buy the craftsmen's produce, which most of them were unable to afford anyway. With the furniture and metalwork markets already saturated, the Guild soon ran out of funds and had to be liquidated in 1907, less than 5 years after relocating to Chipping Campden.

Well, what can I say? 'Location, location, location', as modern real estate agents formulate their three main principles. It is no less important for the searchers of an Arcadia, an Edenic kind of Utopia, heavily focused on the pre-existing natural environment – and that includes the indigenous population of a coveted place. Unlike the modern-day Whiteway colonists (see above) and similar to the followers of the Panacea sect (see Chapter 4), who had

Trucks in the Garden of Eden

grossly misplaced their own Garden of Eden, members of the Guild and School of Handicraft, while being undisputed masters of their trade, were no experts in real estate, which, remembering Mikhail Bulgakov's Voland (see above), had 'spoiled them'. They had gone for a cheap scenario without considering its longer-term implications.

To sum up my personal perception of Chipping Campden's short-lived 'Arcadia' and paraphrasing Alexander Pushkin's famous dictum (from his 'Mozart and Salieri' drama) 'Genius and villainy are two things incompatible,' I can state responsibly that, likewise, Utopia and real estate are two things incompatible, too! Again, like in so many other attempted Utopias, 'the boat of love had crashed against the rock of routine' (pace V. Mayakovsky).

To be fair, Ashbee's Arts & Crafts Utopia, sorry, Arcadia, did have a lasting impact: Utopias often do. Chipping Camden these days is resplendent with art galleries, craft and jewellery shops and such like. Most of them were closed on the evening of our short visit, but their sheer presence made it clear that the town had become a lucrative place for artists and a destination for tourists. And the best proofs of that were the only things in town that remained permanently on display day and night, and even at the height of the pandemic: windows of multiple real-estate agencies featuring local properties worth £1.5 million and more. One thing was certain: it was no longer a Cheap-ish Campden. The town's short-lived Utopia was over. For good.

We did manage, however, to witness a small Utopia in action that very evening, on the campsite where we stayed overnight. Having spent over an hour trying unsuccessfully to put up a small toilet and changing tent next to Alphie (it – the semi-assembled tent, not Alphie – kept suddenly jumping up in the air and then collapsing on the ground), I was distracted by the amazing happenings on the parking slot next to ours, to which a quiet elderly couple had arrived in a battered jalopy almost simultaneously with us. Without saying a word to each other, they produced a huge roll of tarpaulin from the boot of their car and set to work. They obviously knew what they were doing – each attending to their own specific task before proceeding to the next one. In front of our eyes, a miracle was happening: out of a shapeless pile of tarpaulin, a small palace, with several rooms, windows, a door with an anti-mosquito net and its own spacious veranda with a roof, was growing slowly but surely. With every minute, it looked cosier and closer to perfection, and soon the taciturn grey-haired couple, having packed up their tools and switched on the electric lights inside their makeshift mini-palace, walked off towards the bathroom unit, hand in hand!

Stunned by that real-life Utopia unveiling in front of our eyes, all three of us, including Tashi, were looking at them with our mouths agape.

Chapter 9

Ornate Doors to Nowhere

Every Utopia has an implied dystopia.
Damien Rudd, *Sad Topographies*

On the way to Wales, we made a detour to Bournville, a Model Village (life-size, not miniature, like in Burton-on-the-Water, thank God) turned 'Garden Suburb' of Birmingham. Started in 1895, it predated Letchworth Garden City by eight years and was a source of inspiration for Ebenezer Howard, who, on visiting Bournville, to which the *Birmingham Daily Gazette* referred in 1901 as 'the Modern Utopia', stated publicly: 'A garden village (Bourneville) has been built, a garden city (Lechworth) is but a step beyond.'[12]

Bournville was conceived by George Cadbury, a Quaker and a cocoa magnate, as a 'chocolate town', his intentions being noble and praiseworthy, if totally utopian. He wrote in 1907:

> The Founder is desirous of alleviating the evils which arise from the insanitary and insufficient accommodation supplied to large numbers of the working cases, and of securing of workers in factories some of the advantages of the outdoor village life, with opportunities for the natural and healthful occupation of cultivating the soil.

By then, there were over 350 houses in the village, and, to manage his creation, Cadbury founded a charitable Village Trust, which still administers Bournville.

Having driven (or rather crawled) through the drab, dirty and traffic-ridden streets of Birmingham city centre and finding ourselves in the leafy, quiet and lovingly laid-out suburban village of Bournville was like getting out of hell and straight to heaven, created by George Cadbury and a (then) young architect William Alexander Harvey, who designed most of the buildings in the new village. According to his plan, the streets in Bournville were at least 42 feet wide (including pavements), and the houses all set at least 20 feet from the road, so that the minimum distance between the opposite house fronts was 82 feet. Remember Owen Hatherley's 'socialist voids', so familiar to me from the Soviet Union (Chapter 2)? Sorry, I couldn't help the analogy, which in the case of Bournville, didn't seem particularly relevant at the first glance. But let's wait and see...

The houses of different sizes and designs, from Tudor and English Country styles to Dutch Colonial Revival and Arts & Crafts, were not arranged in straight lines, but placed irregularly, even higgledy-piggledy, yet each had all modern (for the early 20th-century) conveniences, including the coveted, but very rare (at that time) bathrooms.

Church bells were tolling musically above the neatest imaginable village green, in which small groups of locals were strolling unhurriedly or relaxing on comfy white benches under the trees. We sat on one of the benches, with Tashi squeezing in between us, and had the most amazing impromptu picnic of cheese sandwiches and dog sausages (I mean the sausages were *for* dogs, not made out of dogs, as – allegedly – some cheap sorts of soap were in the USSR), while listening to the divine bell music, which, as we soon realised, was coming not from the nearby church of St Frances, but from a small rectangular hut next to the terem-like diamond-shaped Visitors Centre in the middle of the Green.

As we found out later, those were the sounds of a Carillon – a musical instrument comprising a minimum of 23 bells, played from a baton keyboard. It is most commonly found in Belgium, France and the US and is a rarity in the UK. The 4-octave Bournville Carillon was installed on the roof of the village school and later taken down to the level of the parapet by George Cadbury himself (to please the workers, no doubt). With 48 bells weighing 17.5 tons, it is adjudged one of the world's finest.

Why a carillon, and not something more familiar, like, say, a grand piano or an organ? My guess is that George Cadbury, a well-disposed and mildly eccentric dreamer by nature, wanted to

Trucks in the Garden of Eden

make his creation, Bournville, unusual, even unique. As we would soon find out, the carillon was not the village's only curiosity.

It was a warm day, and we soon felt like having a drink. Tashi showed his thirstiness by a series of habitual high-pitch whinges, which momentarily droned out the divine bells.

Next to the green, we found a small shopping mall with an alfresco cafe. 'Can we please have a water bowl for the dog, a latte for the lady, and a bottle of lager for myself?' I asked the waitress, who seemed to recoil on hearing my order and gave me a blank stare.

'What? Beer? You are in Bournville, sir!'

Customers at neighbouring tables stopped sipping their coffees and were eyeing me with a mixture of scorn and fear, as if I were a junkie on the loose demanding an on-the-spot crack pipe.

How could I forget that George Cadbury as a Quaker and a health addict had made sure that Bournville was strictly teetotal, just like Letchworth under Ebenezer Howard (who, incidentally, was neither a Quaker nor a teetotaller himself). But, unlike Letchworth, which stopped being teetotal in 1958, when a couple of 'proper' pubs were allowed to open there, alongside the already existing (albeit, not too popular) non-alcoholic The Skittles, Bournville – according to Cadbury's bequests – was to shun alcohol forever.

We all know from history that an enforced prohibition (or near-prohibition) can only lead to an excessive clandestine drunkenness, which doesn't happen in Bournville only because it is effectively a suburb of Birmingham, with lots of pubs and wine bars within a short walking distance. Declaring a unilateral prohibition in a small district in the middle of a large and heavy-drinking industrial city was not effective. It smacked of a similar Bolsheviks' decree in Russia in 1918–1921, or of Gorbachev's decision to limit vodka sales in the late 1980s USSR.

I was always of the opinion that there was something thoroughly totalitarian (and hence, perhaps, perversely utopian) about a nanny state and its manifestations. An unexpected further proof of that was awaiting me in Bournville's Stirchley library, which I visited the following morning (we stayed overnight on the Birmingham University campus) in search of some local history material. It was there that I came across a pocket-size 1924 booklet, with a lengthy and somewhat oxymoronic ('suggested rules') title that sounded like a cross between a code of conduct and a Christmas card: 'Bournville Village. Suggested Rules of Health. With Best Wishes from George Cadbury'. Had it not been for space constraints, I would have been tempted to reproduce it here in full. Here's an extract:

> If you follow these rules, you will be healthier and therefore more cheerful. You will probably live ten years longer than those who ignore them.
>
> Do not take more than three meals a day... Some delicate children need a cup of milk before going to bed.
>
> Do not take flesh meat more than once a day...
>
> Avoid alcoholic liquors, tobacco, pork, aerated drinks, and all drugs as far as possible.
>
> Bring milk to boiling point before using; do not boil.
>
> Never allow water to stand on tea more than three minutes, or tannic acid, which us injurious, is developed.
>
> Be sure that bread and other food is well cooked.
>
> Furnish your sleeping apartments with single beds; double beds are now little used in civilised countries, except in the United Kingdom.
>
> Breathe through the nostrils with the mouth closed, especially at night.
>
> Teeth should be brushed night and morning.
>
> Sleep is much more refreshing when the room is dark...
>
> Do not sleep in any clothing worn during the day...
>
> In a truly happy home the father or mother will conduct family worship at least once a day when the Bible should be read and a hymn sung.
>
> Cultivate a cheerful and thankful spirit.

Reading those 'suggested rules', I kept remembering a slang Odessa expression: 'Are they having me for an idiot, or what?' (translated word-for-word). There was a separate brochure distributed to every resident of Bournville under 21 years of age. The 'suggested rules' in it were along the same lines, yet had some additional 'tips': 'Aim at reading good books... To breathe is to live... To breathe deeply is to live a healthy life... Never spend money for the sake of spending it. And to crown it all: 'If you frequent the picture palace or theatre, remember that yours is the responsibility to decide whether it is beneficial and instructive or degrading or harmful.'

All of a sudden, Bournville has all but lost its attractiveness. To someone like myself, who grew up in a totalitarian state where everything that wasn't explicitly permitted was forbidden (whereas the main rule of a democratic society is the opposite: everything that is not explicitly prohibited, is allowed), all those 'suggested rules' sounded painfully familiar, as if I heard the invisible yet omnipresent Big Brother of my childhood and youth whispering again in my ear: 'Do follow these rules, or else...'

With all due respect to Cadbury's Quaker views – temperance, obsession with health – he had no right to impose them on the residents of Bournville of his own time and of the future. A town dweller or a tourist is unable to buy a pint of beer not because it is not available (like in the former USSR where any kind of beer was one of the hardest to get commodities, and people – including yours truly – were prepared to queue for many hours to get it), but because someone decided it was not good for you. This was a clear manifestation of totalitarianism which made me agree with Isaiah Berlin and Karl Popper, who thought that utopianism was at times the highroad to totalitarianism. Again, I found the toxic remains of the Soviet Union in the most unlikely place – the allegedly utopian former model village of Bournville!

My brief visit to Bournville's main attraction, the Cadbury World emporium-cum-theme park, only strengthened that impression.

'You are entering a Utopia!' ran a sign at the entrance.

'At last!' I smiled.

With my long-time aversion to anything sweet, the result of chain smoking which had ruined not just all my teeth, including the sweet tooth that I remember having as a small child (prior to picking up cigarettes at 16), but also most of my sugar-sensitive taste buds, I was probably not the right person to appraise Cadbury, that chocoholic's Utopia ('choc-ful of history news and tasty treats', according to a promotional brochure), with its 14 'chocolate zones' and numerous 'Chocholatey Rides' and tasting points, where kids from all over Britain, having stuffed themselves with chocolate, were getting hyper and unruly.

My own impressions aside, let's have a quick look at some of the reviews on uk.trustpilot.com: 'Not worth the money. Go to ASDA instead'; 'Costly'; 'Outdated and Overpriced', 'What an absolute waste of time', 'Absolute waste of money', etc.

Ornate Doors to Nowhere

Cadbury as a company, which is no longer UK-owned, is now facing accusations of child labour, environmental damage and excessively high sugar content in its products, so the habitual Utopia-turned-dystopia pattern would appear complete. George Cadbury's health-conscious intentions were indisputably good (at least, in the beginning they were) and most of his 'suggested rules' were useful, but as asserted by an old Portuguese proverb which has become this book's main dictum, the road to hell is often paved with good intentions.

Our quick visit to Bournville had a happy ending, after all. The lucky coda was played out in The Country Girl pub, right outside Bournville's territory and Cadbury's sphere of influence, where prohibition rules were no longer applicable. I can't recall enjoying my pint of lager more than I did then. And Tashi, too, was savouring his meaty sausage provided by one of The Country Girl's chefs.

Wales is the part of the British Isles which I know less than England, Scotland and Ireland, in all of which I have lived and worked at some points in my life, so travelling in it felt almost like exploring a 'foreign' environment. That somewhat outlandish sensation was considerably enhanced by the almost Mediterranean (in all except for the weather)-looking towns and the road signs in Welsh: 'Araf '– Slow; 'Allan' – Exit etc. I joked to Christine that Araf and Allan were two Welsh brothers who were there to welcome us to their country as we were driving across the irregular and erratic border between Wales and Shropshire, like wool thread chased by a playful kitten.

With a handful of utopian settlements to visit, we had to stay overnight at B&Bs and at campsites too. Tuned to spotting utopian (i.e. near-ideal, near-perfect, dream-like) features in the cities, towns and villages, we couldn't help ticking off similar signs in the places where we stayed. The first one was Caer Beris Manor Hotel in Builth Wells, a Grade II listed manor house, set in 18 acres of parkland. We were put up in 'Her Ladyship's Suite', with a 4-poster bed the size of a medieval town square (so large that sleeping in it alone could be classified as a minor offence) and a view of the river.

Views are important. One can change the wallpaper and rearrange furniture in the room, but the view from the window remains the same. I have always believed that views from hotel windows should be graded, in the same way Karl Baedeker used to grade nature walks and vantage points. Touching the old black wrought-iron handle to open the leaded window at Cear Berris was like travelling through time.

Next morning, we took time to explore the grounds of Caer Beris, walking through trees to the river and marvelling at the rhododendron bushes planted by Lord Swansea, who bought the house in 1923. Utopia is a place to where you are always tempted to return, and we did return to Caer Beris for lunch on another day, despite having to make a detour from our 'utopian route', the next stop on which was Hay-on-Wye, the world's first book town on the English-Welsh border.

To be honest, it was I – a book worm and collector of many years standing – who single-handedly declared Hay-on-Wye a Utopia, because for me it was. I used to visit the town often and knew Richard Booth, the book town's founder and its self-proclaimed monarch quite well. Sadly, the King passed away in 2019. As a self-proclaimed, or rather Booth-proclaimed, micronation (an area that claims sovereignty without being recognised by any other sovereign states), Hay-on-Wye was a Utopia by definition, as all micronations are.

Richard Booth opened his first bookshop in the town in 1961. He started by bringing in truckloads of discarded volumes from American university libraries and even now one can see faded stamps of these libraries on many a Hay-on-Wye book. At that time, there were just two hotels and one b & b in town. Booth was determined to turn Hay into a book town, but for many years his efforts went unnoticed. The bookshops had neither appropriate light and temperature conditions nor cataloguing systems, so finding any particular title was almost impossible. Thousands of volumes piled in cardboard boxes were rotting in dark and damp cellars.

In 1976, publicity-desperate Booth launched a 'Home Rule for Hay' campaign. His slogans included: 'God save us from the Development Board for Rural Wales' and 'Balls to Wall's, eat Hay national ice cream!' As the self-proclaimed ruler of Hay, he hurried to appoint his horse, Caligula, prime minister. On 1 April 1977, Richard Booth declared Hay-on-Wye an Independent Kingdom with himself as 'King Richard, the Book-Hearted'. Because of that, the village was soon noticed by the media and its popularity grew by the year. Some major antiquarian booksellers moved in and tourists, mostly bookworms, began trickling in, too. Soon,

Hay became the venue for an annual literary festival. The number of bookshops reached 39 and the number of visitors 500,000 a year. Pubs, hotels and all 108 b & bs were thriving and the locals were singing the praises of King Richard. Thus, books and Booth changed the face of the town.

When I first visited Hay in 1990, old books were strewn all over. They were generously displayed not only in numerous second-hand bookshops but also on self-service stalls, exposed to the elements and often soaked with rain. Booth, dressed in rags and with a makeshift crown on his head, was trudging around the book piles, stopping occasionally to pick up a cigarette stub from the ground and light it up (occasionally, two at a time).

He shared with me his far-reaching and thoroughly utopian plans for a global book empire, with the capital in Hay-on-Wye. At that time, it was easy to dismiss them as 'haywire' (pun intended). Thirty years on, there were more than 50 places throughout the world – from Belgium and Norway to Japan, USA and Australia – describing themselves as book towns or villages, all modelled on Hay-on-Wye.

I interviewed King Richard for my *Daily Telegraph* travel column in the late 1990s. We spoke in one of the grim and unheated 'state rooms' of the partially restored Hay Castle, which he owned. 'Can someone bring in the heater?' the King shouted to no one in particular from his wobbly wooden 'throne'.

The King's brass and cotton, wool-lined crown was lying on the table next to him. His moth-eaten cotton-and-wool mantle was hanging on the back of a chair. The room was chilly and unkempt. The king's monologue lasted for almost an hour. He unveiled his plans to expand book towns to eastern Europe. He assured me that France alone will soon have at least 200 of them 'to supplement their goat cheeses'. He castigated Welsh local authorities for their neglect of small businesses (his favourite topic). He called himself a 'Huguenot in reverse'. He joked that 'every second-hand bookshop creates a museum of the unsellable'. He praised 'the democratic sunshine of Norway'. He claimed that 'no one reads books in Hay-on-Wye'.

He was simultaneously inconsistent and logical, gentle and outrageous, self-serving and selfless, brilliant and banal – but not for a second was he boring. And I was ready to believe him.

'According to the will of the people of Hay, I am reconstituting the House of Lords in Hay-on-Wye,' he confided. I wanted to ask him where he was going to get the lords from, but couldn't:

Trucks in the Garden of Eden

my tongue was frozen stiff. The answer, however, was obvious: if a horse could be appointed prime minister, then staid and self-important Hay-on-Wye cats could easily pass for a bunch of senile life peers.

In the backyard of Richard Booth's Bookshop, allegedly the world's largest, stood a shabby wooden barn, stuffed with Russian (or rather Soviet) books with titles such as *Socialist Realism Today*, *Scientific Communism* (that, alongside *Scientific Atheism*, was a compulsory subject at my Soviet University) and *USSR-GDR Friendship* Will Grow! There was a thick layer of dust on the shelves.

It looked as though, for once, Booth had committed a blunder and had hastily acquired the library of a provincial Soviet town's communist party committee. It was the proverbial junk-heap of history. Old Soviet guidebooks were there, too. One of them, *A Moscow Excursion* (1959), extolled the merits of the monument to Felix Dzerzhinsky, the founder of the Soviet secret police and the co-inventor of the Gulag, opposite the KGB HQ in Moscow's Lubianka Square: 'The monument is made of metal, which has an artistic logic, if we remember that comrade Dzerzhinsky was lovingly referred to by the people as 'Iron Felix'.'

Thirty-odd years later, in August 1991, the people would drag their 'much-loved' Iron Felix, a sadist and a cool-blooded executioner, from his desecrated pedestal. When books, especially guidebooks, put themselves at the service of rulers, they are bound to end up on a rubbish dump.

Now, in 2021, two years after the King's death, Booth's famous bookshop was a pale imitation of the original. Well, it was actually far from 'pale', but gleaming and spotlessly clean, and that was the problem! The wooden shed with Russian books was gone, and the main shopping area had neat bookshelves, lined with nicely bound and thoroughly catalogued volumes. In the same shop where throughout the years I stumbled upon such gems as the first 1935 edition of A. G. Macdonell's hilarious and insightful *A Visit to America*, the English translation of the mauvist novel by my favourite Russian/Soviet writer Valentin Kataev, *The Mosaic of Life* and many others, no more unexpected treasures were to be found, With the sheer joy of search and discovery removed, Booth's treasure trove had become an ordinary large bookshop,

And Hay-on-Wye itself was no longer a bookworm's heaven, with 'honesty bookstalls', where the customers were invited to pay as much as they wanted for a book by putting the money in the honesty box. at every street corner. It was now a gentrified and

Portmeirion – a touch of the Italian Riviera in North Wales. (Photos by Christine Bohling)

On a guided tour of Spielplatz, a naturist resort in Hertfordshire.

Town centre of Stevenage, AKA Silkingrad.

Brutalist architecture in Stevenage.

Stapleton Colony in North Yorkshire, the only remaining settlement of the Brotherhood Church.

Right: Letchworth Garden City's sleeping towers – the Cloisters building.

Below: Broadway Gardens – Letchworth Garden City's central square, with the fountain in the distance.

Bottom: The UK's first roundabout in Letchworth Garden City.

Above left: Cottages for miners' widows in Shilbottle.

Left: Honesty bookshop Hay-on-Wye.

Below: A house in Port Sunlight used in the filming of BBC's *Peaky Blinders*.

Above right: New Earswick, reportedly Britain's most successful model village, during lockdown.

Right: View of Saltaire.

Below: Workers' cottages in Saltaire.

Dinosaurs at large in New Lanark, Scotland.

Tremadog in Wales, one of Britain's earliest planned settlements.

Right: Remains of the ancient Utopian settlement on the Island of St Kilda, Outer Hebrides.

Below right: Foula. View from the playground of the island's primary school, presently with four pupils. MV *Greg Mortimer* is in the background.

Below left: One of the last four Sterwartby Brickworks chimneys to be demolished in 2021.

Above: Sunset on Rutland Water.

Below right: On the lookout for Utopias.

Below left: Pegasus Cottage, Vitali's writing shed.

Ornate Doors to Nowhere

prosperous festival town, with gastro pubs and al fresco cafes, full of Chardonnay- and Latte-sipping literati. Richard Booth's Utopia was gone, and the spirit of discovery and adventure had been replaced with an attractions-listing page from the latest edition of a Lonely Planet Guide.

But, luckily, not entirely gone! We found the last of Richard Booth's unsupervised 'honesty bookstalls' still surviving on the grounds of the old Hay Castle. All books there were priced at £1. And wasn't that a utopian miracle that there I spotted and acquired a true bibliographic rarity – a somewhat faded, yet otherwise well-preserved, copy of *The Sunlight'Year Book* for 1899. 'A Treasure of Useful Information of value to all Members of the Household'. With a special contribution by the 'eminent London historian Sir Walter Besant', it was published by Lever Brother Ltd in Port Sunlight, a utopian settlement near Liverpool, which was on the itinerary of our continuing quest.

That was not the last 'honesty shop', with a regulation honesty box we found. There was another in the grounds of the Fforest Fields Camping site, a 15-minute drive from Hay-on-Wye, where we stayed overnight.

An 'honesty box', or 'honesty shop' is a distinctly 'utopian' concept, for complete honesty, so hard to encounter in real life, has been one of the main principles of all Utopias, starting with the 'no place', invented in 1516 by Sir Thomas More. No wonder Fforest Fields has been called the Shangri La (a synonym of 'Utopia') of campsites by previous visitors and it was hard not to agree with that, albeit I would rather call it 'Arcadia' – the correct term for a rural or sylvan Utopia. And it was not just the honesty shop, a small general store with all the basics needed for an enjoyable camping night that you could help yourself to any time of day or night having left the money in the honesty box, but the general level of camping comforts that were not much different from Caer Beris. Except for the four-poster beds.

Our next camping night was at Daisy Bank Caravan Park, not far from Newtown, the birthplace of one of the world's greatest utopian thinkers, Robert Owen, whose museum was closed to the public due to the pandemic but was briefly re-opened specially for us.

Newtown, which, according to the omniscient Adrian Room and his *Dictionary of Place-Names in the British Isles* 'was already a 'new town' or new settlement in the 13th century, when its name was recorded as Newentone', had the misfortune of being officially designated a New Town in 1967, which meant that most of the grace and beauty it might have possessed until then was buried under ugly residential beehives, multi-storey car parks and multiple 'socialist voids' (to quote Owen Hatherley again). It was unimpressive, to say the least, and had Robert Owen known that his ideas would – even if indirectly – lead to that mini-Stevenage of Powys, he would have turned in his grave.

We met Councillor Rex Shayler, who had the keys to the Robert Owen Museum and had kindly agreed to let us inside. The arts-and-crafts Museum building, now also housing – very much in the spirit of Owen the educator – a free lending public library, was across the road from the spot on which the house had stood where little Robert was born in the room above his father saddler's shop on the 14 May 1771. That house was demolished in the 1920s, and in its place now – hardly in keeping with the ideals of Owen the socialist – was a branch of the HSBC bank. In fact, one small, yet important and evocative part of it had survived and adorned one of the walls of the Museum.

'A good memorial museum starts with authentic door handles,' Yuri Avdeev, director of Anton Chekhov's house museum in the village of Melikhovo, about 50 miles from Moscow, once told me as I was touching with trepidation the gleaming authentic door handles that Chekhov himself used to touch...

The organisers of Newtown's Robert Owen Museum went one step further by putting on display not just the door handles from the house of Owen's birth, but the whole oak door, complete with a handle, a knocker and even a keyhole, which the eight-year-old future social reformer had once stuck his historical finger into!

Here is how Owen himself describes that episode in his detailed and beautifully written autobiography *The Life of Robert Owen Written by Himself*:

> I have narrated my narrow escape from being killed by the scalding of my stomach. Shortly before this event, I was doing something with the key-hole of a large door in a passage between my father's house and that of our next neighbour, and by some means I got one of my fingers fast in the key-hole, and in my attempt to get it out it was twisted so painfully that I fainted, and I know not how it came loose, for I was found in a swoon, lying on the ground.[13]

Ornate Doors to Nowhere

Little Robert was obviously one of those knowledge-hungry and inquisitive children who want to find out for themselves how everything works. We spotted that massive door the moment we crossed the threshold of the dimly lit, musty-smelling museum (with no other visitors, Tashi was granted entry too) built into a wall and leading nowhere. It seemed an apt metaphor for Robert Owen's wonderful utopian ideas, destined to hit the wall.

Owen was an archetypal Renaissance man. A child prodigy who started working and teaching others at the age of 10, he was preoccupied with the ideas of wellbeing, education and equality for everyone. Himself a businessman, a factory manager and proprietor, he abhorred child labour, exploitation and poverty and was full of optimism about human nature. 'There is but one mode by which man can possess in perpetuity all the happiness which his nature is capable of enjoying, that is by the union and co-operation of all for the benefit of each,' he wrote in 1826.

While being a humanist, Owen was also a practical industrialist, who firmly believed that the exploited workers' productivity was bound to be much lower than that of the happy and educated ones. 'The character of a man is without a single exception formed for him,' he wrote in the article 'New View of Society' in 1814 – a view diametrically opposite to the 'Social Darwinist' ideas of Herbert Spencer et al that came later. A 'socialist capitalist' by nature, Owen was wealthy enough to put those ideas into practice by laying the foundations of the global co-operative movement and by creating a 'material climate for happiness' – the near-ideal utopian workers' communities, with free schools and kindergartens, sanitary working conditions, social centres and other benefits, first in Scotland's New Lanark (see Chapter 12) and then in New Harmony, Indiana, both of which were temporarily successful.

To the end of his days, Owen remained an incorrigible idealist (he was also into spiritualism), a dreamer, and a staunch proponent of the ultimate goodness of human nature. 'By teaching the influence of surroundings, the earth will gradually be made a paradise and its inhabitants angels,' asserted he.

With lots of followers, called Owenites, all over the globe, why didn't Owen succeed in making the earth a paradise? The short answer is because its inhabitants, in their majority, were not angels!

In the end of our tour of the museum, Rex Shyler showed me a bulky brochure with the soporific title 'Robert Owen. A Resource pack for KS2 and KS3'. Despite the title, it was an instructive and

Trucks in the Garden of Eden

well-designed interactive manual (in English and in Welsh) for school kids on everything related to Robert Owen, published – coincidentally? – by the Wales Co-operative Centre (whatever that could be). The pupils were introduced to their great compatriot's life, ideas and works in an unobtrusive, almost playful, manner, with lots of fun tasks and exercises; like, for example, applying for a position of a Victorian factory manager and preparing questions for an interview with Robert Owen himself.

Alongside all those fun tasks, the brochure contained some sobering conclusions: 'Unfortunately, the world today is in many ways all too similar to world of the 1770s. According to the World Bank, 1.4 billion people are living in extreme poverty, defined by the Bank as earning less than $1.25 per day. This is nearly a quarter of the world's population. And inequality seems to be on the increase.'

The clever and honest manual tried to explain why Owen's noble ideas had eventually failed: 'Despite Owen's enthusiasm and hard work, not many mill owners followed his lead and improved conditions for their workers, and even today the living and working conditions for many people around the world are still very poor.'

One wouldn't be far away from the truth to assume that the anonymous authors of the manual shared my profound conviction that, at the end of the day, it was imperfect human nature that stood in the way of and subsequently ruined all Utopias in history.

In Owen's case, a good illustration of the above can be found in *History of American Socialisms* by John H. Noyes, published in Philadelphia in 1870 and referred to by Robert S. Fogarty in his 1972 monograph *American utopianism*. Summing up a first-hand witness's impression of New Harmony, Owen's American venture, he quotes the latter as saying: 'It is certain that there was a proportion of needy and idle persons, who crowded in to avail themselves of Mr Owen's liberal offer; and that they did their share of work more in the line of destruction than construction.'

Does that remind you of something? Yes, Manea Fen Colony (see Chapter 4) – an Owenite community in Cambridgeshire Fens, which collapsed due to the corruption, dissipation and selfishness of most of its members.

Back in Newtown's Robert Owen Museum, I felt an almost magnetic attraction to the nowhere-leading door, built into a wall – a solid oak symbol for all Utopias that ever existed. Like little Robert all those years ago, I had an urge to stick my finger in the keyhole. It was only the vague memories of a similar 'experiment' I conducted at the age of 6 by sticking my two fingers into an electric socket and being thrown across the room by an invisible force as a result, that stopped me. But I could not resist taking a quick peep through the keyhole, knowing only too well what I was going to see, yet with a naive utopian hope of getting a glimpse of the future (or of the past). Pitch darkness!

Our 'Safari Tent' at the Maesmawr Farm Resort in the Black Hills area of mid-Wales included a capacious Jacuzzi, that epitome of luxury (in Britain, if not in Australia) on the porch, and a four-poster bed. It was glamping at its best. Tashi had his own little bedroom, with a bespoke custom-made cradle, and a choice of two special dog-walking fields.

Reclining in the warm and bubbly Jacuzzi until late at night, I was lucky to get a couple of glimpses of the stars, normally invisible under Welsh clouds. I remembered the words of Jan Morris, a brilliant Welsh writer, when she invited me to visit her legendary abode Plas Trefan in the village of Llanystumdwy.

'Welshness is a contradictory concept, for we don't really know who we are,' she told me. 'We live in this beautiful country which for a large part of the year is suicidally awful, grey and lacking in light. In short, Wales is a muddle.'

I thought of her observation while luxuriating in the warm Jacuzzi in Caersws, looking at the stars winking at me from behind the leaky curtain of the Welsh sky...

While in Wales I wanted to revisit Jan Morris's dream village of Llanystumdwy and to look again at Plas Trefan (or Trefan Morris, as it is often called), which, as I knew, now stood empty: shortly after Jan's death in November 2020, her wife Elizabeth (who remained James Morris's wife after the latter underwent gender reassignment in 1972) was moved to a nursing home. I also knew that Jan's son Twm lived in the house across the road and was hoping to have a word with him.

We never reached Plas Trefan though, and for that I am inclined to blame SatNavs, with their dubious ability to make no distinction between a class A motorway and a permanently deserted country road, simply because they tend to calculate your route by distance alone.

From my meeting with Jan Morris, who picked me up at a train station nearest to her place, I had a vague recollection of her driving us uphill in her ancient jalopy. Our SatNav was notoriously useless on hilly terrain, for in its obsessive passion for shortcuts, it kept stubbornly directing us towards some precarious unpaved bridleways that ran via hilltops. Those miracles of modern electronics had not been programmed to differentiate not just between national highways and narrow mountain paths, but also between Minis and limos. As a result, having passed through a number of seemingly deserted hilltop villages, some of which, as we were told later, used to be home for the utopian hippy communities of the 1970s (no wonder, being so hard for the police to get to). As it was more diplomatically put by Clive Aslet, writing about one such village, Ystumtuen, a formerly thriving mining settlement still remembered by many as 'something of a paradise', in his excellent book *The Villages of Britain*: 'Some of them valued the privacy that existed at the end of muddy farm tracks; this was particularly the case for those associated with the drug culture.'

We actually did visit Ystumtuen at a later stage of our Welsh journey and spoke to Anthony, an ex-Londoner, who had moved there with his wife several years earlier. Anthony was busy painting a garden fence (the garden of an empty neighbouring house was full of pieces of rusty motoring junk) and pretending he was enjoying it Tom Sawyer-style. The only living soul in sight, he agreed that the village could represent a Utopia 'for those seeking out a quiet life', particularly in winter when the roads become unusable and 'the only thing you can do is lock yourself in your home and stay warm... Utopia for some but hell for others,' he concluded with a wry smile. Next to his fence, there stood a K7 red phone box, still in working order – probably Britain's last working public phone box, not turned into a mini-library, a defibrillator closet, or, as they did in one English village, a functioning mini-disco for one, complete with a rotating disco ball. I lifted the phone off the cradle and it gave out a thick low-pitch hoot. It was easy to imagine being connected to a 1970s police station to complain of the hippies' anti-social behaviour.

In short, in search for Trefan Morris, we lost all track of distance and time and ended up in a true 'bear's corner', a Russian idiom for a remote and God-forsaken place, on top of a small mountain (or was it a large hill?) from where the only way forward was a steep drop, which would have definitely constituted the shortest (and the fastest) way to reach the valley as campervan fragments and the remains of two humans and a dog. The uncompromising SatNav kept egging me on to press the accelerator and dash forward, which meant down.

Balancing precariously on the five-square-metre top of a hill, I finally managed to turn Alphie 180 degrees and gently steered him down. Revisiting Trefan Morris therefore had to be postponed.

Our stay in Machynlleth turned out longer than we had expected, the reason being my own absentmindedness. While we were hastily packing up Alphie at our latest glamping campsite in the morning, I mistakenly put a barbecue rake inside the leisure battery compartment. What followed was a mini-explosion and a small fire, which I was quick to extinguish. Yet the leisure battery, powering lights in the cabin, water flow from the tap in Alphie's onboard mini-kitchen, and most importantly, the fridge, was dead. That effectively made overnight camping impossible, and we opted instead for a two-night hotel stay in Machynlleth, known as a historic market town and the one-time capital of Wales – yet much less known for its own small Garden Suburb!

Modelled on Wrexham Garden Village and designed by T. Alwyn Lloyd, a follower of Parker and Unwyn (see Chapter 2), Machynlleth Garden Suburb, completed in 1913, consisted of nineteen gabled cottages grouped around a large, leafy green, which, in the words of Lloyd himself, was meant 'to give local Welsh character to it'.[14] Well, he succeeded, if only partially: the cottages were indeed all grey (and 'greyness', as Jan Morris confided, was one of Wales's most distinctive features) and looked rather dull as opposed to the cheerful and unorthodox arts-and-crafts cottages of Letchworth, What was missing to make the 'Welsh character' impression complete was rain, or a rotating water sprinkler in the middle of the green.

Looking for a non-existent sprinkler, I did not immediately notice several ferocious-looking dogs being walked off-lead by their owners, probably the Garden Suburb dwellers. One of those dogs (due to the unwritten rules of canine political correctness, I am not allowed to reveal the little monster's breed, but you can probably guess), without any reason or provocation, dashed at Tashi with his mouth agape. Within a fraction of a second, he had Tashi's wailing head deep inside his mouth. I had to protect our pet by sticking my bare hand into the brute's gaping gullet – not a clever thing to do (I was told later that I should have instead stuck a finger up the beast's anus), but I had no time to consider tactics. As a result, the ogre bit through my thumb (I still carry a scar on it), but Tashi escaped unharmed. For him, our time in Machynlleth was far from a utopian experience.

An agreeable local vet, having examined my bitten palm before injecting me with an antibiotic, or whatever it was in the syringe, told me that from the nature of the bite I might have saved Tashi's life, whereas I myself, in my habitual writer's fashion, was inclined to regard that incident as a warning to stop intruding into other people's Utopias – a message I was going to ignore.

We stayed at the Wynnstay – a traditional coaching Inn right in the town centre, just a couple of blocks away from the 15th-century Welsh parliament building; as they say in America, smack downtown. Charles Dark, owner of the Wynnstay, was passionate about presenting his hotel as a traditional inn for people to meet, have good food, hospitality and wine. The latter at Wynnstay was not just good, but truly outstanding. Charles, my fellow Italophile, who had lived in Italy for a number of years, had arranged for regular supplies of Italian wines, and one could drink them by the glass straight from a barrel, something I had never experienced anywhere else in Britain. And at dinner, we all (except for Tashi) tried an exceptional Italian Frizzante, a cooled sparkling red wine – a treat in the uncharacteristically hot Welsh weather. The delicious and aromatic Frizzante reminded of the Crimean wines of my Ukrainian youth. Not even in my wildest dreams could I imagine then that 40-odd years on I would be able to taste a similar wine in an old inn in the centre of an ancient Welsh market town, and that it would make me – if only momentarily – feel young again. A bibulous Utopia!

There was another improbable (utopian?) outcome of our two-day stay in the old Welsh capital. At our farewell dinner with Charles Black on our second (and last) night, I mentioned how much I enjoyed browsing in each of Machynlleth's four second-hand bookshops – quite a lot for a town of just over 2000 people. Then, after another glass of Frizzante, I delivered the following diatribe: 'Why don't you declare Machynlleth a book town, like Richard Booth once did in the neighbouring Hay-on-Wye? That is bound to bring more visitors to the town and more guests to your hotel. For starters, why don't you try and organise a book festival in

Machynlleth and dedicate it to Jan Morris and travel writing in general?'

Charles did not seem to embrace the idea on the spot (or if he did, he didn't show it), but a couple of months later, to my surprise, he phoned me and said that he might try and raise some money for the festival. Five or six months after that, the First Jan Morris Travel Writing Festival was firmly on its way. And in November 2021, having taken a three-day leave from Cambridge University, I returned to Machynlleth as one of the participating writers. I gave two talks there, one of them, coincidentally, had the same topic as my Hay-on-Wye Big Ten talk over 20 years ago – about my travels through the drinks of Eastern and Central Europe based my book *Borders Up. Eastern Europe Through the Bottom of a Glass*. Twm Morris was among the guests of that Festival, which since then has become an annual event and is now called Amdani – 'about her' in Welsh – meaning of course Jan Morris,

Chapter 10

The Bridge that Crosses Nothing

> Planned as part of the metropolitan city, the garden suburb is the best template yet devised to achieve a habitable earthly paradise.
> Robert A.M. Stern et al, *Paradise Planned*

At times, driving along precariously winding Welsh roads through rain and mist felt like moving inside a huge, chilled wine glass. I soon got used to Welsh road signs, and even started coming to grips with some names on the map by simplifying them to recognisable English words. Thus, the town of Betws-y-coed, which, for some reason, seemed to be on my way wherever I went, became Co-ed Betsy, Porthmadog – Port Mad Dog, Criccieth – Cricket and so on.

Purely for the sake of Tashi, still recovering after his gruesome Garden Suburb experience, we decided to stay away from 'Port Mad Dog' (just be on the safe side), but made a short detour to the beautifully laid out town of Tremadog in Gwynedd, blending gracefully and symmetrically with the surrounding hills. Both Tremadog and Porthmadog were founded by one and the same 'dog', i.e .William Alexander Madocks in 1798. But if the eminent British politician landowner and 'agricultural improver' took a lot of effort to plan Tremadog, his second child (as sometimes happens in families), Porthmadog, was neglected and ended up a tasteless architectural pile.

Coming back to the Welsh road signs, what made me a bit apprehensive of them was a bad experience I once had in Ireland, or to be more exact, in Rath Cairn – a predominantly Irish-speaking town, where almost all signs were in Gaelic only. It was there that I learned (under duress) my first two Irish words: 'Mna' and 'Fir' at times, misleadingly designated by just two letters, M and F, when

The Bridge that Crosses Nothing

looking for a toilet inside the local community centre. What can I say? There's no better way of mastering a foreign tongue than when confronted with everyday basic needs. To my great relief (in more than one sense), I spotted a blurred lady's silhouette above the 'Mna' (M) sign, which saved me from proceeding by trial and certainly error. There was no silhouette of any kind on the 'Fir' (F) door.

While preparing for the Wales part of the trip, I learned to my sheer horror that in Welsh there were 10 (ten!) different words and expressions for 'toilet' – from 'TY BACH' and 'LLE CHWECH' to 'LAF', 'GEUDY' and even 'CLOSED', the latter originating from the English word 'closet'. It was only when already in Wales that I was (again) hugely relieved to see that the most widely used Welsh word for 'toilet' was 'TOILED'.

Guided by my old Soviet-childhood habit of eating the yummiest bits of a meal last, I deliberately saved a visit to Portmeirion for the very end of our Welsh journey.

That highly eccentric and unusual Italianate dream-town was the creation of an equally eccentric (he famously wore breeches and long yellow socks still in the 1970s) and unorthodox architect Clough William-Ellis, or simply Clough, as he was known, On the surface of it, the place had little, if anything, to do with the utopian fragments I was looking for. Neither a model village nor a socialist-leaning workers' settlement, it was – as far as I knew – just a product of a nostalgic dream.

I gleaned that impression (which turned out to be correct in the end) when reading about Clough's long-term obsession with the Italian fishing village of Portofino, as well as with the Mediterranean lifestyle and architecture in general. Stuck for most of his life in rainy and windy Snowdonia, he was often dreaming (quite literally) of the sultry Mediterranean coast and its graceful sun-drenched architecture. With the 'general improbability of Portmeirion's very existence' in mind, here's how Clough himself explained the reason behind his life's main project: 'Why? Because the building of such a place to my own fancy on my own chosen site had been a dream at the back of my mind since the age of five, and never left me.'[15]

Nostalgia is one of the most creative human emotions. Particularly, nostalgia for a place. Not necessarily the place where you were born and grew up in. It can easily be a town, or a country, or even a continent, which you had never visited, but were still in love with.

I know that feeling only too well. As a travel-hungry little boy I was obsessed with Paris which I was sure I would never be able to see. An old tattered map of 'the City of Light' was the pride of my ever-growing collection of guide-books, atlases and train timetables. I would stare at it until my eyes started hurting and I was able to discern behind the threadbare rumpled paper the outlines of the Eiffel Tower; until I could smell the aroma of freshly made coffee in the Rue de Rivoli. In a self-induced dream-like state, I could walk, with my eyes closed, from Saint-Germain-des-Pres on the Left Bank to Montmartre...

I felt a similar bitter-sweet longing after a year in Australia, when I started missing my old beloved Europe, with such pain and passion that I was sometimes worried about my sanity. And I was not alone in my craving. I realised it having discovered Battery Point – a historic centre of Hobart, the capital of Tasmania. Both architecturally and in spirit, it was a smaller version of a 1950s English village recreated by the first settlers, mostly British convicts exiled to Tasmania, the so-called secondary prison, while already doing time in continental Australia. From there, as they knew, there was no return, so they decided to recreate their England down under: by planting chestnuts, oaks, limes and poplars etc in the reluctant Tasmanian soil; by building English- (and Scottish- and Welsh-) looking cottages and churches. One of Battery Point's most moving features is Arthur Circus – miniature copy of a Georgian London square.

For one man, Roelf Vos, a long-time immigrant from the Netherlands, a resistance fighter during the Second World and a self-made Tasmanian millionaire (whom I had the honour to meet in 1991, one year before his death) this nostalgia for Europe went even further: he lovingly recreated a whole Swiss village, complete with chalets, chateaux, Kirchen, and rosti-serving *Kneipen* under the gum trees, right there in the Launceston region in the middle of Tasmania. He named the village Grindelwald – and it is still there, now as a Swiss-style holiday resort and a living monument to the power of human nostalgia.

Having arrived down under with his family in tow, yet with not a guilder in his pocket, in 1951, Vos eventually made a fortune and started his own 'Roelf Vos' supermarket chain (known locally as 'Vossie's'), which gradually spread all over Northern Tasmania and beyond. Having sold the chain to Woolworths in 1979, he made his nostalgic dream come true.

The Bridge that Crosses Nothing

The town's construction began in 1980 around an artificial lake. Grindelwald is a truly unique place, with houses built in Swiss style creating a dream-like ambience throughout the entire village. Those houses have the authentic features of Swiss chalets, and visitors feel as though they are being teleported to Switzerland. The settlement is surrounded by glassy lakes and views of the Tamar Valley, somewhat reminiscent of the Swiss Alps. On the edge of the town is the 40-hectare Tamar Valley Resort, opened in 1989, which shares the Swiss architectural style.

A talented woodcarver, who decorated the town generously with his peculiar abstract wooden sculptures, Vos spoke of attracting hundreds of Swiss people to Grindelwald, and despite the fact that the Swiss are probably the world's most unlikely migrants, several families did indeed settle there during his lifetime.

Remembering Jan Morris's description of Portmeirion (in her book *The Matter of Wales*) as 'designed not just as a folly, but as a statement of aesthetic principle', I was half-expecting to find there another Tasmanian Grindelwald, which I had come to admire, with a strong Mediterranean touch.

Alas, our visit to Portmeirion proved less inspiring and shorter than we had expected – all because of Tashi. Or rather not because of him, but due to the new draconian regulations of the 'Portmeirion Village Resort', according to which 'Pets are not allowed on site, with the exception of Guide or registered assistance dogs/animals.'

The reasons for that? Here we go: 'One reason for the rule is the conflict pets (particularly dogs) produce in natural areas.' Conflict? Don't know about other pets, but Tashi only produces one thing in natural areas. That thing quickly gets picked up by the parents – sorry, the owners – and, having been placed in special plastic bags, is disposed of in the no-less special bins.

Let's read on. In a further attempt to justify their decision, the Resort administration has come up with the following pseudo-philosophical statement: 'Dogs, by nature, can damage sensitive habitats as well as harass or kill vulnerable wildlife.' Judging by the recent Garden Suburb episode Tashi represented the most vulnerable, even if domesticated, and not too wild, life. I am sure that Clough William-Ellis, with his passion for Portofino, would have been appalled by those regulations, for an Italianate – or any Mediterranean – village without dogs and cats is like a wedding without a bride, or a campervan without wheels.

And yet, we all – except for Tashi who hadn't been given a chance – fell in love with Portmeirion, despite the fact that we had to take turns visiting it: while one of us was enjoying the beauties of the resort, the other had to walk Tashi up and down the huge – and not at all utopian or dream-like – overflow car park.

The first thing that impressed me about Portmeirion the moment I passed between the two Palladian tollbooths marking the village's tollgate was how compact and versatile it was. A seemingly eclectic medley of different epochs and architectural styles, Gothic, Arts-and-Crafts, Colonial, Georgian, Tudor, Romanesque and more, the place did not look at all messy. On the contrary, all those different structures miraculously formed into a perfect architectural ensemble, enhanced by the stunning and nearly Mediterranean sea views. Yes, the presence of the village on its coast had somehow made the normally grey and dull Irish sea appear Mediterranean-like: deep-blue and aquamarine. An architectural Utopia of sorts.

I knew that Clough was not rich, and that most of the structures in Portmeirion were built not from scratch but rather ingeniously from existing ruins and semi-ruins, in danger of demolition, rescued by him and brought to the site of his village from all over Britain and Europe. The massive Renaissance fireplace in the village's Victorian-style hotel was removed from the Great Exhibition of 1851. The Italianate Campanile ('We have the need for a campanile,' Clough was reported as saying repeatedly) is surrounded by houses that came from some 18th-century English villages. The Arts-and-Crafts Town Hall contains a splendid 17th-century plastered ceiling rescued from a demolished mansion in Flintshire. There was also an impressive colonnade designed by James Bridges, carefully transported from Bristol and a Norman Shaw facade. No wonder Cough liked to refer to his creation as 'Home for Fallen Buildings'.

The abundance of carefully landscaped gardens and green spaces, and the proliferation of exotic 'Mediterranean' plants and trees – rhododendrons, azaleas, palms, cypresses, gingko and eucalyptuses – also added to the ineffable charm of the place.

I was particularly thrilled to spot a Battery Cottage of a Kentish character – a flashback to Hobart's nostalgic Battery Point, if only in the name. To me, it was the proof of a mysterious connection that appears to exist between nostalgic places in different parts of the globe...

I was getting an almost physical pleasure from wandering up and down Portmeirion's narrow lanes and cobbled squares, which made me think again that in my previous life (if any) I must have

The Bridge that Crosses Nothing

been a cat in a medieval European, most likely Mediterranean, town. Alas, in the village, cats (as well as dogs) were conspicuous by their absence. Unlike tourists, of whom about a quarter of a million visit each year. Being completely immersed in the place's nostalgic beauty and in my own Portmeirion-triggered reveries, I hardly noticed their rambunctious presence. It was with reluctance that I had to return to the car park: we had to drive on. Christine then went to the village to take photos while I was left to guard Tashi who was by then fast asleep in his makeshift bed inside Alphie. We thought that Portmeirion was an incredible achievement by the eccentric, persistent and not very wealthy architect, who – being unable for all sorts of reasons to live in his chosen landscape and environment – made that very landscape come to him!

It reminded me of yet another little-known utopian project of the mid-1960s, when British architect Ron Herron introduced to the world his concept of a Walking City – a metropolis consisting of a series of mobile structures (multi-storey buildings) that could move about on enormous telescopic steel legs, pretty much like the Martians from the *War of the Worlds*. The most famous (and rather scary, I have to admit) Walking City drawing I could find showed those self-propelling 'structures' to be at least thirty storeys high. They were designed to shift from one site to another in case the former proved unsuitable or didn't have a nice-enough view. A serious challenge to Motopia (see Chapter 6).

Luckily for us all, Ron Herron belonged to Archigram, a group of British dreamer architects, who didn't aim at having their projects realised and their robotic giants constructed. They were quite happy to simply produce disruptive, trailblazing and outrageously utopian ideas, among which we could also mention the Plug-In-City, a framework into which standard dwellings could be easily fitted, and the Instant City, a moveable airborne settlement hovering above the ground suspended from balloons.

It was the Walking City that appealed to me the most. Probably because of one of my childhood's favourite rhymes by Agnya Barto (Chapter 1) 'The House That Moved' about a slum-like Soviet *khrushchioba* – a city slum built under Khrushchev's rule – on wheels which travelled across the country to Leningrad to take part in the First of May parade.

Without a doubt, the Portmeirion Utopia, so lovingly nurtured and brought to life by Sir Clough Williams-Ellis, could have been even more complete without the unreasonable ban on dogs and cats, one of the basic components of the very environment Cough wanted to recreate.

But, as we have seen already, Utopias never reach completion. Otherwise, they wouldn't have been Utopias, or 'no places'.

As we progressed further North, our previously non-existent camping and campervanning skills kept improving.

Gone were the times when it took us over two hours to set up camp. We came to discover the advantages of a concerted team effort, with me unloading Alphie, putting up a storage tent and starting the fire; my wife turning around the seats inside the salon (easier said than done) and making them into a Pavarotti-size bed. Each of us knew what to do and, just like that taciturn elderly couple we had admired in the Cotswolds, we hardly spoke until everything was ready for an unhurried evening feast around the bonfire. Packing up in the morning was a tad more cumbersome, but not half as tricky as finding our next camping place. Most campsites were located in the middle of nowhere. They were connected to the rest of the world by narrow and often unpaved, unnamed paths, consisting almost entirely of bumps and potholes.

'Wow!' – that was how all three of us reacted to driving into Port Sunlight on a sunny September afternoon. To be honest, Tashi's interjection sounded closer to 'Bow-Wow!', but that did not change the nature of the shared emotion that caused it.

The contrast with the rundown suburbs of Liverpool, through which we had just driven, could not be greater. In Port Sunlight, we drove along the broad, sunlit and leafy avenues lined with beautiful arts-and-crafts cottages punctuated here and there with small parks and squares with flowerbeds and playgrounds – the 'public voids' that, miraculously, did not seem superfluous and out-of-place in that thoroughly idyllic townscape. Apart from slow moving, as if himself mesmerised, Alphie, there were no cars around. The only other 'vehicles' in the streets were pushchairs, steered by young mums in colourful dresses to the accompaniment of the melodious birds' chorus. Calm and happiness could be felt in the air...

The Bridge that Crosses Nothing

As we were crawling ahead, I could not help the acute feeling of déjà vu, as if I had already been exposed to this live epitome of quiet prosperity. The first thing that came to mind was the front cover of a 2014 issue of *E&T* magazine (of which I was then Features Editor) focusing on Utopias. We commissioned an artist to draw a picture of an ultimate paradise on earth and urged him to have a look at Letchworth's Broadway Gardens (Chapter 2) for inspiration. I could now see that he must have ignored our advice and visited Port Sunlight instead.

Port Sunlight, conceived by Lever Brothers in 1887 and started in 1888, was at least 15 years older than Letchworth Garden City, and Ebenezer Howard had borrowed some of his architectural and design principles from the already thriving Merseyside model village. We could now see very clearly that Letchworth's best aspects (Broadway Gardens, the Broadway itself and a handful of original streets) were actually modelled on (if not to say copied from) Port Sunlight.(The imitation went both ways: at later stages of Port Sunlight's development, all its 30 architects hired by the founders, including the celebrated landscape designer Thomas Mawson, were under the strong influence of Letchworth Garden City, which, unlike Port Sunlight itself, kept growing).

My other – somewhat disturbing – associations brought about by Lever Brothers' utopian creation were much less distinct and involved the notorious make-believe 'Potemkin Villages', built by the 18th-century Russian Prince Grigoriy Potemkin to impress Empress Catherine the Great when she came to inspect his domains (see Chapter 1), that had become a byword for window-dressing; as well as the Soviet Union's 'Exhibition of Economic Achievements' in Moscow, not far from which I had the misfortune to live in the early 1980s. As I have already noted, most of those much-publicised 'achievements' were fake or non-existent, or rather only existed on the Exhibition grounds (designed, incidentally, by the followers of Vladimir Semyonov, a great fan and champion of Letchworth Garden City, who became chief architect of Moscow under Stalin in the 1930s, see Chapter 2).[16]

The cocktail of emotions I experienced on entering Port Sunlight, a curious mixture of admiration and apprehension, was like the feeling one might have after a reunion with a long- estranged abusive parent, an encounter both desired and feared.

It was interesting to see that the first glimpse of Port Sunlight caused similarly controversial (albeit different in their essence) emotions in Jacqueline Yallop, the author of *Dreamstreets*, a fascinating paean to Britain's utopian villages:

> When I turn into [Port Sunlight] from the main road, the sudden arrival is a surprise: broad avenues and long vistas, peaceful village greens, trees organised into disciplined copses that draw in the eye ... the industrial detritus of beyond [the Liverpool suburbs] is completely invisible: it's easy to believe that I've been transported many miles into the ancient tranquillity of rural Cheshire.

Just like in my case, however, after the first glimpse of Port Sunlight, Yallop's initial fascination and astonishment quickly give way to bemusement, uneasiness and even a bit of claustrophobia: 'But paradoxically, there's also an impression of enclosure, created at least in part by the uneasy sense of artifice... I recognise the unsettling feeling of having stepped into a beautifully crafted video game or a film set.'

Precisely! The striking unreality and the sheer compactness of Port Sunlight were those of a lovingly constructed film set! Still under the impression of the filming of *The World's End* in Letchworth several years earlier, when the whole town was used as the film location, and just like Jacqueline Yallop, I could not help the uneasy premonition 'that at any moment the illustration might be shattered by the arrival of canteen lorries, an elaborate explosion, a high-speed car chase'.

Port Sunlight was founded in 1888 by politician and industrialist William Lever, who was looking for somewhere in Britain to build a new soap works and to house its employees. The site on the Wirral peninsula (north of Bromborough Pool, which already housed a 'model village' for the workers of Price's Patent Candle Company) that attracted his attention was then just marshy farmland criss-crossed by tidal creeks. But Lever saw the potential in it: the area allowed for expansion, plus Liverpool, the infinite source of labour, was nearby.

In building the village, Lever used the best architects, town planners and house designers of his time, with bricks for some houses, done in Flemish style, imported from Belgium. Using the examples of New Lanark, Saltaire, and the neighbouring Bromborough Pool, Lever also made sure that his workforce enjoyed some welfare provisions.

Today's Port Sunlight is largely unchanged since 1925, when William Lever died. And not just in its outward appearance: 900

residential dwellings, 12 public buildings, including Gladstone Theatre, as well as a number of monuments and memorials. The village still has 2000 residents in over a thousand households. Only a small minority of 'Sunlighters' work at the soap factory (now part of Unilever), which has been moved outside the village, a designated conservation area in its entirety. Port Sunlight has repeatedly applied for UNESCO World Heritage Site status, which has so far been withheld.

Our first hours in Port Sunlight were full of quiet admiration. I even went as far as mumbling (to no one in particular) that we should seriously think of moving to that amazing Garden Village, where Utopia had become reality.

As we found out later, unlike in the 1970s and 1980s, when the tenancies of all Port Sunlight homes used to be tied to the soap factory and could only be purchased or rented by its workers, now out of the 900 houses in the village (nearly all of which are Grade II listed), 300 are rented out by the Village Trust – a charity which effectively runs Port Sunlight – and most of the rest are privately owned. As a number of Port Sunlight dwellers assured us, there was no vetting procedure for potential house buyers, contrary to what they thought in neighbouring Liverpool and Chester, still unsure of how to react to the Utopia on their doorstep.

According to John Spilletts, a pensioner and a volunteer village guide who grew up in Port Sunlight where both his parents worked at the soap factory, certain rules, or rather 'convenances', still applied to all house owners. They were free to decorate the insides of the houses, but any structural changes to the interiors, let alone exteriors, needed to be approved by the Trust. Painting of the external walls should be in keeping with the street's approved colour scheme. 'For Sale' signs, satellite dishes, outside gates and brick walls were all strictly prohibited. In John's own words, the Trust controlled everything – 'from the house to the curb'.

Does it remind you of anything? Like the enforced prohibition in Bournville, say? In Port Sunlight, which also started as a model village for workers of one particular factory, the associations with Cadbury's Bournville were numerous. But as we found out, Lever's totalitarian ways went much farther than Cadbury's...

In Letchworth, to get permission to build my writer's garden office, aka Pegasus cottage, we had to submit to the Heritage Foundation an 'essay', explaining how the new structure would fit in the Garden City's architectural ensemble. We did it – and the permission was given. I doubt if the same procedure would be as simple in Port Sunlight.

Because of the ongoing pandemic, we were unable to visit a couple of sample Port Sunlight cottages, normally open for inspection. We did, however, joined John's guided tour and learned, among other things, that Port Sunlight had indeed been chosen as a film set (mine and Jacqueline Yallop's impressions were proving correct) for a number of movies and serials, including *Peaky Blinders*. As our small tourist group, led by John, was trudging through the village's parks and boulevards, the ever-so-friendly denominal Sunlighters – sitting on benches, cycling, or playing ball games on grass lawns – would wave to us amicably. A couple of them even shouted: 'Welcome to the world's best village!' Were they genuine or just a bunch of specially hired impersonators on the Village Trust payroll?

In the local Museum I managed to get a glimpse of the 1916 'Rules for the Regulation of Tenancies', the very tone of which was much more uncompromising than that of George Cadbury's 'Suggested Rules of Health' and was reminiscent (to me at least) of the curt no-nonsense style of the Criminal Code of the USSR:

Rule 1. Persons to be eligible for dwellings must have their applications approved by the Directors of Lever Brothers Limited.

Rule 2. The tenancies are from week to week...

Rule 5. No one may lodge in the Village who is not in the employment of the Company, or their sub-contractors.

Rule 6. Lodgers in one house must be of the same sex.

Rule 7. The following regulations will be strictly enforced. Tenants with families of more than two children must not have lodgers.

Rule 8. An authorised official of the Company may visit any house in Port Sunlight at any time, for the purpose of seeing that due regard is being paid to order and cleanliness... This will be strictly enforced.

These rules make the 'utopian' Village appear a bit like a prison. In fact, in the Netherlands and in Australia, I had a chance to visit low-security prisons with much less strict-sounding inmates' codes of conduct. In one such penal institution in Haarlem (Holland), for

The Bridge that Crosses Nothing

example, prison officials (unlike those of the Lever's 'Company') were not allowed to visit the inmates' rooms without an advance warning and had to knock at the cell's door before entering.

One would assume that these days, when the omnipotent company no longer ruled the village and all the power was in the hands of Port Sunlight Village Trust (PSVT), founded in 1999 by Unilever Plc, such Edwardian regulations were no longer in force. Well, I also thought that until I had a chance to browse through the village's website featuring, among other things, a downloadable 'Tenants Handbook'.

Don't get me wrong: the language and the tone of the Handbook, starting with 'Dear Tenants', are much friendlier that that of the above-quoted Rules. Yet certain rules sound disturbingly similar: 'PSVT will not give permission to keep a pet in an apartment'. The Handbook also explicitly prohibits 'hosting a community event' without PSVT's approval and explains how and to whom to report other tenants' 'fly tipping and anti-social behaviour'. encouraging informing on neighbours.

The latter, again, reminded me of the old, yet not so good, Soviet Union, where, above the doors of every village's or town's 'Soviet' (Council), there was a KGB-administered pillar box for written (mostly anonymous) denunciations of one's fellow citizens' 'anti-Soviet misdemeanours'. 'Please drop your reports here!' was the invitation on the box.

Too harsh a comparison, perhaps, but as an old Taoist wisdom goes, every long journey (including the way to totalitarianism) starts with a single step...

Adam Macqueen's revealing book, *The King of Sunlight – How William Lever Cleaned Up the World*, (it wasn't on sale in the Museum), and other sources (like, say, *Lord Leverhulme*, Lever's biography by W.P. Jolly and *The Dark Side of Sunlight* by David Hollett) show how the factory workers' lives were policed from the head office. Here's what William Lever himself once wrote: 'The private habits of an employee have really nothing to do with Lever Brothers providing the man is a good workman. At the same time, a good workman may have a wife of objectionable habits, or may have objectionable habits himself, which make it undesirable to have him in the Village.'[17]

To me, such a statement smacks heavily of Stalinism.

Among the peculiarities of Port Sunlight's planning that struck me most were the near-absence of cars, which were all parked at the rear of the houses in the former garden allotments (similar to the 'utopian' cul-de-sac town of Radburn in the US, see Chapter 6) and the complete absence of any kind of shops. But there was a single excellent old pub, the Bridge Inn. It was there that we invited John Spilletts for drinks on our first evening in the village.

The Bridge Inn was cosy, welcoming and down-to-earth, its only distinctly 'utopian' feature being the prices. A meal for two cost £8, and a bottle of house wine £11, half the price in the South East. A piece of cold sausage for Tashi was free.

Yes, as John told us, there was much more about that pub than met the eye. The Bridge Inn opened in 1900 as a temperance inn. As a lifelong teetotaller, Lever wanted it to be 'dry'. Having survived a couple of abstemious years, the soap factory workers started demanding the Bridge Inn changed its status to a licensed establishment, and Lever, who – unlike Bournville's George Cadbury – was fond of democracy games, agreed to hold a village referendum on the matter. In a cunning political move, he proclaimed himself a supporter of women's suffrage and insisted that the female population of the village took part in the voting alongside the men. His hope, obviously, was that women would support the pub's non-alcoholic status. To be on the safe side, he imposed a 75% majority in favour as a precondition of the change. One can imagine his surprise when 80%, including most of the women, voted for the license!

Lever had to comply, which, to me, signified two things: 1. He was not quite a Stalinist and could be made to uphold some democratic principles. As John himself put it, unlike Letchworth's Ebenezer Howard, Lever was a capitalist not a socialist. 2. He did not know his own workforce very well. The latter point can be illustrated by the fiasco of his operations in the Belgian Congo, where Lever Brothers routinely used slave labour at their Leverville plantations, and in Stornoway in the Outer Hebrides, where he alienated local workers by behaving like the 'monarch of the Western Isles' while neglecting the locals' beliefs and traditions.

What William Lever – a 'benevolent despot', in the words of architectural historian Clive Aslet – was definitely good at was below-the-line marketing and advertising. He claimed in all seriousness that his Sunlight soap would not only wash clothes by itself, but would also keep the housewives who used it, perennially young. I found more proofs of his marketing genius on the same night, prior to going to sleep in our Travelodge hotel right outside Port Sunlight, so full of dogs and so dog-friendly that it should have been renamed Howliday Inn

The Bridge that Crosses Nothing

I was browsing through the old book I bought in the last remaining 'honesty bookshop' in Hay-on-Wye (Chapter 8) – the 1898 *Sunlight Year Book*, with what looked like the world's longest book title – *A Treasury of Useful Information of value to all Members of the Household. Including Calendar and Kindred Matter, British Colonies and Dependencies, Geography, Literature, Science, Fine Arts, Commerce, Architecture, Agriculture, Army and Navy, Sports and Pastimes, Cycling Maps, The Household, Medical, Port Sunlight, etc.*

I wondered what other obscure field of knowledge could be hiding behind that promising 'etc.', for if one were to believe the subtitle, the omniscient and 'profusely illustrated' 480-page almanac was covering the lot, except perhaps for Agnoiology – the highly esoteric study of the quality and conditions of ignorance.

On top if it all, the almanac ran an original story by Conan Doyle, the creator of Sherlock Holmes, Brigadier Gerard and Professor Challenger. I can only guess how much he had (rightly) charged the publishers, Lever Brothers Ltd, for the right of the first publication of 'Burger's Secret' – a 18-page story 'Specially written for the Sunlight Year-Book', according to the subtitle.[18]

What was the point of such a weighty foliotome (there were five annual editions, from 1895 to 1899), effectively echoing all those countless Victorian dictionaries and encyclopedias already in existence? The answer is simple: Sunlight Soap advertising! At the bottom of every single page there was a punchy bold-type ad for Sunlight Soap. The long Conan Doyle story, for example, carried the messages such as: 'SUNLIGHT SOAP is worth its weight in gold'; 'Take life easy use SUNLIGHT SOAP'; 'Don't worry! Use SUNLIGHT SOAP', and (as if specially targeting Tashi), 'Prize Dogs and Poultry should be washed with SUNLIGHT SOAP'.

Thank God, Tashi, who was by then snoring gently in the far corner of the hotel room, was unable to read. Otherwise, he would have been hugely upset by being equated with poultry. He had an instinctive dislike of soap, triggered perhaps by the fact that in the Ukrainian city of my childhood, we tended to believe that soap was made of the fat of stray dogs. Disgruntled football fans' favourite call from the terraces of Soviet football stadiums was 'Referee – for soap!' A football match was the only public event when people had a chance to express themselves freely.

But back to the *Sunlight Year Book*, which, incidentally, devoted just 10 pages out of 480 to Port Sunlight itself. Free copies of the almanac were widely distributed to churches, schools

Trucks in the Garden of Eden

and libraries all over the UK. No wonder that the British Soap Makers Association kept issuing protests against such blatant and all-permeating advertising, the likes of which most of its other members could not afford.

The use of factual reference-book-style subject matter as a background for soap ads was astute. Firstly, that kind of material was easy to get and cost nothing. Secondly, and most importantly, the predominantly encyclopaedic nature of his Year Books added credibility to their overall contents, including the ads. The *Sunlight Year Book*, just like Port Sunlight itself, was an impressive, clever, attractive, yet largely futile, gimmick. Like most Utopias...

During our farewell drive around the neat, spotless and habitually deserted Port Sunlight the following morning, I was mentally rereading the closing paragraphs of the Port Sunlight Chapter of Jacqueline Yallop's *Dreamstreets*: 'Here (in Port Sunlight) residents were often discontented or resistant ... the village was seen by some as an imposition, an autocratic step too far, and an anachronism. Here there is a bridge, a pretty English country bridge, that crosses nothing and leads only to the factory floor.'

Similar to the Door to Nowhere in the Robert Owen Museum in Newtown (see Chapter 9), the Bridge that Crosses Nothing in Port Sunlight (it used to cross the long dried-up creek) can serve as a vivid metaphor for all failed (all that have been attempted so far) Utopias.

Chapter 11

'Do Not Tell Titus!'

An acre in Middlesex is better than a principality in Utopia. The smallest actual good is better than the most magnificent promises of impossibilities.

Thomas Babington Macaulay

No matter how fast Alphie was carrying us further north, we were unable to escape from the persisting Covid pandemic, which seemed to be spreading around much faster than I could drive.

I was able to watch its progress by spotting more and more shops and offices on our way that seemed either temporarily or permanently closed; by the increasing number of people in 'Elons' (the must-wear face masks – as in Elon Musk), and by the growing number of video clips taking the mickey out of the spreading pandemic that kept arriving on WhatsApp. If several weeks earlier, I would receive just one or two memes a day, tentative and half-hearted, like perch biting in April, as if the internet itself got fed up and apathetic with the protracted Tier 2 lockdown, now their daily count was approaching 50 and they were getting more bizarre and more sardonic by the day.

Another worrying sign was that it had become routine for undertakers and funeral directors to bombard me every morning with emails on the 'great' and 'secret' (from whom?) offers of how to bury or cremate myself with the lowest possible expenditure. The number of such offers had grown tenfold since I took out a new life insurance policy. It appeared as if all those 'Do us the Honour' funeral parlours wouldn't rest until I finally kicked the bucket under their relentless pressure – so much so that I had to pay my email provider to stop those vultures circling my computer screen!

To me, all of those echoed the latest government pandemic-related decisions, most of which sounded like sad jokes (or memes, if you wish), too. The only difference was that they were all supposed to be dead serious. The pandemic was obviously gaining momentum, and one day it was announced that, among other things, new travel restrictions, strictly enforced by police, were about to be tightened to the Tier 4 level, which simply meant no travel at all outside a 3-mile radius from home. And the fact that we all (with the notable exception of Tashi and Alphie) got recently vaccinated with two different vaccines (by the sound of their names only, I chose to refer to them as 'wine-cines' ('AstraZeneca', dry white, and 'Pfizer', sparkling) was not going to lift that ban. It all meant that we only had a tad more than one week to wind up our journey and to return home. A Covid dystopia had got in the way of our peripatetic quest for Utopias.

With a lot of 'utopian' ground still to cover in the north of England and in Scotland, we had an emergency impromptu coffee stop near Saltaire (with all the pubs and cafes closed, we had to make coffee in Alphie's own tiny kitchen) to discuss the changed situation and decided that we would still try to visit as many places as possible, in a kind of a whistle-stop tour. With most of offices, museums etc. shut down, we would focus on accumulating the maximum number of first-hand impressions and personal contacts (while wearing Elons, no doubt) that we could later, when safely back at home, interview on Skype or on Zoom. After that, having put on our Elons (just in case), we hit the road again.

Our reactions to the first sight of the giant Salt's Mill building in Saltaire, a Victorian model village in Shipley, near Bradford, was similar to the 'wows' we voiced in Port Sunlight, if only in sound and not in intonation. If the latter in Port Sunlight was one of admiration, the Salt's Mill textile factory building was awe-inspiring. Architecturally, it was a cross between a giant Elizabethan mansion and a Stalinist wedding-cake-shaped skyscraper of the Moscow University type. In all its disproportionate hugeness, it reminded me of a typically oversized and heavy grey Catholic church dominating many a small Irish village. It also had a Pisa Tower effect, as if about to collapse on top of you any moment, so much so that I instinctively steered Alphie away from it. It appeared as if Saltaire's founder, industrialist Titus Salt ('Salt' as in animal, not mineral) built it with just one aim – to intimidate. And that first impression proved correct.

'Do Not Tell Titus!'

Larger than St Paul's Cathedral, Salt's Mill was the world's biggest factory when it opened in 1853. Driven by the supposedly noble and humanistic (utopian) principles, Titus Salt was in reality a control freak and an egomaniac, who had not only named the new industrial village after himself ('Saltaire' from his last name and the River Aire which flows through the village), but also almost all its streets (20 out of 22) after his relatives and family members, a strong reminder of Turmenbashi (the 'Father of All Turkmen'), Saparmurad Niyazov (1940–2006), the former dictator-president of Turkmenistan, who named everything, including months of the year and days of the week after his relatives, and the country's biggest pig farm after his own mother. (He was a self-absorbed tyrant, with no sense of humour.)

Italians have an interesting way of describing the size of buildings, without adjectives, with the help of suffixes alone. For example, if casa means just a house, casetta is a cottage, or a small house; casaccia – a large house, and casuccia – a large and ugly house! Well, to me, Salt's Mill building was an archetypal casuccia, or a più grande casuccia.

I am still not quite sure whether we were in luck or not to have discovered that despite the pandemic, the building was still open for visitors. It was about to shut down from the following morning, yet still open on the afternoon of our brief visit. Again, like in Portmeirion, Christine and I had to take turns popping in, for dogs were not allowed inside. And this time round, I was happy to accept the ban: if Tashi went off-lead inside the building, the chance of finding him in the endless labyrinths of winding corridors would be close to zero. As I was walking, or rather running (keep on reading!) along the endless empty (and, if I may say so, totalitarian) corridors, with bared pipes and ventilation shafts under the ceilings, I was reminded of the description of 1920s Moscow's "House of the Peoples', as seen by Ilf and Petrov – a brilliant duo of the pre-WWII Soviet satirists – in their novel *The Twelve Chairs*.[20]

> The corridors of the House of the Peoples were so long ... that people walking down them inevitably quickened their pace. You could tell from anyone who passed how far they had come. If they walked slightly faster than normal, it meant the marathon had only just begun Those who had already completed two or three corridors developed a fairly fast trot. And from time to time it was possible to see someone running along at full speed; he

had reached the five-corridor stage. A citizen who had gone eight corridors could easily compete with a bird, racehorse or Nurmi, the world champion runner.

Alas, the progressing arthritis stopped me from becoming a new Mo Farah, but by the time I reached a spacious hall where a cafe (now closed) was located, I could have probably overtaken a notoriously slow-moving Amsterdam number one tram.

Apart from the cafe, the hall was home to the largest open-access bookshop I had ever seen. Countless stalls, piled with books, were stretching to the corridor's end, i.e. to the horizon. Unfortunately, the bookshop – like everything else in Saltaire, in the whole of the UK and in the rest of the pandemic-dominated world – was about to close down, and I only had a chance to notice an amazingly wide choice of poetry and Buddhism books displayed on the stalls.

To me, that thoroughly utopian (out-of-place, or out-of-no-place) bookshop and the adjoining David Hockney Gallery inside the totalitarian casuccia of a building were the best features of the whole heritage site (factory and village), adding some reason to the UNESCO's decision to award Saltaire a World Heritage status in 2001.

I wasn't half as impressed by the village itself. A Titus Salt's retirement project, it was built to accommodate the factory's workers and comprised 820 buildings on 26 acres of land. What struck me initially was the uncharacteristic proliferation of pharmacies and hairdressers, including a salon, with the name 'Salt Hair'. Again, Ilf and Petrov's associations proved helpful and I cannot refrain from quoting here the iconic opening sentence from *The Twelve Chairs*:

> There were so many hairdressing establishments and funeral homes [of which pharmacies can be regarded as precursors – VV] in the regional centre of N. that the inhabitants seemed to be born merely in order to have a shave, get their hair cut, freshen up their heads with toilet water and then die.

As most of Saltaire's historians note, Salt's main objective, thinly camouflaged by his philanthropic ambitions, was to keep his workforce under constant control – both at the factory and at leisure. His unlimited 'paternalism' (the word, most frequently used by Titus's biographers, to describe the industrialist's character) is still reflected in the name of one of Saltaire's bars – 'Don't Tell Titus'. This is explained by the fact that not only Salt was a convinced teetotaller himself, but – similar to Bournville's George

Cadbury – he insisted that his workers followed his wishes steadily (as opposed to a drunken 'unsteadily'), allegedly in the interests of their health, but in fact just out of fear of their reduced productivity. He was always ready to enforce the edict by sacking the disobeying drinkers or evicting them from his village.

Why is it so that the majority of history's dictators (with one notable exception of Stalin) were either teetotal, or worse, claiming to be teetotal? The best example of the latter category was the late Romanian leader Nicolae Ceausescu, who posed publicly as a complete teetotaller and preached abstention in his speeches, whereas in fact he was a chronic alcoholic, who had his favourite plonk, the sunflower-oil-tinted Galbena Odobesti, delivered to all his 30-odd palaces by special pipelines. I tried that horrible 'wine' myself in Romania and can confirm that not only it had the look and the consistency of sunflower oil, but it also tasted like it. It was as kitschy, bland and mediocre as Ceausescu himself.

I am of course far from equating Titus Salt, who just like William Lever, could be described as 'benevolent' despot, with the dumb and bloodthirsty Romanian tyrant. And yet, the witty name of that unremarkable bar in the centre of Saltaire was a powerful reminder that every Utopia imposed from above (or by decree), be it the blood-soaked and tyrannical 'socialist paradise' of the Russian Bolsheviks, or 'model villages' for the workers, created with the aim of squeezing them (the workers) dry in the most effective manner, will cause resistance and will eventually fail.

Walking the cobbled streets of Saltaire village, I kept silently repeating the words of Alexander Galich, an émigré Soviet bard, murdered by the KGB in Paris in 1977: 'Do not be afraid of war; do not be afraid of poverty; do not be afraid of prison, but always be afraid of anyone who says: "I know what you should do!"'

We stayed overnight in the Abbey Lodge Hotel in Shipley. Unable to find an open eating place anywhere in town on that pre-lockdown Sunday evening, we had a picnic on our hotel room bed. Our new schedule showed that we had overstayed in Saltaire and, if we still wanted to get home before travel restrictions came into force, we had to accelerate. Luckily, our next place to visit, New Earstwick, was less than 40 miles away.

The feelings at entering New Earswick, a pretty model village on the edge of York, were again similar to those we had in Port

Sunlight: fascination and recognition. Only the latter sensation here (I mean similarity with Letchworth) was much stronger. No wonder: the main architects of that Yorkshire model village, founded in 1902, were Barry Parker and Raymond Unwin, both of whom would be hired to design Ebenezer Howard's future Garden City a couple of years on.

The similarities were so obvious that we all momentarily felt at home – as if driving along a curtailed version of Letchworth's Broadway, only instead of the fountain and the iconic 'UK's First Roundabout, circa 1909', the street was lined with garden allotments. Joseph Rowntree, a chocolatier, a Quaker and a philanthropist par excellence, who founded New Earswick, was – like Robert Owen – an idealist, a dreamer and a genuine champion of social reform, deeply involved in improving the quality of life not only of the workers of his own factories but of all working people in Britain. In stark contrast to Titus Salt and George Cadbury, Joseph Rowntree, son of a grocer, rejected the traditional Victorian paternalism in relation to his workforce and created a general welfare structure that did not depend on discipline and productivity. That explained the multiple garden allotments, still there in New Earswick. And whereas Howard's designs for Letchworth included an obligatory apple tree in every back garden of the workers' arts-and-crafts cottages, Rowntree went one step further and insisted on *two* regulation fruit trees in each garden, as well as an allotment.

Unlike in Bournville, Port Sunlight and Saltaire, only open to the workers of the respective local factories, any person of modest means from anywhere in Britain was allowed to buy a cottage in New Earswick, which shows that unlike George Cadbury, William Lever and Titus Salt, George Rowntree's philanthropy went beyond his immediate interests as an industrialist.

The village was all but empty, with very little traffic in its broad and leafy ramp-ridden streets (they do love their ramps in garden suburbs and model villages), in which children were playing unsupervised, a sight that has become rare almost anywhere else in Britain.

New Earswick was obviously a very safe place. And not just to live in, but also, according to the sign above a neat and small office we were passing by – 'Last Wishes Funeral Parlour' – to die in, too. I was again reminded of 'Do Us the Honour Funeral Home' from Ilf and Petrov's fictitious 'regional centre of 'N'. The laconic wooden signs in the deserted Garden Square pointed to 'Bakery',

'Do Not Tell Titus!'

'Station', 'Cobbler', Hairdresser'. There was some old-fashioned charm about them.

We parked Alphie in an absolutely empty car park next to the Community Swimming Pool, right behind the Folk Hall – a peculiar local community hub which housed a cafe (closed), a souvenir shop (closed), and a handful of meeting rooms and offices, including those of the local newsletter, *The New Earswick Bulletin* (closed).

There's a certain paradoxical advantage in exploring utopian (or any other) settlements during a pandemic, with most of the traditional public places shut down and out of reach, and the true peculiarities of the place laid bare. There are very few distractions for a keen observer willing to look under the community's skin. The only problem is that there are very few locals around to talk to, so instead of people, one has to interact with 'silent witnesses': buildings, monuments and landscapes.

'When everything else fails – read signs and notice boards!' My experience showed that it was no less effective (at times, much more effective) than interviewing local bureaucrats and/or dignitaries, whom I could always contact by phone or email afterwards, if there was a need. I started with the sign at the entrance to the swimming pool building across the car park:

> Friends of New Earswick Swimming Pool (FoNESP) are a small group of volunteers formed in October 2017 in response to the news that the Joseph Rowntree Housing Trust planned to close the Pool. After a successful campaign FoNESP took over the running of the Pool in January 2019. Our Pool has a unique history, having been opened in 1967 by the Rowntree Trust with the support of the local community, notably children being asked to donate 'Half a Crown' and the villages joining a 'Buy a Brick' scheme. As part of the Garden Village scheme, it was built to enhance the health and wellbeing of the local community.

I was very touched by that sign testifying to the fact that the Joseph Rowntree-inspired community spirit of charity and 'carefully considered informality' was alive and well in New Earswick. Remembering another sign I spotted while driving around the village earlier, I wondered if there was also a FoLWFP (Friends of the Last Wishes Funeral Parlour) group in the community.

Inside the empty and echoey Folk Hall there were numerous notice boards and information windows. I was drawn to the one targeting children and containing stacks of colourful 'do not remove' information leaflets. One of them – richly illustrated and written as a diary of a little girl – told the story of the 1905 New Earswick 'Snowden Family': 'Hello! My name is Alice Snowden. My Dad got a job working for Mr Rowntree. He helps build the houses. And after all the houses are built he will look after them and do repairs.' It felt like interviewing a ghost. Another leaflet was 'Getting a Job at the Rowntree Factory':

> As early as 1920 Seebohm Rowntree [Joseph Rowntree's brother and business partner] set up a psychological Department at the Cocoa Works, possibly the first of its kind in the country. They had fully trained staff, whose job was Vocational Selection and Time and Motion Studies.

Hmm... I hadn't realised that some modern HR clichés (e.g. 'vocational selection') were already in use in 1920. Further down, the leaflet carried a quote from Seebohm Rowntree himself:

> The new process may show increased profits, or it may produce less waste, but unless it also enables those working on it to be contented and healthy citizens, the Psychological Department does not consider the process really efficient. A process must be efficient from both the workers' and the Management's point of view to be truly efficient.

Mr Seebohm Rowntree was obviously very fond the of the word 'efficient' – a fact that had made his pronouncement much less 'efficient' than it could have been had he not been so fond of the word 'efficient' (it's infectious).

There was also something vaguely Orwellian in the seemingly omniscient and omnipotent 'Psychological Department' (with capitals) and 'the Management' (with capitals, too). Seebohm Rowntree's excuse was that in 1920 he couldn't have possibly read *Nineteen Eighty-Four*, first published in 1949, and was therefore unfamiliar with the sinister concepts of Big Brother and the Ministry of Truth, let alone Room 101. The leaflet ended on another disturbing note: 'Across the world today, personnel departments and employment tests can trace their history back to the early practices at the Rowntree factory. Most importantly, Rowntree & Co always put "the human factor" and well-being of the workers at the heart of their industry.' (Here I should be forgiven for recalling Donald Trump's mantra, 'America first!')

'Do Not Tell Titus!'

So that is where all those insipid and meaningless, politically correct, terms, 'human resources', 'human factor', 'head of wellbeing' (I knew a person who actually was the 'head of wellbeing' at a large bank), originated. That nearly spoiled my so far largely positive impression of New Earswick. On reflection, however, I decided that cliches aside, the methods practised by the Rowntrees' 'Psychological Department' (including 'The Moores Formbard', 'Smarties Sorter' and 'Buzzer Test' – no time to describe them here, but do look them up if interested) were both interesting and innovative for their time.

The most laconic and the most evocative sign inside the deserted Folk Hall was attached to a totally empty multi-tiered wooden stall in one of the corridors. 'FREE FOOD'. That sign above the empty shelves looked disappointing – as if it was an epitaph (installed by the Last Wishes undertakers?) to yet another Utopia that had failed, despite all the good intentions behind it. Writers such as Clive Aslet, the author and compiler of the magnificent *Villages of Britain* concluded that New Earswick's 'model of an architecturally well-tempered community' did fail in some respects.

On this occasion, allow me to disagree. Despite (or, possibly, because of) not being able to meet a lot of the villagers, except for the kids playing in the streets and coming in and out of the swimming pool, all three of us (including Tashi, who was happy to keep stumbling upon generously filled-up water bowls, scattered all over the place) could feel the special – warm, welcoming and happily democratic – community spirit of New Earswick. The village, emptied and silenced by the pandemic, was still able to talk to us via its buildings, notice boards and street signs.

I very much wanted to believe that in its carefully considered informality, it was a Utopia still in progress.

The view from Alphie's windows was un-English: mountains, moors, pastures enclosed by drystone walls, narrow winding roads. And if we looked down, we could discern handfuls of gritstone houses, not 'nestling' (I hate this cliché) in the narrow valleys, but rather clinging to the hills, as if in danger of sliding down.

The scenery appeared more Swiss than English, yet we were not in the Swiss Alps, nor even in the Slovak Tatra mountains, but in the Pennines, also known as either the backbone (probably if observed from the hilltops), or the roof (if viewed from the valleys?)

of England. Whatever the sobriquet, they looked superfluous and excessive for the England we were used to in our flat rural Hertfordshire. Without taking my eyes off the increasingly precarious road, which Alphie, judging by the angry undertones of his engine, did not feel like climbing, I kept repeating (silently) one of my favourite pronouncements from Ostap Bender, the acerbic 'smooth operator' of *The Twelve Chairs* by Ilf and Petrov, which I know almost by heart and, as you might have noticed already, love to quote: 'Ostap did not like the mountains. 'Too showy... Queer kind of beauty. An idiot's imagination. No use at all.'

As an acrophobia sufferer, I was ready to agree with Ostap.

We stopped for lunch in Blanchland, a medieval Alpine village in the North Pennines. From 1721, it had been run by the Lord Crew Trustees – a charity started by the eponymous Lord. From the leaflet I picked up in the Lord Crewe Arms, the local pub, I learned a new word – 'Premonstratensian'. 'In 1165 Blanchland Abbey and thus Blanchland itself was founded as a Premonstratensian (it took me some time to type it!) priory.' In case you don't know, this tongue-breaker denotes a junior monk of sorts. The monks, who left the village in 1539, used to wear white – 'blanche'– robes, hence Blanchland. They told us in the pub that the ghost of a white-robed monk can often be seen crossing the bridge over the Derwent Reservoir on a moonlit night. 'The latest signing was last week,' an amicable barman told us and added that the pub itself was the former Abbot's Guest House and therefore was full of ghosts, too. On hearing that, Tashi began to howl loudly at a huge period fireplace in the corner, as if one of the Abbot's Guest ghosts was about to emerge from it. With our aim being places utopian, not ghost-(or guest)-infested, it was a signal we had to get going.

Thirty miles on, or rather on and up, we arrived in Nenthead, one of England's highest villages (1,437 feet) and home to the country's highest parish church. It was also Britain's very first purpose-built model village for workers, boasting, among other things a Reading Room, the first free lending library in England – a particularly pleasing landmark for a bibliophile like myself. Nenthead's thoroughly 'utopian' nature was enhanced by the fact that it was located in Eden! Not in the Biblical Garden but in the more down-to-earth (if not to say boring-sounding), eponymous 'local government district' of Cumbria.

Built in 1825 by the Quaker-owned London Lead Company, Nenthead contained 2000 people by 1861 – the year serfdom was officially abolished in Russia. It is not by chance that I remembered that date while preparing for my visit to that peculiar North Pennine village, which by 1861 – as opposed to Tsarist Russia where peasants had just stopped being the property of the landlords – had good housing for workers, a school and a washhouse for the miners and their families – all built by the Quakers.

After lead mining fell into decline in the 1880s, Nenthead was taken over by the aptly named Belgian Vielle Montagne ('old mountain') Company, which started mining zinc in the Pennines and kept doing so more or less continuously for the next 80 years, when the last mine closed down and the village was briefly taken over by 'people seeking an alternative way of life' (according to a modern tourist brochure) – the hippies of the 1960-70s, who as we had already observed in Wales, always had a propensity for remote uphill areas, where they could practise their favourite habits in relative safety. The hippies of Nenthead, however, were more into music than drugs, so many of them had eventually settled down in the village and started an annual music festival, which is still held. So, when in Nenthead, one can now – quite literally – dance to the music of time.

The first thing we noticed on arrival was that unlike most of other English mountain villages, Nenthead was not 'nestling', nor even clinging to, but was literally embedded into the North Pennine Hills, with the River Nent running right through it.

It was thanks to Britain's first free library (aka the Reading Room) that I had developed an *a priori* positive attitude to Nenthead: indeed, it was the first 'utopian' community on our itinerary that made books and reading its first priority. I wanted to learn more about the village, but the blasted pandemic got in the way again. There was no one around I could talk to. Even the visitors' centre was unmanned, albeit, luckily, open. I picked up a couple of fliers and maps of the village and, with Tashi straining at the lead, set off for a circular walk. To get to our first site, we did not have to go too far. To be honest, we didn't have to go anywhere at all, for the Village Community Shop and Post Office, formerly the Reading Room, was right next to the visitors' centre.

There was nothing much left in the shop to remind one of its past. The sign at the entrance said 'Snacks', instead of books, and inside – instead of book stacks – there were stacks of snacks. I closed my eyes trying to visualise miners and villagers of 200 years ago gathering there after their shift to borrow books and read the papers. But instead, I suddenly had a flashback to the favourite Reading Room of my childhood. Located in a quiet corner of the magnificent 'Public Park of Relaxation and Rest' (not to be confused with a cemetery) in the my native city of Kharkiv in Soviet Ukraine, the Reading Room (or 'Chital'nya', in Russian (Kharkiv was and still is – predominantly Russian-speaking), was a flimsy wooden structure, resembling a large shabby gazebo, or a roofed veranda, open to the elements. At the age of 6 or 7, I would come there often with my 'Old Bolshevik' granddad. And while he was carefully studying the latest issue of *Pravda*, staring at it intently through the thick lenses of his spectacles (he had cataracts in both eyes), I would get immersed in a dog-eared book by Arthur Conan-Doyle or James Fenimore Cooper. One little detail of that ramshackle, yet surprisingly cosy, Reading Room is still firmly ingrained in my memory – a curt, handwritten sign on top of a thick folder with old newspapers. 'NEWSPAPERS ARE FOR READING!'

When I share that small recollection with my ex-Soviet compatriots, the mention of the sign inevitably (if not immediately) causes an outburst of laughter. To my younger Western readers, not too familiar with the daily realities of the 'Ustopian' (utopian-turned-dystopian) USSR, I must explain that the strict and seemingly nonsensical sign has to be considered in the context of chronic shortages of nearly all basic commodities in the Soviet Union, one of which was toilet paper.

Sure enough, people had to find substitutes for the latter. I remember how a couple of years after the official demotion of Stalin by Khrushchev in 1956, the multi-volume collection of Stalin's articles ended up in the toilet of our communal flat. Due to the thick glossy paper Stalin's works had been printed on, the collection was not very fit for purpose. Newspapers would have done a much better job.

Significantly, several years later, the same fate befell the works of Khrushchev himself, demoted and exposed by Brezhnev. In the mid-1980s, it was time for Brezhnev's writings to head for the country's uncomplaining loos after the latter was demoted and exposed by Gorbachev, under whose rule toilet paper shortages reached their all-time height, and the sight of an overjoyed man or woman running in exaltation through the streets of Moscow with toilet paper rolls wound around their torsos like machine-gun-cartridge belts, became common. 'Where did you get it, buddy?' the envious passers-by would ask him?'[20] 'Just round the corner, in Prosperity Lane,' they would reply proudly before adding: 'But hurry up! They are about to run out!'

'Do Not Tell Titus!'

By the time Gorby was demoted, however, the Soviet Socialist Utopia had collapsed, and the Wild-West Mafia-style capitalist dystopia came in its stead. Shortages of daily basics, including toilet paper, came to an end to be replaced by the general lack of decency, honesty and common sense, which is still dominant in Russia. This is how far I ended up in my vicarious travels from a small community shop-cum-Post Office in Nenthead!

I was shaken out of my reveries by Tashi's high-pitch howling – a signal of thirst. He was dragging me towards the colourful drinking fountain across the road. Built in 1877, it had a practical purpose for the villagers (and for their dogs, no doubt), unlike the numerous decorative fountains in most of the Garden Suburbs and model villages, from where 'the workers' joyful laughter can often be heard', pace *Korea Today* magazine (see Chapter 2).

We walked past The Miners Arms pub and took a gravel track up the hill towards Hillerdon Terrace, featuring cottages with disproportionately large gardens, which, as we already know from Letchworth, Bournville and Port Sunlight, are sure signs of utopian village-planning, only in Nenthead they appeared decades earlier. Those houses, now looking abandoned, with their residents driven deep inside by the pandemic, were built by the London Lead Company for their key workers: miners, smelters and overmen (supervisors).

We continued along the mountain path to St John's Church, the highest parish church in England. With his broad furry paws, ideally suited for negotiating snow-ridden tracks in the Himalayas (as his Tibetan Terrier ancestors used to do), Tashi felt very much in his element and was trotting happily in front of me. The breathtaking near-perfect view from the hilltop across the valley was only slightly marred by the steep-sided grassy mounds – spoil heaps from the mine workings – sticking out here and there as silent reminders of the fact that perfection as such does not exist, and all Utopias come at a cost.

Further up the track stood the large present-day Nenthead Village Hall, formerly the village school, built by the Lead Company in 1864. That school was unique in a utopian kind of way: attendance was compulsory for the miners' children, or else their dads risked losing their jobs.

Now, let's pause for a moment and try to understand why temperance, imposed from above (which was, incidentally, *not* introduced by the founders of Nenthead, despite their Quaker views) smacks of totalitarianism and never works, whereas compulsory

Trucks in the Garden of Eden

primary education is not just acceptable, but also highly desirable and even democratic.

To be honest, I do not know the answer, which, most likely, lies somewhere deep inside the same mysterious 'human nature' that makes all Utopias eventually fail. In my defence, I can only say that, in my view, creative non-fiction, of which travel writing is a part, is not about providing answers, but rather about posing more and more questions, the answers to which (if any) may be found by the readers. That, I think, is the essence of literature.

We headed downhill, with Nenthead's most utopian feature lying right underneath our feet and paws. To make our descent as safe and non-slippery as possible, the steepest part of the hill was carefully cobbled. As I found out later, it was done not for people but for the mine's 'staff' ponies as they pulled heavy carts of goods and mining spoil up and down the hill. But humans and dogs were able to take advantage of the cobbles, too. Comfort, not imposed from above, but brought about by practicality. Take it as another of my self-coined definitions of a true Utopia.

To complement that unexpected feeling of a Utopia, as we were making our way down the cobbled track, we could hear in the distance the distinctive mellifluous chimes of an invisible pandemic-defying ice-cream van.

Those chimes floating above the Pennines did turn out pretty utopian (or shall I say prophetic?) during our last stop in England before the Scottish border – in an ancient mid-Northumberland village of Shilbottle. For Tashi at least, they did: in the local Running Fox cafe, where we were having lunch, they were selling special ice-cream for dogs! And ice-cream, alongside cheese and pizzas, has always been one of Tashi's favourite foods. Ice-cream for dogs. It did sound excessively consumerist for someone like myself, who had grown up in the USSR, where most basic foods (for people, not for dogs), let alone delicacies, had been chronically hard-to-get.

Can foods be utopian? I wasn't sure about it until recently when I first laid my hands, or rather my teeth and tastebuds, on *Ikra Stolnaya*, an imitation Beluga caviar, made of seaweed and packed in cute and compact glass containers by a Belarus-based company, Santa Bremor. Not being able to afford the real Beluga caviar, which now costs around £400 per 100 grams, I could not believe my tongue when I first tried Stolnaya, which costs less than £3 per 100 grams. Believe it or not, the taste was better than the real caviar, and the tiny (and cholesterol-free) caviar balls kept bursting in my mouth, as if they were the real Beluga sturgeon eggs. So, in a way, that amazing ersatz caviar ticked all imaginable boxes by clearly outperforming its authentic variety in 1. Taste. 2. Texture. 3. Colour. 4. Environmental friendliness (saving the lives of rare and protected sturgeons). 5 Healthiness, and lastly, 6. Price! A Utopia on all counts!

I started ordering Stolnaya by crates from an online shop at a price of £4 per large tin, and it had become an essential part of my daily breakfast. Eating real black caviar every day, like a gluttonous oligarch, was the ultimate Soviet Utopia. I refer you to the 100 per cent true story of my dying granny whose last wish was to try Beluga caviar, of which my Mum did manage to get a tiny amount at the Kharkiv Intourist Hotel for foreigners, having spent half of her monthly salary on it.

So, yes, foods can be utopian too. As well as dystopian, like, say, the hard-to-get in the USSR so-called 'poor man's 'caviar', made of aubergines, which was more readily available in Kharkiv, from where my father would send it to me by cratefuls when I first studied and then lived and worked in Moscow.

Sadly, the story of *Stolnaya* had an unfortunate, yet entirely utopian, conclusion. When I was finishing the first draft of this book, that incredible product suddenly disappeared from all online and off-line stores which – as if on command – had suddenly run out of stock. It could have had something to do with the ban on most Russian and Belarusian imports due to the invasion of Ukraine (albeit *Stolnaya* had been distributed in the UK by a German company). Or (less likely) the rumours about *Stolnaya*'s great taste and super-low prices had finally reached the beleaguered British food shoppers and they started frantically stocking up on that edible wonder. Whatever it was, *Stolnaya* is no more, and that only supports my description of it as a utopian food. As we have seen many times already, true Utopias – edible or inedible – do not last!

Apart from the ice-cream for dogs, there was another little-known utopian touch to Shilbottle, a historical centre of coal mining which began there in 1728. In the early 20th century, the local colliery was purchased by the English Co-operative Wholesale Society (ECWS) for the sum of £50, which these days would only get you about 15 grams of the coal-black Beluga caviar. The Society also built a model village for miners, who – like in some other utopian model villages we have already visited – were provided with a paid week's holiday. But the lucky Shilbottle miners were among the very first in Britain to be also given a pension scheme! The village can be safely regarded as the UK's age-care pioneer, for on top of the pension, the generous ECWC had built in Shilbottle a row of cottages for elderly miners and, in what I regard as a somewhat defeatist gesture, another row for the elderly miners' widows, a scenario not dissimilar to a street in Letchworth where a health food store is located right next to a funeral parlour. To quote Rev. Colin Gough, the author of *Church and Community in Shilbottle. A Chronicle of 900 years*, the Shilbottle colliery 'provided the best working conditions for any miners in Britain at the time'.

After the protracted decline of coal production in the 1970s, when the National Coal Board took over the colliery (as history shows, whenever the name of an organisation starts with the word 'National', it means danger; National Health Service, National Rail etc.), the pit finally closed in 1981. But the Widows Row was still there, and we had a chance to walk along it, for it was indeed a 'row', and to take photos of some of the drab-looking and seemingly abandoned cottages.

All that ECWS TLC resulted in Shilbottle coal being highly regarded and even, reputedly, used to keep Buckingham Place warm during the pre-WWII years. Call me naive, but I found that 'natural circulation of warmth' quite symbolic (utopian?), as if the miners, treated with tender loving care by the establishment, had passed on that metaphoric 'warmth' to the powers-that-be. A more cynical person, however, would probably sum it up in the old British Navy way: 'You scratch my back – and I'll scratch yours.'

'What's in a name? That which we call a rose by any other name would smell as sweet.' Yet the name does matter sometimes. 'What's in a name? That which we call a Shilbottle by any other name would smell as sweet.' But would it? Since the times of Sir Thomas More, the concept of Utopia has been expressed and described in such melodious terms as 'Arcadia', 'Accordia' (a new area of Cambridge), 'Eden', 'Paradise', and so on. How about a 'Shilbottle Utopia' then? Doesn't sound that good, does it? Despite the fact that in reality, that small Northumberland village had probably come closer to a Utopia than any of the others. And yet, a 'Shilbottle Utopia' never went down in history.

According to Rev. Colin Gough: 'The name of Shilbottle suggests a Saxon origin – Shil's botel or home – someone who in his own

'Do Not Tell Titus!'

day was respected as a leader.' So, a chap called Shil was obviously a 'respected leader', and his cosy 'botel' (read home) had gradually evolved (or rather devolved) into a more familiar 'bottle'. Nice and clear. I seldom, if ever quote Wikipedia, but on this occasion I'll break that unwritten rule. Here's what Wiki says at the end of its short article on Shilbottle: 'In recent years, road signs to the village have been altered by the method of 'crossing' the first 'l' in 'Shilbottle to make it appear as 't', thus making it read as Shitbottle.' That last clause was self-evident, superfluous and unnecessary, from my point of view. 'Although signs have been restored and replaced over the years, this continues to be a problem.'

Again, my beloved literary duo of Ilya Ilf and Evgeny Petrov provide yet another relevant street scene from the deeply dystopian regional centre of N:

> When the moon rose and cast its minty light on the miniature bust of [poet] Zhukovsky, a rude word could clearly be seen chalked on the poet's bronze back. The inscription had first appeared on June 15, 1897, the same day that the bust had been unveiled. And despite all the efforts of the police, and later the militia, the defamatory word had reappeared each day with unfailing regularity.[21]

Chapter 12

The Case of Negative Nostalgia

...this your island, which seemed as to this particular the happiest in the world, will suffer much by the cursed avarice of a few persons.

Sir Thomas More, *Utopia*

For someone like myself, who has spent half of his peripatetic life away from the county of his birth, there exist two distinct types of nostalgia: positive and negative. The former is a bitter-sweet longing for the happy moments of your past, like that for the 'Ukrainian Venice' town of Vilkovo (see Chapter 8); the latter – a somewhat darker attraction to (or even a near-obsession with) the environment you grew up in, no matter how restrictive, or even sinister, it was.

It was the second type of nostalgia, enhanced by the Shilbottle-triggered interest in unusual place names and road signs that prompted our 50-mile detour on the way to New Lanark. In my continuing quest for Britain's utopian places, how could I miss a village, named Moscow, deep in the Scottish county of Ayrshire? The detour in question was not in fact entirely accidental or impulsive. I had even done some homework on the village which was easy: there was only one mention of Moscow, Ayrshire, that I was able to find in library books: the 1992 *Illustrated Architectural Guide to Ayrshire & Arran* described it as an 'oddly named village and telephone exchange beside the Volga Burn, for the motorist on the main road no more than two unnecessarily large signs drawing attention to the name, and a sprawling untidy garage'. The guide explained the origins of the village's name, which, apparently, had no connection with Russia, but derived from the Old Scots 'Moss haw' meaning a marshy ravine. As for the Volga Burn, it was but 'a facetious nomenclature coined to strengthen the putative link' or in plain English, it was simply a joke.

I also browsed through newspaper archives. In two faded 1884 issues of the *Kilmarnock Standard*, I came across a description of the mysterious Moscow murder, obviously the first, last and only village event of any distinction during the last 160 years:

> Mr Robert Rankin, a well-known Kilmarnock gentleman, who has lived for some years in retirement at the hamlet, had been found dead in circumstances which demanded enquiry. The body of Mr Rankin was found lying in a pool of blood, and even a casual glance was suggestive of foul play... In the right hand, was an ordinary nail hammer which at first was suggestive of suicide, but a closer examination showed that the hammer was not at all grasped by the hand, having evidently been placed in it after death.

I contemplated the challenge of committing suicide by hitting one's own head with a hammer...

A battered road sign, 'Waterside 13, Moscow 3', was the first real-life proof that the Scottish Moscow actually existed. It was not long before the view in our windscreen was blocked with a large sign, the size of a billboard, 'Moscow. Please Do Not Stop', it ran. Only joking. In reality of course the sign said: 'Please Drive Carefully', but it could have just as well been the former, for the passing cars did *not* drive carefully and made sure they roared through Moscow without slowing down. In a way, I could not blame them: 'You blink and you've missed it,' as one Ayrshire Muscovite put it to me later. At a first glance, modern Moscow did not differ greatly from the 1884 crime-scene description in the *Kilmarnock Standard*:

> Moscow, lying quite apart of any main road, consists of only a single row of small houses extending for rather less than a hundred yards. On the other side of the road is Volga Bank Cottage, in which Mr Rankin resided... Such is the scene of the tragedy. A novelist could not choose one more fitted to excite the imagination with a sense of loneliness and awe.

One didn't have to be a novelist to deduce that 'loneliness' was still there. The village was entirely deserted, except for a flock of sheep grazing dispassionately next to a 'sprawling untidy garage'. A florist's van pulled over next to me. 'Are you from Moscow?' the driver asked me. 'Yes, I am,' I replied honestly. 'Where is Dykescroft Cottage?' he then enquired. I was perplexed.

Yet the very fact that flowers were to be delivered to someone in Moscow, unless it was a funeral wreath, was reassuring. I decided to keep exploring the place by locating first a public toilet and then a post office -- in that order. The total absence of public facilities of any kind was probably the only feature shared by the Scottish Moscow with its Soviet namesake, as I remembered it. The village did not have a telephone exchange any longer and never had a post office of its own, the nearest one being in Galston. One positive sign though was that unlike in Soviet Moscow, there were no queues, which could be explained by the lack of such essential queue-forming components as shops and people.

There was nothing else left for me to do or to explore in the Scottish Moscow, which despite (or maybe, because of) its minuscule size was still much more attractive and human than the other one – the scene of not just one, but of millions of unsolved murders throughout its history; the dystopian, sinister place from where the orders to invade my native Ukraine had been issued. With relief, I drove away from Moscow never to return.

Heading for Dumfries, we were driving through the long-suffering Anglo-Scottish Border Country, which H V Morton once described as a 'queer compromise between fairyland and battlefield'.

'You are over the speed limit!' George, our deranged and cranky SatNav, would crackle from time to time in his rasping voice.

'Oh, George, here you go again!' my wife would exclaim. 'Don't you see that we are actually standing in a queue and not even moving?'

'Yes, George, why don't you shut up once and for all!' I would echo from the driver's seat.

'At the roundabout in eight hundred metres, take the third exit and turn right.' Liz, George's more reliable Google Maps counterpart, would butt in. She spoke with a posh London accent, which made her sound permanently annoyed.

We inherited 'George the SatNav' as part of an outdated sound system that bore more than a passing resemblance to the original Game Boy and was firmly embedded into the dashboard of our Toyota Alphard. Operated via a series of buttons and with no touch screen, the system was ancient. With his favourite mantra being the cantankerous and crackling 'You are over the speed limit!',

The Case of Negative Nostalgia

often voiced when the car was stationary, George was useless. No wonder that soon we started referring to him as 'our SatNag'. George's other annoying eccentricity was to triumphantly announce 'Route recalculation!' at the most inappropriate moments, such as when negotiating a seemingly endless roundabout – an unasked-for intervention that could easily lead to an accident.

Why didn't we get rid of George straight away, you may ask? Well, that was much easier said than done. George proved to be extremely resilient and – like the courageous voice of a determined political opposition in a totalitarian country – utterly irrepressible. Not just us but a number of experienced audio technicians were unable to silence him completely.

Not quite defeated (read silenced), George remained grossly unreliable, so we started using a Google Maps talking SatNav from my wife's smartphone instead. 'Liz' was how we christened the pleasant female voice so unlike George's, best described as the half-hearted drawl of a geezer. Liz was precise and matter-of-fact, her only eccentricity being an unbridled affection for bridleways and semi-abandoned trails where she would send the not-so-tiny Alphie without the slightest hesitation, as if directing him to a toll-free flyover or an autobahn. As a result, I once had to back down a super-narrow dirt track for about a mile to give way to a farm tractor.

Two vociferous and mutually incompatible SatNavs inside one campervan, with George's demented 'route recalculations' in the middle of Liz's instructions on how to negotiate yet another octopus-like giant roundabout, was not conducive to successful navigation. To paraphrase J.K. Jerome, Four Voices in One Campervan (To Say Nothing of the Bark). And yet, whether you want it or not, you end up forming an almost intimate relationship with your SatNavs, for how can it be otherwise when they become directly responsible for the lives of yourself and your campervan companions?

In my utopian dreams, I often see a new generation of SatNavs that could be interviewed before you buy them to allow you to decide whether you like their voices, accents and manners. Ideally, you should be able to take them on a test drive to see if you could work together as a team. Because, as we had deduced already, teamwork was a guarantee of successful campervanning. Today of course, you can select a variety of voices and accents.

Unlike that of George, Liz's speech had always been formal. It therefore came as a surprise when at some point on our trip to Scotland I heard her say: 'In five hundred metres, turn left towards Devil's Porridge.'

I spotted a road sign 'Devil's Porridge'. Had it been meddled with by some unknown wrongdoer in the middle of the night, like in Shilbottle? Propelled by curiosity, we followed it.

'Devil's Porridge' turned out to be the nickname coined by Sir Arthur Conan-Doyle for the peculiar product of the former H.M. Factory Gretna – cordite, a highly effective dry explosive, resulting from mixing nitro-glycerine and nitro-cotton and indeed resembling a kind of white and gooey porridge-like paste. As we were told in the 'Devil's Porridge' Museum on the site of the former factory, the toxic blend was mixed by women in special 'porridge pots', Thomson Nitrating Pans, often with their bare hands.

Founded in 1915, when Britain was losing the war through lack of ammunition, H.M. Factory Gretna, with its buildings stretching for over nine miles, was then the world's largest enterprise of its kind. The factory employed 30,000 people, mostly the 'munitions women', who worked under the supervision of qualified male and some female engineers.

The H.M. Factory's workers lived in relatively isolated and unmapped townships: Eastriggs and Gretna Garden City, which constituted the only 'properly' utopian settlements in the Dumfries & Galloway area. To me, they evoked the strongest feeing of negative nostalgia that I experienced on that trip.

In the US's National Atomic Museum in Albuquerque, New Mexico, which I visited while researching a book on America, I once saw a map of Soviet so-called 'secret cities'. Collectively, these secret cities were known as *zakrytye administrativno-territorial'nye obrazovaniia* (ZATO – don't even try to pronounce it aloud), or 'post boxes', and many were built by slave labour from the Soviet GULAG. During the Cold War, many of the USSR's towns and cities, including some of its largest, were 'closed'. Anyone with a foreign passport was forbidden to enter, and many were even out of bounds to Soviet citizens. These closed cities provided the technical foundation for Soviet military technology including chemical, biological and nuclear weapons research and manufacturing, enrichment of plutonium, space exploration, and military intelligence. Large numbers of highly qualified scientists were concentrated in them, developing new technologies but totally isolated from the global research community. Such 'secret cities' were known only by a postal code, identified with a name and a number.

To me, the map seemed incomplete for one simple reason: I spent the first three years of my life in one of the 'secret cities' near Moscow, to where my parents, young scientists (Mum — a chemical engineer, Dad — a nuclear physicist) and the newly-married graduates of Kharkov University, were dispatched in the early 1950s to work at a top-secret Soviet government facility developing nuclear and hydrogen bombs. The town of 40,000 people — both unmapped and unnamed (it was referred to as 'Military Unit BA/48764', or something similar) — was definitely not on the map.

I approached the Atomic Museum's Director and told him about the omission. He got very curious and asked how I could prove 'my' secret town's existence. Of course, I didn't remember much from those distant years; I was too young.

But strangely enough I could recall some smells, vague impressions and feelings. I remember the chiming of church bells (the nearby town of Zagorsk was the centre of Russia's Orthodox Church — then heavily corrupted and KGB-controlled), black-robed priests, holy water springs in which the area abounded, and brand-new portraits of Stalin (who died one year before I was born), displayed in the windows of log-cabins next to faded icons of Holy Mary. I can clearly remember a walk in the wintry forest when I for the first time in my life saw a wild hare jumping away from us along the snow.

We lived in a so-called 'communal flat' having to share bathroom and kitchen with several other families. One of our neighbours, an engineer who worked at my parents' laboratory, used to keep his motorbike in the corridor (our apartment was on the fifth floor of a standard block of flats, and there was no lift, so the motorbike owner had to drag his vehicle up the stairs every evening). That mechanical monster once fell on top of me as I was playing in the communal corridor. My screams must have been heard all over the town.

Because my parents were at work all day, they had to hire a child-minder to look after me. She was an ancient woman (babushka) in a kerchief and looked very much like Baba Yaga, a long-nosed witch from Russian folk tales who lives in a hut standing on chicken's legs.

Once, coming home from the laboratory, my parents saw the Baba Yaga with me in a bundle standing near the church and asking for alms to feed 'the poor little orphan' – that was me. It was the 'orphan' bit of her whining mantra that must have offended my parents more than anything else (I don't blame them), and the contrite Baba Yaga was sacked the same day.

I visited the town with my mother shortly before my defection from the USSR in late 1989, after thirty-three years. The devilish 'facility' was still there. It was still located in the grounds of the old monastery, only instead of crosses, the factory buildings had faded metallic red stars mounted on the onion domes. The town was still surrounded by the thick concrete wall with barbed wire. You could only get in through a couple of checkpoints, provided you had an invitation from someone living inside the compound.

A young military guard, having carefully scrutinised our credentials, gave us a one-day pass into my childhood and Mum's youth – equally constrained and repressed.

We were invited by a woman who worked with my parents many years before. She was the only person still alive of those who had worked with my father. The treacherous effects of radiation, dormant for many years, finally came to the surface and destroyed them all (including my Dad) one by one. And the woman herself? Yes, she was alive, but was no more than a skeleton covered with skin. In her late fifties, she looked at least eighty years old. Her hands were trembling incessantly, and her skull was practically bald. What a far cry from the smiling plump laboratory assistant on the old yellowish photo my mother had shown me. And, God, what a miserable life she led. Alone in the whole world, without any relatives or friends, she was dwelling in a tiny one-room kitchenette. Books were piled everywhere, on the bedstead and under the table. Among them not a single romance or thriller, nothing that could pass as pulp or easy reading, but almost exclusively art, history or philosophy. She offered us tea and produced a small packet from the drawer saying it was her monthly ration. Having wasted all her life for the sake of the system, what did she get in return? A seventy-five-rouble pension, a tiny hole of a flat and one packet of tea a month.

But she said she was happy. 'I have lots of books and lots of memories – what else do I need?'

'The place hasn't changed a bit,' my mother noted sadly on the way back.

The early 1950s were tough. Stalin wanted to develop nuclear weapons by hook or by crook to achieve military parity with the West and then, ultimately, superiority over it. My parents had to work for twelve hours a day and there was practically no protection against the radiation.

My mother recalled how skin peeled off her palms when she was pregnant with me (so I must have got my share of the stuff too).

The Case of Negative Nostalgia

According to her, some of her colleagues literally expired in front of her eyes from overdoses, and my father was particularly affected, since he dealt directly with radioactive substances and often used to travel to 'Lemonia' – a secret nuclear weapons testing range in Kazakhstan. He died of a heart attack at the age of fifty-six. None of his co-workers lived to see his or her 60th birthday.

How could I prove it?

I said to the Atomic Museum Director that I'd ask my mother to pen her memories of the place and post them to him. My Mum was then living in Australia. She agreed to write some notes on the 'secret city' of her youth and started working on them. Shortly after that she fell ill and had to be moved to a hospital. Sorting out her papers in her miniature Melbourne bed-sit which she had left forever, I found several notebooks with her characteristic scribbles. Some of them were the notes she had written for the Atomic Museum. I've translated them:

Zagorsk, 1951.

Winter. Early morning. I open the door to my laboratory. The room is lit up with some strange fluorescent light. Where is it coming from? The lead-lined fume cupboard contains retorts with radioactive substances, and it is they that emanate this weird light. My first thought is: 'How beautiful!' A colleague arrives, and together we admire the sight, not realising immediately that those fluorescent solutions carry colossal radioactivity doses. They were sent to us for research purposes from a range in Kazakhstan, where nuclear bombs are being tested. This highly radioactive glow accompanies us on most of our working days. The only 'protection' we have is a pair of rubber gloves...

Midday. We are staring at Geiger counters showing the quantity of radioactive particles in the substances that we analyse. Suddenly, all the counters go into 'red' indicating a massive radiation dose. Where did it come from? People from other laboratories complain in the corridors that their counters show the same picture, and everyone is concerned about the source. At this point, in the end of the corridor there appears Major Gramolin, a young and capable scientist, a recent graduate of Moscow Chemical Defense Academy. He is short, muscular and has a noble 'aristocratic' face of a Pushkin era hussar. He is dressed in a protective suit he wore while working in the contaminated (or 'dirty', as we used to call it) zone of increased radioactivity. It was the radioactivity of his suit that has made our Geiger counters go crazy — despite the 'special' decontamination shower he had to take before leaving that horrible zone. His suit had to be incinerated. As for Gramolin himself, he died suddenly of a heart attack in his early 40s.

Olya and Raya – two girls from Ukraine – worked as our laboratory assistants. They were sent to us straight from a Poltava comprehensive school. Olya was a tall green-eyed blonde, and Raya was a plump, short and brown-eyed joker. They both worked in a Drinking Water Decontamination Laboratory. Radioactive water was decontaminated with the help of a chromatographic column, and that was why they always kept three separate vessels with normal drinking water, radioactive water and water decontaminated in the column. Once – in a rush to get to the factory's canteen during a lunch break – the girls mixed up the vessels and drank some radioactive water. It was tragic. They were soon diagnosed with radiation sickness. Hospitals, disability and slow painful deaths followed.

I will never forget it, never!

A young colleague of ours, with whom we shared a communal flat, once brought home a Geiger counter to measure the radiation background. It transpired that all our personal belongings, clothes in wardrobes, cushions, blankets, even handkerchiefs were radioactive, a fact that, however, did not worry us in the least. We were young and naïve, despite being scientists. Besides, what was the point of worrying when we lacked effective means of protection; our clothes and bodies were not properly decontaminated after work. Protection of the staff was never the authorities' concern: the only thing that mattered was the order of 'our great leader and teacher Comrade Stalin' to come up with the Bomb as soon as possible. After that, several of our co-workers, having armed themselves with dosimeters, measured radioactivity levels in the forest outside the factory (formerly, the monastery) walls. All the trees, the grass, the flowers and the ground were emanating the invisible deathly rays. It was the same in the residential part of the town only half a kilometre away.

My mother passed away in Melbourne in 2006.

Now can you see the similarities? Just like with the 'closed town' of my childhood, the very existence of Eastriggs and Greta Garden City, built to accommodate the workers of the 'secret' munitions

The Case of Negative Nostalgia

factory, was supposed to be *sub rosa*. Just like the former, they were home to over 30,000 workers, yet didn't feature on any maps. But in the case of Eastrigg ad Gretna it was pretty much a Polichinelle's secret: everyone in the vicinity knew what was happening on the site. Likewise, my parents recalled that if one asked for directions in the streets of their 'closed' town, it was not unusual to hear in response: 'Cross the road, turn left, walk past the A-Bomb-making facility behind the old monastery gates and you will see the post office.'

The differences were also striking. Unlike in my town, the residents of both Eastriggs and Gretna Garden City were free to come and go without a hard-to-obtain special pass. Also, as testified by the name of the latter, the living conditions in them were much better, although the Soviet town had one indisputable advantage: unlike the two Scottish 'secret' settlements, declared totally teetotal and without a single pub between them, it was not alcohol-free!

Despite (or, more likely, because of) being officially teetotal, there was a serious drink problem in Gretna and Eastrigg, as there was nothing to stop their dwellers from 'smuggling' alcohol from elsewhere. Forbidden fruit is always the most coveted. As it has been shown countless times in different parts of the world (1920s US, Norway, the Faroe Islands, Gorbachev's USSR etc.) sobriety by decree only leads to excessive drinking. David Lloyd George who visited H.M. Factory Gretna and the settlements in 1916 commented that drinking amongst the workers did more damage that 'all the German submarines put together'.[22] The same year, Sir Arthur Conan Doyle, when visiting the area as a war correspondent called Greta Garden City and Eastriggs 'The Miracle Towns.' But, while impressed by the workers' 'regular and comfortable' living conditions, he also noted that '…there is the perennial question of the drink in which the girls have an enormous advantage.'

While in Gretna and Eastrigg, Conan Doyle did observe (and was even accosted by) numerous drunken women, which didn't stop him from being impressed by their bravery in dealing with Devil's Porridge, when 'the smallest generation of heat may cause an explosion… Those smiling khaki-clad girls who are swirling the stuff round in their hands, would be blown to atoms in an instant if certain very small changes occurred,' he wrote, in what reads as an attempt to justify the women's propensity for booze.

Trucks in the Garden of Eden

Walking in modern Gretna, now an ordinary commuter town, I had repeated flashes of superficial recognition. Only not of the Soviet 'secret town', as you might have thought, but of Letchworth Garden City and London's Hampstead Garden Suburb. No wonder: both Gretna Garden City and Eastriggs were laid out and built by Letchworth's and Hampstead's chief architect Raymond Unwin, the only difference being that in Gretna he was commissioned not by private do-gooders, like Ebenezer Howard and Henrietta Barnett, but by the British Government.

The familiar-looking arts-and-crafts cottages, neatly balancing both formal and informal architectural elements, had electricity, running water and – innovatively for 1915 – in-house toilets, one for each family. The latter constituted the closest proximity to utopian luxury at the time. Forty-odd years later, in the officially non-existent 'secret city' of my childhood, which enjoyed much better food supplies than most mapped Soviet towns, we still had to share toilet and bathroom with the neighbours. Utopias are not immune to the influence of the countries, governments and social systems under which they had been created.

Readers of my travel books may be familiar with a habit of mine – travelling with old vintage guide-books: Baedekers, Murrays, Bradshaws and such like. In the late 1990s and early 2000s, I even had a column 'Baedeker Raids' in the *Daily Telegraph*, in which I recounted my travels around Britain armed with the 1893 edition of the quirkily meticulous *Baedeker Great Britain Handbook*, an idea that was later borrowed by the BBC and Michael Portillo, in his orange trousers. Vintage guidebooks never failed to provide me with what I call a carcass of time which I could then revivify with my own experience and imagination – two main components of creative writing, M. J. B. Baddeley's 1908 *Thorough Guide* to Scotland is among my all-time favourites. Unlike many other classic guide-book writers, Baddeley never minces his words. 'An hour is amply sufficient to comprehend Berwick,' he states categorically in the end of his short entry on one of the most history-rich Scottish Border towns. Or how can you argue with the following peremptory assertion: 'Edinburgh is, without doubt, the finest city in the kingdom.' As for Gretna Green, which even as far back as in 1908, had that romantic association: 'Gretna Green, now little more than a prosaic railway station.'

In its categorical tone, the latter reminded me of the title of one of the how-to-write books by American author Ben Yagoda (I use it sometimes in my tutorials) 'When You Catch an Adjective, Kill It'. Or of the famous Zen pronouncement: 'If you meet the Buddha – kill the Buddha.'

To me as well as to thousands of other visitors from all over the world, (albeit for different reasons), Gretna Green was anything but prosaic. Kitschy and superficial with regards to its souvenir stalls and shopping malls, mythical maybe, but not prosaic. Why mythical? Because of Gretna's reputation as a place where an eloping couple could quickly get married by a local blacksmith, with the ensuing consummation (without which the marriage could, allegedly, get annulled) in one of the village inns.

With the possible exception of the 'consummation', this is nonsense, particularly misleading since 1857, when a law was passed in Scotland requiring 21 days of local residence before a marriage could be officially registered. This regulation probably had something to do with the fact that in 19th-century Scotland girls could legally get married at 12 and boys at 14. Being stuck together for 21 days in a God-forsaken Scottish village and without their favourite toys for a period might cool the ardours.

As for the myth of being married 'over the anvil' by the agreeable Gretna blacksmith (and there was indeed a blacksmith in Gretna prior to the First world War, just like in any other small British village), according to the 1844 edition of the *Chronicles of Gretna Green* by Peter Hutchinson, 'In spite of all our inquiries, and searching, and scrutiny, we could not discover that a blacksmith had of late years performed the ceremony, nor indeed that a blacksmith had ever done it at any period whatever.'

As often happens with utopian concepts, the myth had proved stronger than reality: thousands of couples from all over the world still come here to be confronted with bagpipe music, overpriced souvenir shops (with the 'Famous Blacksmith Shop' among them) and no-less-kitschy eateries and shopping malls. 'A Big Wee Shop', displayed a banner saying 'Courtship is a Maze' at the entrance. I thought it could have said: 'Marriage is a Maze: Easy to Get in, but Hard to Get out!' I liked the way it was all summarised in the headline of an article on Gretna Green on one Italian travel website: 'SPOSARSI A GRETNA GREEN, L'ULTIMO & SUPER KITSCH VILLAGIO DI SCOZIA'

No translation required, except 'Sposarsi', which means 'getting married'. I am not quite sure why, but to me it sounds punchier, more cadent, and, yes, a tad more romantic (for kitsch can be romantic too) in Italian than in English.

To enhance my 'negative nostalgia' even further, several miles away from Gretna we stumbled upon the gruesome remains of Chapelcross, Scotland's first nuclear power station, constructed specifically to churn out plutonium for the British Nuclear Weapons Programme. It used to generate some electricity too. Opened in 1959 and closed in 2004, when the decommissioning commenced, Chapelcross had, reportedly, contributed to the significant increase of the background radiation levels in the area.

Of course, I'm going to associate the abandoned Chapelcross with Chernobyl, which I visited in 1994. Yes, Chapelcross had managed to avoid a similar catastrophe, but the sight of its rusty pillar-like rods and dead funnels piercing the uncomplaining Scottish skies was sinister enough to complement the pang of negative nostalgia caused by H.M. Factory Gretna's museum.

We needed some positive impressions to balance my persisting black reveries. So we went to Moffat – a name which sounded soft and fluffy, like some undiscovered Australian marsupial. According to the Guinness Book Records, Moffat was home of the world's narrowest detached hotel, the Star, recently – for obvious reasons – renamed the Famous Star. Built by William Norman in 1860 and made as narrow as possible for tax reasons, it measured just 20 feet from side to side and was located in Chapel Street – officially the shortest one in Scotland. We managed to squeeze inside and had coffee in its narrow, elongated bar. Contrary to expectations, the hotel did not feel at all claustrophobic. It was warm and cosy, and therefore homely enough to generate the tepid feeling of a Utopia I had been craving so much all through the trip.

That elusive sensation was further enhanced by an accidental find on the road. Driving through the ill-fated town of Lockerbie, where Pan Am Flight 103 crashed in December 1988, I spotted a signpost, 'Ukrainian Chapel', next to an abandoned bus depot. Not inclined to put too much trust in road signs (not after 'Shilbottle' and 'Devil's Porridge'), but definitely intrigued, I followed the arrow and soon arrived at a small, Lego-like structure, neatly assembled out of corrugated iron and roof tiles, with a large rickety cross above the entrance. The hut

The Case of Negative Nostalgia

was locked, but from a notice on its doors I gleaned that it was 'Hallmuir POW Chapel'. Through a tiny window, I could discern an unexpectedly ornate church interior, with mosaics, icons and candelabra.

That very evening, having made enquiries at our hotel, I was given the name of Peter Kormylo, an academic and a local historian of Ukranian origins, whose father was one of the Chapel's builders. Mr Kormylo has kindly sent me the information about that highly unusual structure.

The story of the Hallmuir Chapel goes back to 1947, when Ukrainian prisoners of war arrived on the Clyde from Rimini on the Adriatic coast of Italy, where they had been interned on surrendering to the British. Miraculously, unlike hundreds of thousands of other Soviet POWs who had changed sides and chosen to fight with Germany against Bolshevism and after the war ended were forcibly repatriated back to the USSR, where most of them faced execution, the Ukrainians avoided that fate. To my knowledge, that was only the second post-WWII case when Soviet POWs were not handed over to Stalin by their Western captors. The first one was in Liechtenstein, where over 500 Russians who had crossed into it from Austria, asked for political asylum in May 1945.

Eventually, over 400 Ukrainians ended up at the camp near Lockerbie and were sent to work at local farms and forests. They were granted civic status and got a three-year contract. Mr Kormylo's father was among them. Since most of the Ukrainians were deeply religious, they needed a place to pray. The camp at Hallmuir had forty single-storey huts made of corrugated iron, and Sir John Buchanan Jardine, the landowner, allocated one of them to be used as a chapel.

The Ukrainians had transformed the hut's interior with some amazing hand-made objects: candlesticks crafted from old shell casings; a large chandelier, ingeniously engineered out of coat hangers and fencing wire; hand-painted icons. The Chapel was now a grade B listed building and regularly hosted church services attended by locals. Since the start of the Russian invasion, they had been praying tirelessly for Ukraine's impending victory and for the thousands of innocent victims of the horrible war.

If you find yourself driving in the vicinity of Lockerbie, do make a detour and visit that modest Ukrainian – and positively utopian – Chapel, propping up the grey Scottish sky with its

Trucks in the Garden of Eden

worn-out wooden cross to symbolise the inevitable victory of faith and creation over treachery and destruction.

To save time while in Scotland, we didn't camp. Instead, we stayed for a couple of nights at Rockhall Tower, a historic and, reportedly, haunted old mansion. As we drove unhurriedly towards Rockhall up the little road off the motorway to Dumfries through fields, grazing livestock and trees, I kept imagining that I was an armoured medieval knight astride a thoroughbred stallion who had just eloped with a beautiful maiden (my wife of course) and was on his way to the nearby village of Gretna to formalise his marital union. The tall castle-like L-shaped mansion, rebuilt and further fortified in 1690, with turrets and embrasures, fitted the reverie.

We were lucky to be staying in a bright and airy room under the roof of the 'castle', from where we had panoramic views of the Border Country. Looking down at the longsuffering landscape, I remembered that when on a research trip as a columnist for the *Glasgow Herald* in the early 2000s, I happened to stumble upon the last remaining border markings – a truly historical find of which I claim to be the discoverer. That obscure landmark in the shape of an old stone wall ran between two farms – English and Scottish – in the outskirts of Berwick-upon-Tweed. Built with a purely practical purpose, to stop the cows from either side trespassing onto the neighbour's land, it was still there 400 years after 1603. The Union of the Crowns had obviously had little effect on the continuing Disunion of the Cows...

The 5-star view we could admire through the binoculars kindly provided by the Rockhall owners had no reminders of the battles: just hills, green-and-yellow fields, and – felt, if not quite seen somewhere in the distance – the white-caps of the open sea of the Solway Firth.

It was from Rockhall that we ventured on a one-day trip to Robert Owen's New Lanark – the World Heritage Site of Britain's iconic industrial Utopia. We drove 70 miles to the north only to be faced with yet another 'closed' sign. I did not realise that although still operating (unlike many other heritage sites, shut down due to the pandemic) New Lanark's multiple museums were only open for visitors three days a week. At least no one could shut down the impressive view of New Lanark from the top of a hill: a scattering

The Case of Negative Nostalgia

of multi-storied sandstone tenements and mills in the classical industrial architecture style.

I found a slight consolation in the fact that I had visited the village several times in the past with my kids, although the only thing I could still remember clearly was a hologram of a late-18th-century schoolgirl at the entrance to Robert Owen's favourite creation, the New Lanark School for Children. The site's vast territory was still open for accidental strollers, and we could wander around it freely without entering any of its buildings.

Besides, as I have noted earlier, there was a certain creative challenge in the shut-down, deserted, and even permanently abandoned sites, villages and towns where, for lack of interviewees and interlocutors, you had to converse with the walls, the streets, the parks and the houses, all of which had their stories to tell.

In New Lanark on that occasion, I didn't have to strain my hearing, Instead, we had to protect our ear-drums from the piercing all-permeating roar of animatronic dinosaurs. Tashi's astonished barking in response to the giant creatures' mechanical twitching was immediately absorbed and recycled by their guttural bellows, which made the few little kids visiting the site by accident, just like we did, scurry away in tears.

With all of its shops and museums closed, the World Heritage Site was still wide open for those skilfully engineered and scarily vociferous prehistoric animals as part of 'the Jurassic Lanark Free Family Trail', according to a leaflet I picked up at the gates. According to the map, the 'Trail' passed through Lanark Town Centre and the 'New Lanark World Heritage Site' as well as Robert Owen's garden. Dinosaurs in the Garden of Eden!

The same leaflet encouraged visiting families to 'walk in the footsteps' (it didn't specify whose, the dinosaurs' or Robert Owen's) to 'follow the Jurassic Lanark trail and live to tell the tale'. 'Dinosaur hunting can be exhausting,' it went on. 'Don't forget to take time out and explore the many excellent shops, cafes and eateries in Lanark town centre and New Lanark.'

I wondered what Robert Owen himself would have thought about such ferocious (in the true sense) PR promotion of his favourite creation – New Lanark?

And you know what? After some shilly-shallying, I decided that as someone who loved animals and ordered the display of a set of his own colourful drawings of elephants, tigers, lions and giraffes in the Assembly Hall of his New Lanark school (as testified by the famous 1825 engraving by G. Hunt), Owen would have loved it!

And although it would, most certainly, differ considerably from the intentions of the creators of that rather tacky and openly commercial 'Jurassic Trail', to me the dinosaurs in Owen's 'Garden of Eden' were a moving reminder of Robert Owen's pure, almost childish, idealism that manifested itself in his noble, yet hugely utopian, deeds and ideas, and of his own childhood, when at nine he already worked as a factory undermaster, and at ten as a teacher.

Yes, it was probably due to his skipped childhood that all his life Owen had remained the proverbial boy who never grew up. I realised it very clearly looking at the huge toy dinosaurs in his garden.

Owen's perennial boyishness had also added a new meaning to one of his most idealistic manifestos, with the protracted title 'The Twelve Fundamental Laws of Human Nature on which Robert Owen predicates a change of society that will form an entire new state of existence, as read in the debate between him and Mr. Campbell, at Cincinnati, Ohio, on the 13th April, 1829', a copy of which I picked up in the Owen Museum in New Town (it now adorns one of the walls on my writing shed). All 12 points of this impressive, yet naive and childish in its essence, document, idealise 'the individual', with a 'superior creative organisation'.

I hugely respect Owen for trying to tackle that eternal and, sadly, impregnable barrier on the road to all past and present Utopias – human nature, a perfect 'individual', or 'a new man', as it was referred to in the intentionally misleading document from the rubbish heap of history, 'The Builders of Communism Moral Code'. Issued in the USSR in 1961. It proclaimed that the 'creation of a new man' one of the Communist Party's main tasks on the road to Communism, would be achieved 'within the lifespan of the present-day generation'. I have referred to that deceitful document earlier.

By taking over the cotton-weaving mills of New Lanark, Owen had embarked on a great philosophical and social experiment – trying to change his workers' character and attitudes, a next-to-impossible task. In his own words, 'For two years it was a regular attack and defence of prejudices and malpractices between the manager and the population, without the former being able to make much progress, or to convince the latter of the sincerity of his good intentions for their welfare.'[23]

The Case of Negative Nostalgia

In return for such understanding, Owen offered his New Lanark workers some real benefits: free schooling for their children, an excellent co-operative village store, where they could buy things on credit, shorter working hours and many more. 'The population could not resist a firm, well-directed kindness... They were convinced that a real desire existed to increase their happiness... They were taught to be rational, and they acted rationally.'

That can sound cynical by modern standards, but Robert Owen was not a hypocrite. One of history's great humanists and utopians, he remained a devoted capitalist (I see him as a 'socialist capitalist') and a successful manager. According to John Hatton Davidson, the compiler of a succinct, yet insightful and informative brochure, 'The Life of Robert Owen', 'What Owen had achieved was to remoralise the society. As a result, the establishment became much more profitable.' So, it was not by chance that he named the new school building, opened in New Lanark on 1 January 1816, 'The Institution for the Formation of Character'.

The school register for 1816 shows 80 pupils from three to six and 190 from six to ten. Their parents paid 3d per month for each child, which was just 1% of the average wage. There were no rewards, or punishments in the school: learning was to be made a pleasure.

This rhyme, compiled for the pupils by James Buchanan, one of the schoolteachers, is representative of the highly unusual, gentle and informal approach to education advocated by Robert Owen:

The Cow
Come, children, listen to me now,
And you shall hear about the cow.
You'll find her useful, live or dead,
Whether she is black, or white, or red.
When milkmaids milk her morn or night,
She gives us milk, so fresh and white,
And this we little children think,
Is very nice for us to drink.

Why did I choose that particular rhyme, and not, say, another one called The Sheep ('Hark now to me and silence keep,/And you will know about the sheep')? When my malfunctioning aortic valve was replaced in 2017, I opted for a biological, as opposed to a mechanical valve, either porcine or bovine. They found out they

Trucks in the Garden of Eden

had run out of the former, and so used the latter. Since then, my friends joke that I suddenly start mooing for no reason. To which I say: 'Think yourself lucky that I moo, and do not grunt!' Since the surgery, I do feel special affection for cows grazing in the fields, and that probably influenced my choice.

From cows – back to the dinosaurs.

As it happens, Robert Owen's New Lanark project was successful for as long as Owen himself was there to supervise it. His 1824 departure for the US, where he tried (and failed) to recreate his community experiment in the village of New Harmony, Indiana, was the start of New Lanark's slow decline, which culminated in the formation of the New Lanark Conservation Trust in 1974 – 'the last throw of dice before the bulldozers moved in to raze the whole site, or rather what remained of it, according to 'The Story of New Lanark', a brochure published by the same Trust that concludes: 'New Lanark had not so much fallen behind; rather it was the rest of the world which had caught up.'

I would have put it differently though: New Lanark had not so much fallen behind. It was human nature that had failed to catch up with Owen's 'factory of dreams'. The 'useful' 19th-century cows had evolved into the impressively scary, yet useless, 21st-century dinosaurs. Until the 'New Man' is finally created (and that means never), all extinct and not-quite-extinct Utopias are destined, like the dinosaurs, to extinction. Despite the museum's closure, our trip to the modern Jurassic Park of New Lanark was not a waste of time.

Having returned to Rockhall Tower on the same day, we had to make an important decision on where to go next. It was only a couple of days before the draconian tier-4 lockdown restrictions were to come into force, so we had to head south, back home, and fast. We had to skip mainland Scotland's last utopian settlement we had intended to visit – Findhorn, a model eco-village on Moray coast, 30 miles east of Inverness – a thoroughly utopian community of new-age environmentalists, with, allegedly, the lowest CO2 footprint of any settlement in the developed world. I heard that many of the houses in Findhorn had been built of recycled materials, including whisky barrels, and that the village even had its own local currency, the Eko, with 1 Eko equal to one

The Case of Negative Nostalgia

pound sterling, which made it a kind of a mini-state in its own right. Sadly, we had no option but to put off the visit to Findhorn until after the pandemic.

Alas, that was not meant to happen either, because in July 2023 it was announced that Findhorn was no longer financially viable and was facing closure. The fascinating eco-village had joined a long list of failed Utopias.

Chapter 13

Per Insulae Ad Astra!

I found paradise, drew a map, and within 15 years it was ruined.
Costas Christ, editor for *National Geographic Traveller* on the

Thai island of Koh Phangan.

I always loved islands, and in the course of 30 years of my travel writing career visited dozens of them, including the Faroes, the Falklands, the Ascension Island in the Pacific, the Hebrides (both Inner and Outer), the Channel Islands (all of them) and a number of islands and islets off the coast of Australia and Tasmania, including the obscure Three Hummock Island. The latter was then populated by hundreds of giant red kangaroos, thousands of poisonous snakes and one elderly English couple, who had their food and mail dropped from a plane once a week. Separated during the Second World War, they vowed never to leave each other again and lived on the island until their deaths (within a month of each other) several years ago.

An island's relative isolation from the rest of the world had always had a calming effect on me and made me feel at home on almost all of them. Visiting an off-shore island has always been a near-utopian experience: travelling 'abroad' without having to cross the border.

The islands of Scotland are among the most fascinating features of Britain's geography. Having visited many of them, I can conclude that most (I am talking here only about the islands that are still populated, or were inhabited in the past) constitute, or used to constitute, near-ideal models of a utopian society.

Below you will find an often-disrupted non-chronological reportage of my post-pandemic expedition to the remote Scottish

Per Insulae Ad Astra!

islands on board MV *Greg Mortimer*, during which I had multiple flashbacks to previous visits to those far-flung places as a roving columnist for the *Glasgow Herald* during the 2000s.

Looking back at those exciting journalistic assignments, I could still recall random details: spending days at the Gaelic College on Skye; posing as a potential buyer of the island of Soay (it was then on sale for just £200,000), complete with its feral sheep and tame otters, immortalised by Gavin Maxwell; discovering the UK's best Indian curry house in Lerwick, the capital of Shetland; and breakfasting alone in my Stornoway hotel on a Sunday morning, when the only thing that moved on the whole of the still strictly Sabbatarian island were the bubbles in the glass of mineral water in front of me.

I fell in love with the Scottish islands there and then and couldn't wait to rediscover those I had visited already and to explore the ones I hadn't.

I wake up from the characteristic rattle of an unwinding anchor chain, followed by the suave and cheerful voice of David Berg, our Swedish Expedition Leader, wishing his fellow expeditioners 'a very good morning'. David's loud velvety voice, coming from a carefully concealed (like a KGB bugging device) intercom, is filling my spacious cabin. It is 6 am, and initially everything in me rebels against getting up. I want to stay in my super-comfortable king-size bed; to keep being rocked gently by the ocean waves, soothed even further by the ship's cutting-edge stabilisers.

My first instinct is to switch David off as I habitually do at home to my intrusive alarm clock. But the source of the voice is nowhere to be found . I realise then that I am already fully awake and ready for another day of adventures and close encounters with the Scottish Islands. The question that is bothering me now is whether the Zodiac landing on the island of St Kilda (or Foula, or Staffa) is going to be 'wet' or 'dry', which would dictate a dress-code for the day: water-proof pants and rubber boots, stocked in the ship's 'Mud Room', or jeans and trainers.

The Wild Scotland expedition on board the purpose-built brand-new MV *Greg Mortimer* was like nothing I had experienced before.

To begin with, I had never sailed on a ship named after a living person – this one named after an acclaimed Australian mountaineer and engineer Greg Mortimer, God bless him! Perhaps it is a peculiar and rather agreeable Australian tradition (she is run by an Australian company) to name sea vessels after the living rather than the dead (another expedition ship that joined the company's fleet in 2022 was MV Sylvia Earl – a still very much alive and active American marine biologist). Unveiling a floating monument to a living person was something that I had thought only Russian oligarchs, dictators and royalty could get away with. Americans tried it in the early decades of their independence, but soon gave up.

And what an incredible small ship she is. Built in 2019, she is the first passenger vessel ever to feature the inverted Ulstein X-Bow to ensure that her farthest forward point is not at the top, which increases the ship's fuel efficiency, stability and safety. In combination with Rolls-Royce dynamic stabilisers, this offers unrivalled steadiness, reducing both pitching and rolling.

To be honest, I am not a great sailor and have always been prone to sea sickness. That is why I was carrying with me an impressive supply of travel sickness tablets, most of which listed 'dizziness and nausea' as their most common side-effects. Despite crossing some of the roughest parts of the North Atlantic, including the notorious Cape Wrath, named so for good reason (or so I thought), I hadn't taken a single pill and felt the *Greg Mortimer*'s tremors only once, on the very first night of the voyage, when we were sailing past the Western Isles. The sensation was close to the one experienced by my favourite Soviet writers Ilf and Petrov during their journey from Europe to America on board the SS *Normandie* in 1935:

> In the stern where we were located everything trembled. The deck and the walls and the easy chairs and the glasses on the washstand and the washstand itself trembled. The ship's vibration was so pronounced that even objects from which one did not expect any sound made a noise. For the first time we heard the sound of towels, soap, the carpet on the floor, the paper on the table, the electric bulb, the curtain, the collar thrown on the bed... If a passenger became thoughtful for a moment and relaxed his facial muscles, his teeth at once began to chatter of their own free will.[23]

In my case, a similar chorus was joined by the throbs of the iPhone on my bedside table and the stubborn flap-flapping of the open door of the safe hidden inside the wardrobe. It took me a while to locate the latter and to stabilise the door with a no-longer-needed map of Edinburgh, where our journey had commenced.

Alongside the stabilisers, my favourite onboard gadgets were two Jacuzzis on the upper deck, right under the radar. Sitting in them (alternately), I kept imagining myself a fulmar or an albatross (at times, even a puffin) whooshing forgetfully above the waves.

MV *Greg Mortimer* carried 15 Zodiacs – inflatable shuttle boats, made of flexible tubes with pressurised gas, which we could board from the four dedicated sea-level launching platforms to explore the coastline, the grottos and the wildlife (including seals and whales) from close-up, or to land on the shore. These platforms were designed by Greg Mortimer himself, and I can testify that even for someone like myself, long past his athletic best, jumping into the Zodiacs was almost as easy as boarding a London double-decker bus.

It was of course an expedition, not a cruise. There was total lack of black-tie (or any other) entertainment, apart from excellent lectures by the onboard experts: ornithologist and historian John and archaeologist Carol, as well as the Zodiacs, the Mud Room and the occasional 'wet landings'.

It was there, in the Scottish Islands – after all the setbacks and tribulations of my long quest for Britain's Utopias – that I finally discovered two surviving near-ideal utopian communities – those of Foula and Fair Isle, as well as the historical utopian settlement that had existed on the now-depopulated island St Kilda,

Accompanied by ranger Sue from the National Trust for Scotland, which now owns St Kilda, I had a chance to wander among the stone remains of the small community that had thrived there in total obscurity and isolation from the rest of the world for about 2000 years, until the remaining 30 or so if its members were resettled on mainland Scotland in 1930.

All St Kildans enjoyed equal rights and until the mid-19th century knew nothing about money. They lived off seabirds, fish, crops and Soay sheep descending from the 100-hectare island of Soay in the St Kilda archipelago (see below). Those dishevelled, wild-looking sheep could still be seen all over the island. Having outlived human settlers by almost a century, they behaved as the island's only remaining masters (which they actually were, not counting the National Trust for Scotland) – jumping over the ruins and bleating belligerently.

Rent in St Kilda was paid with puffins and feathers. Making ropes out of horsehair, using fulmar oil for their lamps and obtaining fishing hooks from the stomachs of gannets that had devoured the fish escaped from the lines of fishermen in Scottish and English waters, were among the unique and truly utopian St Kilda 'technologies'. Unlike the inhabitants of some other Scottish islands, where whisky was considered a cure for all ailments, the inherently teetotal St Kildans regarded fulmar oil as a panacea, which soothed rheumatic pains, coughs and bruises.

The island had no crime and was ruled by a democratic little 'parliament', whose main function was to make sure that every islander got fed, housed and clothed. All significant possessions, such as boats, tools, fishing nets and ropes, were common property. The sense of community in St Kilda was unparalleled and based on mutual trust. The introduction of money in the 1830s and the end of the barter system was a powerful blow to the island's utopian spirit.

According to George Clayton Anderson, an Englishman who visited St Kilda twice in the 1830s, the St Kildans, '...though subject to Great Britain, have no official person among them ... and their knowledge of our laws must be very trifling and of little use of importance in their system of economy.'[24]

The islanders were safe and thriving well until the more or less regular communication with other islands as well as mainland Scotland was established in the mid-19th century. The first tourist ship called on St Kilda in 1834 and that opened the floodgates. Lured by tales of the primitive trusting islanders, all kinds of mainland crooks and fraudsters rushed to St Kilda, where they had been able to cheat the gullible locals of their possessions. Further waves of visitors followed, and with them came infectious diseases, like smallpox, to which the islanders had no immunity. All of this led to poverty and confusion among the islanders, whose condition deteriorated even further in the aftermath of the First World War, by which time most of the young and healthy locals had emigrated. By 1930, all 36 remaining St Kildans, most of whom spoke no English but only Gaelic and had never been off the island, had no option but to agree to being resettled on the mainland. They were leaving for good. Such was the end of Britain's oldest, purest and the most resilient utopian community.

Symbolically therefore (at least to me it was symbolic), it was in a Zodiac on the way from St Kilda back to the *Greg Mortimer* that I and my fellow expeditioners had a chance to take a close look at one of the world's living wonders: the magnificent Minke Whale.

In fact, it was not one whale but three, playing just 20 metres away from our unsinkable Zodiac, adrift near the coast of St Kilda. They were showing their brownish glistening bulks, then diving again and waving at us with the giant fans of their caudal fins. 'Wow! Wow!' all eight passengers on board our Zodiac, including me, were howling in chorus, like a pack of hungry wolves. Having forgotten about our cameras and iPhones, we were watching the amazing creatures knowing we'll remember the scene for as long as we lived.

Call me a fantasist (which, incidentally, I am), but I was ready to believe that those graceful whales had embodied the souls of the bygone St Kildans who had never left the shores of their beautiful once-utopian island.

Revenons à nos moutons, or back to our sheep, as the French say. In this case, I mean the Soay sheep originating from the island of Soay, which actually means 'sheep island' in Norse. MV *Greg Mortimer* sailed past that tiny island with a population of two. To me, however, it signified one of my most challenging and revealing journalistic assignments, which resulted in the discovery of one writer's fascinating Utopia and in the collapse of the over-ambitious Utopia of another writer. Here's the story:

My feet got soaked the moment I stepped on board the moored powerboat, tossed about by the waves, as if we were already at sea. Through the thick curtain of unceasing rain, I could discern the dark, forbidding presence of the Cuillins across the bay. I was about to join the cheerful crowd of 1200 or so Scottish lairds, who jointly owned two-thirds of the country's territory. True, I could not afford the Cuillin mountains, put up for sale for £10 million, and even if I could, what would I do with them? They were a bit too bulky for a paperweight on my desk. I was after something more affordable – an island, on which I was about to land.

It all started several days earlier with a short newspaper report announcing the sale of 'the three-mile-long island of Soay off the coast of Skye (with) no roads or shops', but with a 19th-century two-bedroom 'mission house' and several other buildings thrown in. As a writer, I always dreamed of having an island of my own, where I could pen the most important book of my life.

I contacted Inverness-based Macleod & MacCallum estate agents for an advertising brochure. To my surprise, it referred to 'Soay House & the Owner/Occupancy of South Soay Croft & Common Grazings' rather than to a straightforward island. 'Common Grazings' did not sound very romantic, yet even my rudimentary knowledge of farming was sufficient to deduce a direct link between 'grazings', which featured in the brochure, and 'droppings', which didn't.

The encouraging thing, however, was that, between 1945 and 1951, Soay was owned by Gavin Maxwell, one of the last century's most interesting Scottish writers, who used it as a base for his ill-fated shark-fishing enterprise, described in one of his books, *Harpoon at a Venture*. Gavin Maxwell always struck me as an underrated genius. Best remembered for *Ring of Bright Water*, an internationally acclaimed book about otters, he was not just a naturalist turned writer, but also an artist, a racing driver, an army officer, a secret agent, a fisherman, a traveller, and a poet. Maxwell once complained that he could not write a novel, because he was unable to structure it properly. His own life, resplendent with dramas financial and personal, was itself like a badly structured, yet gripping, work of fiction.

'Rabbits have two habits, breeding, and feeding (the purpose of the second is just to keep them fecund),' he wrote several hours before his agonising death of lung cancer (he was a chain-smoker) in 1969 at the age of 55. What an iron-cast spirit he must have had to crack jokes in the very jaws of death.

Maxwell had lived his short life to the full, and Soay, to which he often referred as a Utopia and 'my Island Valley of Avalon', played a huge role in it. The writer bought it in 1945 for £900, borrowed from his mother, and sold it in 1951, two years before all 30 islanders were evacuated to Mull, except for one family, that of Joseph 'Tex' Geddes, Maxwell's wartime friend and his shark-fishery's harpooner. It was Tex Geddes's Orkney-based son Duncan who was now selling the vacant island croft for 'over £280,000' – then the price of an average two- or three-bedroom flat in London or Edinburgh.

My crossing to Soay could be best compared to a rollercoaster ride under a cold shower. In my borrowed wetsuit, I felt like a U-boat captain who gave an order to submerge and only then realised that he had left his submarine at home.

The weather forecast was right: 'gale-force wind', mixed with rain, was targeting me with what felt like handfuls of prickly deep-frozen shrimps, some of which would stick (and then thaw reluctantly) in my ears and nostrils. Grabbing my seat handle with both hands, I was sinking and flying up in the air all at the same time.

'I had not dared to cross to Soay myself, lest I might be stuck there for an indefinite time,' Gavin Maxwell once wrote. I realised

Per Insulae Ad Astra!

what he meant by the end of the crossing. The powerboat could not approach the shore, and we (Chris, a *Glasgow Herald* photographer, and myself) had to be 'evacuated' from it by a fisherman, Oliver Davies, one of Soay's two remaining permanent residents (his wife Donita was the second) in his multi-purpose inflatable dinghy.

Despite wind and rain, the island *felt* beautiful, although, with my eyes full of water, I could not be quite sure what it looked like and kept conjuring up photos from the real-estate brochure and lines from Maxwell's poems about Soay, 'and the waves crept over the lonely beach' and so on. I thought that Maxwell's quick decision to buy the island could largely be explained by the fact that he first visited it on a hot summer day in 1944.

We 'inspected' the mission house, which was blissfully dry and felt very much alive – as if the residents had just popped out for a ... whatever one could pop out for in Soay. Books were everywhere. In one room, I saw a faded set of *National Geographic* for 1984.

We went inside Soay's one-room primary school, now serving as a 'community centre' (rather bizarre, with no community left). It housed a brand-new and seemingly untouched pool table and a box of library books under a not-too-promising hand-written note: 'Next delivery date October'.

Oliver told me how all the current and former islanders got together to protect the school building from being sold as a holiday cottage several years ago.

'If this house is kept as a school, there is a chance that one day the island community can be revived,' he said.

'Do you seriously believe in this revival?' I asked him.

'Why not? It's a great place to live and to bring up children. Here you don't have to put up a show, you can be yourself, and life itself becomes your only challenge.'

I asked him how he saw a potential buyer.

'We need an active person. Preferably, a writer. He will also have to be a fisherman, for fishing is the only way of making some money here.'

I wanted to tell him that they had found such a person: I was a writer, still fairly active (as proved by the crossing) and once managed to ferret out a couple of perches from a pond at the tender age of six (Appendix 1). But at that very moment, Donita, Oliver's wife, ran into the room and said that we had to dash back to the shore: the weather was getting worse (could it?), and the skipper of our boat radioed her to say that we had to sail off immediately.

'Life is precious, and there are enough beds in my house,' said Oliver somewhat mysteriously. I thought he simply didn't want us to go.

Although vetted (well, almost) as a potential new laird by half of Soay's population (I mean Oliver), I still wanted to clarify the crofting and (particularly) the 'grazing' issues. In Inverness, I was lucky to get an appointment with Derek Flyn, one of Scotland's leading experts in crofting law.

'Can I buy Soay?' I asked.

'First, you'll be advised to finalise your plans as to residency on the island,' Mr Flyn replied This meant that I had to decide whether I was going to live there or not. That came as a shock, for like many present-day Scottish lairds, I would be quite happy to spend a couple of weeks on my croft, and to cruise the globe for the rest of the year (using the change left from my imminent National Lottery jackpot).

Mr Flyn proceeded to tell me that the main purpose of crofting legislation was to protect the land against such absentee landlords. 'You will either have to live on the island, or find a tenant,' he said sounding as weighty and authoritative as the three-volume *Encyclopedia of Value Added Tax* on a bookshelf above his head (I thought that compulsory reading of all three could be a good punishment for absentee landlords like me). He explained that not only would such a tenant have to be approved by the Crofters' Commission, but, in accordance with the new Scotland's Land Reform Act, he (or they) would have an immediate right to buy the croft from me, whether I wanted to sell or not.

'Buying a croft involves responsibilities, and you'll have to demonstrate your commitment to the land,' he concluded gravely and added: 'Soay is a special place for a special person.'

I was obviously not special enough. Besides, I always had a problem with commitment...

But I could now understand Gavin Maxwell, who wrote on leaving Soay:

> I remember it on those glorious summer days when a smooth blue sea lapped the red rock of the island shore and the cuckoos called continuously from the birch-woods; or on bright winter mornings when the Cuillins were snow-covered, hard, intricate and brittle as carved ivory; I remember it with nostalgia for something beautiful and lost, the Island Valley of Avalon.[25]

Per Insulae Ad Astra!

The Hebridean Avalon – Soay – was waiting for its new King Arthur. As far as I know, it still is.

One of the undisputed and eagerly anticipated highlights of my *Greg Mortimer* expedition was a visit to the Shetland Archipelago island of Foula – officially the most isolated bit of British territory and the remotest populated.

Another reason for being so happily Foulish about setting foot on Foula was that I was the owner of the first Ordnance Survey custom-made map of that island, which I received as a gift at the new state-of-the-art Ordnance Survey (OS) headquarters on the outskirts of Southampton while researching an article on that iconic British institution, which celebrated its 225th anniversary in 2016. To mark the occasion, they released the first ever OS map of Mars (of which I was also given a copy) and – no less significantly – the one of Foula, the island which until then was the last remaining OS-unmapped part of British territory. Since then, on the imaginary (and not OS) map of my very much desired yet highly unlikely destinations, Mars and Foula had been on a par.

Indeed, for an average citizen it is hard to come up with a valid reason for visiting Britain's most remote island, with an area of 4.9 square miles and a population of 38, lying on the same latitude as Saint Petersburg, with just one road. It has to be said that since the 1990s, growing numbers of tourists, mostly bird watchers, have been making their way to Foula from around the world to see its puffins, skuas, razorbills, gannets, and more. That was probably why Ordnance Survey mapmakers decided finally to put the island on a separate custom-made OS Explore 1:7500 scale map, published in 2017. Just like the map of Mars, it immediately became a collector's item,

Recalling my happy childhood habits of vicarious armchair travelling, I studied the map of Foula for... I nearly said for hours on end, as was the case with the faded map of Paris from my dog-eared *Soviet Atlas of Geography*, but there weren't enough features on the Foula map to spend hours studying it. But for me it certainly carried a substantial utopian charge.

To begin with, all Foula's place names on the map were in old Norse, a legacy from the island's Scandinavian past. Due to the island's remoteness, that peculiar dialect had been in use there later than anywhere else, until the early 19th century, when it was replaced by 'Shetlandic', a variation of Old Scots still spoken occasionally in Foula and all over Shetland.

Here's an example taken from *The New Shetlander* magazine I found in a Lerwick library: '*Noo bairns. My peerie kist is aa tied up. I'm ready to geng.*' – 'Now, children. My little chest is all tied up. I am ready to go.' I liked both the sound and the message of those three short sentences in the living Shetlandic language.

But what made a visit to Foula even more like a trip abroad without crossing the border was that it was the last part of Europe except for Mount Athos, a semi-independent republic of Orthodox monks in the north of Greece, still adhering to the Julian calendar, which is 13 days behind the Gregorian.

'So what date is it today?' I asked the first 'Fouler' I came across in the small harbour the moment I stepped out of a Zodiac (the *Greg Mortimer* was anchored about a mile away from the ragged and rocky shore) onto the island. It was the 1st of June by our (Gregorian) calendar.

'It is the first of June,' said the slim middle-aged woman. 'These days we only use the Julian Calendar for Christmas and New Year celebrations, when all 38 of us gather in one house on the 6th and the 13th of January.'

I was lucky to have encountered Sheila Gear, an islander and a writer, author of *Island West of the Sun*. She volunteered to show me around the island. Sheila came to live on Foula after graduating from Aberdeen University where she studied zoology. She married an islander and has lived on Foula ever since. As we walked away from the harbour, where the island's only ferry boat was kept in a special compound on top of the pier to protect it from strong south-east winds, she stopped briefly to free a fulmar whose wing was stuck in a thick hedge. The bird flew away with a grateful squawk. 'Foula', which means 'bird island' in old Norse, was home to a quarter of a million birds, nestling mostly on the coastal cliffs, second in their height only to St Kilda's.

We walked past the island's school, which, as Sheila explained, had just five students. It was a relatively new building, which inspired the islanders' hope for the future and was the living proof that Foula was not preparing to become another St Kilda. Ironically, it was on Foula that Michael Powell's well-known film, *Edge of the World*, about St Kilda's depopulation of 1930, was shot in 1936, with islanders taking part as extras. Foula could 'impersonate' St.Kilda perfectly, but it wasn't yet ready to become a film set itself.

Per Insulae Ad Astra!

I was curious about multiple netted stone structures we walked past.

'We call them plantigruds,' explained Sheila. 'We use them as seeding gardens and cover them with old fishing nets to protect the seedlings from birds.'

That reminded me of Lerwick, Shetland's capital, where they covered black rubbish bags left for collection in the streets with pieces of disused fishing nets. The nets, provided by the council, offered the best possible protection from seagulls, those flying pests, which used to rummage through the contents of unprotected rubbish bags with the zest of HM Customs ransacking the luggage of a suspected Colombian drug mule. In a BBC Radio Shetland programme I heard the islanders coming up with possible solutions to the seagull problem – from destroying the birds' eggs to persuading them to fly over Lerwick upside down. Thank God, Shetland ponies cannot fly.

Back in Foula, we soon came to a peat moorland, on which some of the island's endemic Shetland sheep – multicoloured and with short, fluke-shaped tails – were grazing peacefully. Peat was still harvested for fuel in the traditional fashion on the island – cut with a long hand-held blade known as a 'tuskar'.

The ingenuity of the islanders had no limits. As we walked on, Sheila pointed out several old cars parked near houses and serving as wardrobes, storage closets and rubbish bins. She explained that since it was very hard to get rid of old cars in Foula due to its isolation from the mainland, the islanders found other uses for them. She then proudly showed me an airstrip built by the islanders in the early 1970s, when Foula's population dwindled to about 30. It was decided at one of the gatherings (at which all important decisions concerning the islanders were, and still are, routinely taken in a purely utopian tradition, by democratic majority vote) to build an airstrip, a highly unusual endeavour for such a relatively small island, as a gesture of defiance and determination to stay. To build and run the would-be airfield, they founded the Foula Airstrip Trust, which still runs what looked like the world's smallest airport, with a windsock and a tiny hut for the 'terminal'.

To further illustrate Foula's utopian community spirit, Sheila introduced me to the island's unique water supply via an underground pipe network, which, just like the airstrip, the islanders had themselves designed and built. The water is collected at a spring and processed at a water treatment facility in the centre of the isle. The treated water is then pumped daily to two holding tanks, one at each end of the island, from where gravity feeds the flow into each island property. Nice and simple. Yet totally improbable on the mainland where a painless and beautifully straightforward project like that was bound to be nipped in the bud on one of the multiple bureaucratic tiers on its way to approval.

That was of course a fairly insignificant achievement on the global scale, but for the tiny island it was as important as the first water channels built by the Romans over 1000 years ago, on a par with the discovery of electricity, or with the world's first space flight.

As Sheila herself put it in her book "Foula: Island West of the Sun", 'Contrary to popular belief, we (the islanders) do not spend our time sitting in the sun plunking a guitar or wandering through the hills crying 'Dear peerie lamb' to our sheep. The same mad rush that pushes on the rest of the world is just as relentless towards us. Time and tide wait for no man, certainly not for an islander.'

If you happen to miss out on Christmas celebrations one year, don't worry too much, for there's a seemingly utopian, yet quite realistic, solution to your problem. Weather permitting, you can still travel to the island of Foula and join the festive gathering of friendly locals – all in one house, no doubt. Thirteen days should be enough to reach Foula from anywhere in the UK.

Foula's success made me think of another small Scottish island, the residents of which took Utopia in their own hands. I am talking of Eigg. I visited it briefly while researching my *Atlas of Geographical Curiosities*. Eigg, a kidney-shaped island (5 miles by 3) 20 kilometres from the mainland, is one of the Small Isles in the Inner Hebrides. With an area of 12 square miles and a population of 90, it is the second largest of the Small Isles, after Rùm. It looks like a deep groove framed by two small mountains ('Eag' means 'notch' in Gaelic).

Eigg has been known for years for its 'singing sands', a peculiar sound of the wind in the dunes which was compared by one explorer to an Aeolian harp and by another to the noise made by a man walking in corduroy trousers. Historically, the island used to be owned by a series of landlords, some of whom would never bother to visit it, and formalities made the arrangement of public ownership on it near impossible.

Per Insulae Ad Astra!

In 1997, the residents of Eigg, in partnership with the Scottish Wildlife Trust and with the help of a £ 1.66 million investment by the EU's European Regional Development Fund, bought the island from its previous 'laird', an elusive German artist who called himself 'Maruna'. They formed Eigg Electric – a company wholly owned and operated by the islanders through the Isle of Eigg Heritage Trust.

Ten years later, Eigg achieved a global milestone in sustainable development, complete self-sufficiency in renewable energy. Used to relying on diesel generators for a few hours of electricity a day in the past, in 2008 it became the first community in the world to launch an off-grid system based just on renewable sources, the wind, water and sun. This, for the first time in the island's history, gave 24-hour access to power to its residents, despite the local population having risen from around 65 at the end of the 1990s to more than 100. An 11-kilometre network of underground cables distributed energy in households and businesses around the island, with transformers converting the high voltage for domestic use. The power was also connected to a bank of batteries capable of providing electricity to the whole island for up to 24 hours.

Power could flow both ways: if renewables produced more than was being consumed on the island, the grid recharged the batteries. When the batteries eventually got fully charged and accepted no more power, a series of switches would turn on heaters in the communal buildings: the church, the community hall, the public toilet and the pier lobby.

These days the islanders aren't charged a penny for energy consumption, since the whole community benefits from the additional energy, accumulated due to the overabundance of wind and rain in winter. When there's insufficient power, the stored energy in the batteries is used to power the micro-grid. A modern public-ownership Utopia made reality!

All through my short stay on Fair Island, officially the most remote inhabited island in the UK, I felt a gentle – as if coming from the realm of my childhood dreams – touch of freedom and happiness, the source of which was hard to comprehend initially.

One of the locals, a former skipper Neil Thomson, volunteered to drive me around, from the pier to the North and South lighthouses. With an area of just 8 square miles, Fair Isle, situated precisely halfway between Orkney and Shetland (a once-a-week ferry to either takes over five hours), gave an impression of vastness due to the open spaces, invariably culminating in stunning sea views. As we drove, myriad noisy sea birds kept circling above our heads. Neil pointed out a particularly vociferous one. 'It's an Arctic Skua.'

I looked up anxiously, remembering my time in the Faroes, where they warned birdwatchers of the dangers of being attacked by an Arctic Skua, a bird that defends its eggs and young by dashing at any potential threat, including humans. They told me there that the best way to protect yourself was to carry a chair leg above your head: if the bird attacked, it would be the leg, not your head, that would get the bashing. With no chair leg in my shoulder bag, I hoped that the roof of Neil's battered car was enough of a shelter.

Lighthouses have always been essential for the island, situated in notoriously rough seas, with 'merciless rocks and perilous tides' – the cause of hundreds of shipwrecks through the years. The South Lighthouse, now fully automated, looked particularly impressive, with its cylindrical tower, balcony and lantern. During the Second World War, it was a target for German air raids, during one of which (in 1941) the wife of an assistant keeper was killed and his daughter injured.

Now, all is peace and quiet on Fair Isle, with most of its 60 residents living in crofts, Scottish small landholdings held in tenancy, with houses that never get locked, just like in Amaurot, the capital of Thomas More's fictitious Utopia. There is one school, with four pupils and one teacher; one shop; one nurse, and, unusually for a small island, a clear sign of well-being, an evening-only bar inside the bird observatory!

The story of that observatory is quite remarkable. During the Second World War, George Waterson, an Edinburgh bookseller and a keen ornithologist, ended up as a POW in Germany. When he was eventually repatriated and put on a ship back to Scotland, the first piece of homeland he saw from the deck was Fair Isle, with beautiful birds hovering above it. Waterson thought it was a good omen. In 1947, he bought the island and set up a bird observatory on it.

It was the observatory that saved Fair Isle from the fate of St Kilda, i.e. being evacuated, in the late 1940s, when its population dwindled to 44. It started attracting ornithologists and bird-watchers from the mainland as well as offering jobs for the locals. In 1954, Waterson happily passed the island into the care of the National Trust for Scotland, the charity that owns it now.

Thus, the birds and the observatory helped to save Fair Isle from extinction. There could be no better place for the island's only bar!

Too remote to be part of the National Grid, Fair Isle produces its own electricity using a combination of diesel and wind power. The first 60 kw wind turbine, like most other innovations on the island, went up in 1982 as a community effort. Fair Isle made history by becoming the first commercially operated wind energy scheme in Europe.

Yet, the island's biggest claim to international fame is the 'Fair Isle sweater phenomenon' going back to the early 20th century, when the world's golf-playing nobility and *beau monde* began sporting the Fair Isle-knitted V-necked pullovers in geometric banded patterns. It became a global fashion statement for casual wear that has survived the test of time, with the traditional technologies of hand-spinning, weaving and hand-dying still used in the island's knitting workshops. It is largely due to those ancient and perfectly 'green' technologies, helping people all over the globe to keep warm, that Fair Isle was granted Fairtrade Island status in 2004. I like that repetition:'Fair Isle – Fairtrade'.

Neil took me to the community hall, where Fair Isle's famous knitwear: sweaters, hats, gloves, mittens etc., was being sold by a handful of local women, all of whom had open happy faces, with a somewhat mischievous sparkle in their eyes.

'What is it?' I asked one of the women, a newly arrived schoolteacher from Glasgow, who had miraculously already acquired the sparkle too. 'It is contentment,' she said.

In the tiny island's museum, run by Neil Thomson's sister Eileen, I picked up a brochure, 'Standing into Danger. Shipwrecks of Fair Isle' by Anne Sinclair, chronicling the most significant of the hundreds of catastrophes near the island's shores. Reading it when back on board the *Greg Mortimer*, I noticed a strange tendency: most of the featured disasters seemed to have happy endings. The crews and passengers of the wrecked ships and the pilots of the crashed planes would normally survive and stay on Fair Island to recover and to be looked after by the islanders, who, in their turn, would benefit from the shipwrecks, which supplied them with precious timber, invaluable on an island with no trees – a one hundred per cent tit-for-tat utopian scenario.

The islanders' motives had never been purely mercantile, and here's relatively recent example. In 1941, a Heinkel was shot down and crash-landed on Fair Isle. There were no benefits to be had from the plane's remains – a scattering of useless burnt pieces of metal – and yet the three surviving enemy crew members were rescued by the islanders from a steep cliff, given shelter, medical assistance and time to recuperate. One of them, Lieutenant Karl Heinz Thurz, turned 21 during his stay. The islanders made sure his birthday was properly celebrated. Karl returned to the crash site for the first time in the 1980s to meet his saviours, and since then he had been a frequent visitor to the island, his own private Utopia, until his death in 2006.

Needless to say, with its cutting-edge navigating equipment, MV *Greg Mortimer* negotiated the rough seas around Fair Isle without incident. Yet, in my heart I still carry a faint hope that one day I may not crash-land (God forbid), but simply crash out for a few days on that utopian island.

Summing up my expedition to the Scottish islands, I have reasons to assume that Foula's, Eigg's, Fair Isle's and – earlier – St Kilda's little Utopias worked only because they differed substantially from the persisting utopian stereotype of a paradise, bestowed from above. Their own little 'Edens' were built by the determined islanders themselves, with minimal interference from mainland benefactors and powers-that-be.

Perhaps it wouldn't be too preposterous to conclude that Utopias can only work in small and isolated communities, on islands. Was that why Thomas More made his fictitious Utopia a crescent-shaped island?

To paraphrase an old Latin saying, *per insulae ad adstra*! Through islands to the stars!

Chapter 14

In The Eye of The Beholder, or My Utop Ten

> The concept of Utopia seemed to be on its last legs by the 1970s, everyone having had enough of philosophers, architects and tyrants, and their grand visions.
> Jonathan Morrison, *The Times*, 04/03/2023

At last, we were in luck: members of Stapleton Colony, the only remaining community of the once numerous and influential Brotherhood Church, had agreed to see us briefly in their reclusive North Yorkshire forest abode.

For the whole duration of our quest for Britain's utopian settlements, we had been trying to arrange visits to the so-called 'intentional communities', i.e. groups of people who have chosen to live together, normally outside mainstream society, united by a common purpose, idea or ideology.

A weighty 520-page large-format paperback. *Communes Britannica*, released in 2012 by Dreamers & Diggers Publications, lists many dozens of such 'alternative' (read utopian) communities: from New Age and Low Impact Living to religious, agricultural and even 'fictional' (i.e. invented by writers) ones. That list, impressive and puzzling in equal measure, gets regularly updated in the pocket-sized *Diggers & Dreamers Guides to Communal Living* by the same publishers. For an in-depth look at some of those communities, there is *utopian Dreams. In Search of a Good Life* by Tobias Jones (Faber & Faber, 2007). The author had spent a year in a variety of 'alternative' communities: from New Age settlements to old-fashioned farmyards and Christian detox centres. Our aim was to try and visit just a handful of those to get an impression and to convey it to the readers. In that, we were successful only partially.

Spielplatz, the Naturist resort (Chapter 3) for example let us in, and while corresponding to the general definition of an intentional community as having a common purpose, it did not feature in the *Communes Britannica* lists. Apart from that, our requests for a visit, were met with blunt, at times quite brusque refusals, which, although unpleasant, were understandable: the members of those reclusive groups had consciously abandoned mainstream society to be left to their own devices, and not to be intruded on by prying journalists and writers. On one occasion, a forest community in Wales had agreed to see us, but changed their mind when we did turn up: they got visibly nervous on seeing Tashi (or maybe it was me?) and refused to talk to us.

As we were speeding (as much as Yorkshire country roads would allow) towards the Stapleton Colony's sylvan abode, over the radio in Alphie they were talking, rather aptly, about the rate at which we were ruining out planet with CO2 emissions. Approaching our destination was like driving into a secret world. Alphie slowly puffed his way up the forest path, overgrown with bushes and high grass until we came to a clearing with a blue weatherboard house in it. We were met by Jo, Rob and Bracken, three of the four remaining members of the once-numerous pacifist community, fuelled by Quaker ideas and a bit of anarchism, too.

All soft-spoken and gentle, they explained to us *sotto voce* – as if trying not to upset the delicate harmony of nature and beauty that surrounded us – that their main aim was to help the planet in a quiet way, without making a big fuss out of it. They said they were anti-consumerist and were living pretty much outside society: independent from the government and not receiving any benefits, but generating a modest income for themselves by selling their honey and home-grown seasonal veggies. They showed us their 'magical forest' of pine trees. 'It is just like Narnia here when it snows,' commented Rob.

They said they allowed local villagers to cut down some of their carefully selected trees for Christmas to give local kids a chance to bond with nature. They showed us their beehives and introduced us to Calfie – a huge back cow.

From the time of its foundation by John Bruce Wallace in 1887, with its initial base in Croydon and Purleigh, Surrey (the same as Whiteway Colony, see Chapter 6), Brotherhood Church community has been strictly vegetarian and was meant to grow its own food – all natural and organic. Those principles have been kept in Stapleton, where the Brotherhood bought some land in

In The Eye of The Beholder, or My Utop Ten

1921. There was no hierarchy in the community, and everything, including building materials was made from recycled matter. Rainwater was collected in large tanks and whenever possible used instead of the mains.

Just like the residents of Fair Isle and Foula, our hosts, the colonists, looked healthy, happy and at peace. 'Here we feel at one with nature,' Jo told us as we were leaving. Back home, while sampling delicious Stapleton honey, we remembered with fondness that small utopian community, who were trying to make the world a better place.

I started this book's final chapter with a short description of that reclusive Yorkshire community, one of many of its kind, to underline the fact that the concept of modern Utopia is not just extremely vast and versatile ('unembraceable', to quote the unforgettable Kozma Prutkov), but also very subjective and very much in the eye of the beholder.

We all differ in defining Utopia, something which is too good to be true (or like the concept of God in the famous Anselm's definition as 'that than which nothing greater can be conceived'), and yet has been brought about, at least for a limited time. To quote Gregory Claeyes:

> To provide a workable definition of 'utopia' is challenging. The breadth of the genre is bewilderingly large, encompassing positive ideals of much improved societies; their negative satirical opposites, sometimes called anti-utopias or dystopias; various myths of paradise, golden ages and 'fortunate islands' and portrayals of primitive peoples living in a natural state; Robinsonades or shipwrecks; imaginary voyages to the Moon and elsewhere in space; and planned constitutions, model towns and various other visions of improvement.[26]

It was Claeyes who, in referring to dystopias, i.e. 'unpleasant (typically repressive_) societies, often propagandized as being utopian' (pace Wikipedia), came up with 'Malice in Wonderland'.

I can only add to this extensive definitions that, to my mind, most Utopias only work on a personal level and for a limited period of time, for anything that is 'cool' and successful automatically ceases being a Utopia and becomes reality! Sooner or later, all

Utopias (even, sadly, those of the Scottish islands) come to an end and metamorphose into their direct opposites.

Remember the epigraph to Chapter 9, Damien Rudd's 'Every Utopia has an implied dystopia'.

At the end of our journey, I'd like to introduce you to a selection of my *personal* top ten British Utopias, which, for one reason or another, did not fit in the pattern of my quest. They are, in no particular order:

1 *Church Farm, Ardley, Hertfordshire*

This 170-acre non-for-profit organic farm not far from Letchworth is an exemplary 'intentional community', similar to an Israeli kibbutz. Run by my good friend with an appropriate 'utopian' name, Tim Waygood (everyone calls him simply 'Farmer Tim'), an archetypal utopian dreamer but also a graduate of the Harvard Business School. it encourages young people from all over the world temporarily to join its farming community. International volunteers, whom they call 'interns', are paid £50 a week plus expenses. Food and accommodation are provided.

I like coming to the Farm to look at the beautiful animals and birds they keep, to browse through the onsite farm shop, or just to have a chat with Tim about the ideas he keeps generating.

'I am not trying to be normal,' he told me once and added: 'With time, my ambitions have altered from changing the world to creating my own!'

An urban creature to the core, my only connection with agriculture has so far been limited to a traditional one month a year (normally September) in a Soviet Kolkhoz ('collective farm'). All Soviet citizens of working age were obliged to give up their work or studies for a month each year to go to collective farms in their neighbourhood to help harvest potatoes, beetroots, corn, onions, etc. Without that, the much-hyped *kolkhozi* wouldn't have survived in the 1970s and 80s, when they could no longer legally force peasants to work, or tie them to the land by confiscating their passports as they did in the 1920s-30s. The mildly successful peasants had been branded 'kulaks' ('fists', as in tight-fisted) and ended up in Gulag, It was a tragic parody of farming...

Church Farm is the direct antithesis of a kolkhoz. To complement its utopian nature, it even has a small vodka distillery!

In The Eye of The Beholder, or My Utop Ten

2 *Rananim, Zennor, Cornwall*

Whenever I get overwhelmed with the gruesome news from my brutally invaded motherland, Ukraine (and that happens more and more often as the horrible war shows no sign of de-escalation), I recall the 1915 Cornish ordeal of D.H. Lawrence, one of my favourite British writers – the experience which, to me, came to signify an exemplary writer's Utopia.

From the start of the Great War Lawrence had cherished a utopian dream of a place where he could 'sail away from the world at war' and found a little colony of friends. He called that imaginary colony 'Rananim' (he never explained why), and initially wanted it to be based in Florida. His poverty, however, made him look for a place closer to home, in Cornwall.

There is no consensus among D.H. Lawrence scholars as to what exactly the writer meant by calling his imaginary Utopia 'Rananim', which sounds like a Hebrew word meaning 'sonorant' (I've made enquiries among my Israeli friends) that doesn't make sense. 'Rananim' also stands for 'Hello' in Chuukese, an obscure language, spoken in the Philippines, which Lawrence, despite his polyglot abilities, was unlikely to be familiar with. Besides, in Chuukese, 'Rananim' was once the name of a typhoon – hardly an appropriate euphemism for the abode of peace and quiet the writer was striving for. 'He (D.H. Lawrence) called it Rananim after hearing the Hebrew song *Rananim Sadekim Badenol*, which I can't translate,' writes Richard Smith in his blog 'D.H. Lawrence's Rananim: another failed Utopia'.

Well, I am happy to report that, as a keen amateur etymologist, I seem to have cracked the Rananim mystery. Knowing from experience that a quest for a word's origin can often be led astray by an accidental misspelling, I decided to experiment and conducted internet searches for variations on the word, and 'Renanim' turned out to be Ancient Hebrew for 'ostrich'!

Now, that makes perfect sense, if we remember the popular myth that ostriches tend to bury their heads in the sand when frightened or just fed up and pretend that the disturbing world around them simply does not exist. That was exactly what D.H. Lawrence had hoped to achieve by fleeing from all the social and emotional stresses of the ongoing war as well as from the real danger of being drafted (they actually did try to get D.H. commissioned in Cornwall, but he failed medical examination and was left alone).

In December 1915, with his German wife Frieda, also a writer, Lawrence came to the coastal village of Zennor in south-west Cornwall, 4 miles west of St Ives. They first stayed in the local pub, the Tinners Arms, but soon rented a pair of cottages about a mile east from the village – part of the group of houses known as Higher Tregerthen. They paid (for both) an annual rent of £5! On settling down in one of the cottages (they kept the other one for any visiting friends), Lawrence was smitten by the views of the sea, which, he described exaltedly in a letter to Katherine Mansfield as being 'lovelier than the Mediterranean', and by the cottage itself: 'The best place I've ever been in, I think... The world has disappeared for ever. There is no more world any more; only here, and a fine thin air which nobody and nothing pollutes.'[27]

Doesn't this strike you as a head-in-the-sand attitude?

Alas, as we already know, Utopias do not last. Particularly writers' Utopias. Lawrence's dream of a happy community of friends and writers were dealt a blow when Katherine Mansfield and her would-be husband John Middleton Murry, came to stay in the empty second cottage but didn't like it there and soon left, having quarrelled with the Lawrences. One can feel the notes of creeping disappointment in Lawrence's letters to his Russian friend S.S. Koteliansky, whom he addressed simply as 'Kot' ('cat' in Russian):

> 11 May, 1917. We are alone in Tregerthen. I go about in a silky shirt you gave me, & a pair of trousers, and nothing else. Today I have been cutting blackthorn & gorse to make a fence to keep the lambs out of my garden. I loathe lambs, those symbols of Christian meekness. They are the stupidest, most persistent, greediest little beasts in the whole animal kingdom. My garden is very beautiful. But the filthy lambs have eaten off my broad beans.[28]

The writer's angst which he had vented on the innocent and not at all 'filthy' Cornish lambs was, most probably, the result of his bitter disappointment with 'Rananim'.

And there were good reasons for that. The patriotic or paranoid local villagers saw a light accidentally shining in a Lawrence cottage window overlooking a bay where German submarines, allegedly, prowled. Frieda Lawrence was German of course, and that was enough for the villagers to accuse her and her dreamer husband of being spies. In October 1917, the police were called. Having upended the contents of cottage, they ordered the Lawrences to leave Cornwall. The writer's long-cherished Utopia had not simply failed. It had collapsed with a loud bang. Frieda was recorded afterwards as saying that D.H. Lawrence's Cornish experience had changed something in him permanently. D.H. himself described it in his semi-autobiographical novel *Kangaroo*, in the chapter with the self-explanatory title, 'The Nightmare'.

'Hell is other people' is the often-cited line from a play by Jean-Paul Sartre, written in 1944, long after D.H. Lawrence's death in 1930. It was precisely that 'hell' that stood in the way of the writer's heaven on earth.

We made a long detour to visit Rananim. Just like the Lawrences 116 years earlier, we started in Zennor, where we had a ploughman's lunch in the Tinners Arms (still there) and washed it down (I did) with a pint of Zennor Mermaid ale. We then hiked across the fields to Higher Tregerthen.

The landscape was beautiful but bleak. with hardly any sea views from the rough gravel path we were trudging along. Every five minutes or so, Tashi had to be carried over cattle grids. And, yes, the sheep (and lambs) were everywhere, but they were not at all 'filthy' or 'greedy' – nothing like the fearsome feral sheep of Soay and St Kilda (see Chapter 13).

The two cottages of Tregerthen were now remodelled as one large two-storey house, with a high-hipped slate roof. Lawrence's ill-fated Rananim was now in private ownership, and we could only look at it from a distance.

I ticked off the windows overlooking the bay, and for a fleeting moment I thought I could see in one of them Frieda's face under a wide-brimmed sun hat, like the one she – a German writer, not a spy – was wearing in the often-reproduced 1914 photo of herself and her writer husband. But, just like Rananim itself, that was but a fleeting illusion.

3 Tiree, Inner Hebrides, Scotland; My Rananim

At a time of uncertainty and anxiety, it is good to know that there is still a place in the world where a policeman walks his dogs through the stars...

This is also the place where a postman enters unlocked houses without knocking and leaves the mail on kitchen tables;

where people sing psalms to seals resting on the rocks;

Trucks in the Garden of Eden

where low-built thatched cottages squint at you playfully with their deep-set little windows;

where a local remedy for blisters is cotton dipped in whisky;

where in the morning you wake up not from noises, but from silence so deep and deafening that it almost makes your teeth ache...

I am talking about Tiree, the outermost island of the Inner Hebrides archipelago, Not on the itinerary of my Scottish Islands expedition on board MV *Greg Mortimer* in June 2022 (see Chapter 13), it became my utopian Rananim in autumn of 2001, when I spent several relaxing days there in the wake of 9/11, as the whole world held its breath in grief and fear.

The dog-walking policeman, by the way, was a real person, the only guardian of law and order for the islands of Coll and Tiree. He took charge of me the moment I stepped onto Tiree soil after the 4-hour ferry crossing from Oban. Because of a Scottish Bank Holiday, all my local contacts were out of reach and their phones were dead. I stood in a red public phone cabin on the pier listening to dispassionate tones until a uniformed policeman knocked at the glass and asked whether he could help.

'Don't you have answerphones on Tiree?' I asked him.

'No, we don't,' he replied. 'There's no need. People are likely to bump into each other the moment they leave their houses.'

He offered me a lift to my guesthouse, about eight miles away. All roads on Tiree, an island ten miles long and one to six miles wide, were single-track, and the rare passing vehicles waited patiently in special road pockets for our police van to go by. The policeman waved to each of the drivers, and they waved back. It looked as if he knew all 720 residents of the island personally, in fact he did. As we rode, he would often roll down his window to enquire about their health and families. At some point, a boy in his late teens caught up with us on a bike. On his way to take his driving test, he wanted the policeman to certify his photo. The formality was completed in the nearest passing place.

'Bicycle is the best means of transport for Tiree,' my escort remarked as we continued our unhurried progress. 'If you wish, you can hire one from Mr McLane who lives in the croft over there. Two minutes later, my freshly hired bike was rattling in the back of the police van, where drunks and offenders were presumably carried to the mainland, an observation I shared with my new policeman friend.

In The Eye of The Beholder, or My Utop Ten

'Crime on the island is virtually non-existent, and houses and cars are normally left unlocked,' he said. A compulsive traveller spending every holiday overseas, he was on the verge of leaving Tiree several times. But each time he eventually changed his mind. "As I exercise my two dogs on the beach every night I look at the stars – so bright and near you feel you can walk through them. How can one leave a place like this?

My guesthouse, the Glassary, stood in an open field overlooking a rocky bay. As soon as the policeman left to continue his leisurely island beat, I jumped onto the saddle and cycled off 'to where my eyes looked', as they say in Russia, along Tiree's only paved road. The day was surprisingly warm and sunny, and I was ready to believe that, due to the proximity of the Gulf Stream, Tiree indeed held the UK's sunshine record, although I had heard the same claim in several other places.

My previous bike ride was in Amsterdam, where I had to veer among cars, trams and absent-minded tourists. Cycling on Tiree was very different. I rode past grazing sheep and stern-looking cows, who gave me (or was it my red sweater?) disapproving stares. Tiree's answer to Amsterdam canals were numerous little lochs, from where flocks of wild geese would take off noisily on my approach. And instead of gable-topped Amsterdam houses, I was whooshing past Tiree's traditional thatch-covered cottages, their neatly combed roofs held down by large round pebbles on ropes, something that that gave the huts a slightly hip-hop look, as if they were wearing bandannas. With their chimneys canted outwards and away from the roof to minimise the damage of collapse in a storm and to divert sparks from thatch, they also looked like dare-devil Russian Cossacks in their sheepskin hats.

I dismantled near a detached parish church built of local pink granite. On its gate, there was a plaque commemorating a Tiree family who emigrated to Canada in 1893, a time when the population of the island was in the region of 7,000. It has been declining ever since.

'There is not a single tree/On the island of Tiree.' I was humming this doggerel of my own making (variant: 'Life is totally stress free/ on the island of Tiree'), to the accompaniment of the wind whistling in my ears like a hooligan, all the way back to the guesthouse. Not counting three smallish hillocks, Tiree was flat and treeless, due to the tireless winter winds ranging between point 8 ('Fresh gale') and point 12 ('Hurricane') on the Beaufort Scale. 'Tiree', 'treeless', 'tireless', I was savouring the melodious alliteration of Tiree, which in Gaelic, a nice-sounding tongue with just 18 letters in the alphabet, means 'Land of Corn'.

Agitated seagulls were screaming something in Gaelic that evening as I sat at the conservatory of the Glassary's small restaurant. The last tinges of red were lingering in the dark sky like the taste of malt whisky on my palate. On the plate in front of me, one could observe the fourth 'natural' landmark of Tiree – a hillock of haggis, topped with a sharp-edged carrot rash.

The whisky was excellent, and I came to understand why many islanders had flush faces. 'Whisky helps us to beat the wind,' a local woman told me. So their complexions were probably the result of the combined effects of whisky and the winds it was supposed to beat.

When darkness fell and the piercingly bright stars popped out above the sea, I looked up: there, between the Great Bear and the blinking little light of the international space station, was my new friend, the Tiree policeman, walking his dogs along the Milky Way.

4 Ely Place, London, Cambridgeshire (not a typo!)

Ely Place, a quiet little cul-de-sac off Holborn Circus, is my favourite utopian spot in London.

Passing through the ornate iron gates, separating it from the hustle-and-bustle of the city, is like entering a mysterious 'fourth dimension', the name of which is 'dislocation'.

Very few people know that this gated road, the former residence of the Bishops of Ely, is not by jurisdiction a part of London. It is a little corner of Cambridgeshire, still enjoying freedom from entry by the London Police, except by the invitation of the Commissioners of Ely Place — its own elected governing body. The results of the latest elections, dated and certified by the 'Clerk to the Commissioners', are duly displayed on the noticeboard of the magnificent St Etheldreda Chapel — the oldest Roman Catholic church in Britain, where certain liturgies are still held in Latin, half-way up the street.

As a linguist, I was fascinated to discover that it was there, at the entrance to the Chapel of St Etheldreda, popularly known for centuries as St Audrey, or simply Audrey (much easier to pronounce than the tongue-breaking 'St Etheldreda') that the word 'tawdry' originated at a small flea market, selling trinkets and 'tawdry' knick-knacks, right at the 'Audrey's' doors!

Another undisputed attraction was that the little lane, now given over entirely to law offices and company premises, was once a separate 'liberty' – a sanctuary where law-breakers could take refuge and where the civil authorities had no right of arrest. There were a number of such 'liberties' in Elizabethan London.

One of London's best-kept secrets, Ely Place is a living anachronism from the 16th century, when the influential Bishops were determined to remain in their Cambridgeshire diocese even while on ministerial missions in the capital. They bought the patch of land in Holborn, then on the outskirts of London, built a palace on it and declared it part of their native Cambridgeshire, so that they could carry out their ministerial functions unhindered.

They also started growing fruit and vegetables in their gardens and were rumoured to produce the finest strawberries in the whole of England. A 'Strawberry Fayre' is still held in Ely Place every June. In Shakespeare's Richard III, the as yet uncrowned Gloucester tells the Bishop of Ely: 'My Lord of Ely, when I was last in Holborn, I saw good strawberries in your garden there. I do beseech you send for some of them.'

The lane's Ye Olde Mitre pub, claimed to be the second oldest in London, features London's smallest pub lounge, where the licensing hours were until fairly recently set by the justices of the Isle of Ely. One could view a stack of letters addressed to 'Ye Olde Mitre Tavern, Ely Place, Holborn Circus, London, Cambridgeshire'. The letters were first shown to me by the pub's former owners John and Sheila, who used to be very proud of the remains of a Methuselah of a small cherry tree, marking the border with Cambridgeshire in one of the pub's corners.

I often ask myself why this place agrees with me so well. Why does it evoke in me the peculiar feeling of being elsewhere — the sensation both calming and disturbing? Is it due to the fact that as a Ukrainian, with Australian and British citizenships, I am a thoroughly 'dislocated' person myself? Who knows. But the fact remains: regular visits to Ely Place and meditations in St Etheldreda's Chapel had become essential for my spiritual equilibrium. When working on my fantasy novel *Granny Yaga* about the adventures of a benign East European witch in the West, there was no debate about where to locate a magic time portal, connecting modern London to the mythical 'Yesterdayland' – the witch's 'normal' abode one day behind our time. Walking through the dark narrow passageway past Ye Olde Mitre Tavern and crossing into Cambridgeshire had always struck me as travelling through an imaginary, utopian, time portal.

5 Rutland – the county of cheek and charm

'No other county in England surpasses Rutland for unspoiled quiet charm,' wrote W. G. Hoskings, the acclaimed English landscape historian, in 1949.[29] He could have just as well written that today. To me, the main attraction of Rutland, England's smallest and least populous county, is that it doesn't seem to change with time. Just like in 1949, its roads remain quiet and semi-deserted, reminiscent of those in provincial France. It is the only county in the whole of Britain where the dawn chorus easily drowns out the muffled din of a distant motorway; where one can wander in the fields for a whole day without spotting a single human being.

Rutland is unlike any other place in Britain. With its picturesque old villages and sandstone country houses, it resembles a smaller version of Provence, without harbours and vineyards but with its own man-made sea, Rutland Water, Europe's largest man-made reservoir, with surf, sandy beaches, and its own small passenger vessel – *The Rutland Belle*. It features the semi-submerged St Matthew's Church, sticking out its long-deconsecrated head above the water near the village of Nortmanton –the best place in Britain for watching sunsets, when the burning disc of the setting sun slows down for a fleeing moment as it gets impaled on the church's belfry before sliding down into the water to be dissolved.

Within an hour's drive from where I live, Rutland has become my favourite weekend destination, the closest proximity to an overseas weekend break. Indeed, even the suffix 'land' in the county's name signifies it as a unique toponymic entity, on a par with Finland, Holland, Switzerland etc. And half an hour spent on the shore of Rutland Water listening to the surf, with my eyes shut is enough to quench my never-ending nostalgia for the Black Sea coast and the Mediterranean.

I would have moved to Rutland to live years ago, but where would I go then for my utopian 'overseas' forays? To me, Rutland is not a place to permanently reside in, but a destination. Even if the journey only takes a bit over an hour.

My favourite Rutland 'destination' is Whitwell –probably the world's cheekiest village. Why? The answer is on the large road signs at the village's edges: 'Whitwell. Twinned with Paris,' they read. Whitwell, a tiny hamlet of fewer than 20 houses with thea population of just 41 is officially twinned with the City of Love, the City of Light! Does that make Whitwell the Village of Love and the Village of Light? I am sure it does! To an extent.

That utopian idea was born in 1980. It was prompted by Whitwell's only French-style open-air public toilet, which the locals referred to as 'a pissoir'. The villagers decided to write to then Mayor of Paris and future French President Jacques Chirac, asking for a 'twinship' with the French capital and saying that if he did not reply, they would assume the city had accepted their offer.

Naturally, no response came. So the self-styled committee duly organised a French-themed parade to mark their twinning, during which a local French teacher sporting a Napoleonic hat, the only French person to attend, was driven to the pub in an open-top Citroen, A local legend has it that eventually the French did reply, with a firm 'non', pointing out that the twinship was *'pas possible'*, because they were already twinned with Rome! But the road signs declaring Whitwell a twin of the City of Light had already been made, so the village had no choice but to unilaterally declare itself to be twinned.

For Paris, after all is a 'moveable feast' (pace E. Hemingway), so no matter where you feel feisty, you are in Paris. And that's how I feel not just in Whitwell, but in the whole of my utopian Rutland, too!

6 Sark, Channel Islands

'*Haro, Haro, Haro! À mon aide, mon Prince, on me fait tort.*'

With my eyes closed, I am muttering this medieval mantra in Patois, or bastardised French, standing on the old stone pier. The sea is rough, and the boat is late. I hope it never comes.

Haro! Haro! Haro!

Is my desperate, whispered call capable of delaying the boat? It should be, according to the acting Sark Constitution, which assures that under Norman custom, a person can obtain immediate cessation of any action he thinks is an infringement of his rights. At the scene, he must, in front of witnesses, recite the Lord's Prayer in French and cry out '*Haro, Haro, Haro! À mon aide, mon Prince, on me fait tort!*'

All actions must cease until the matter is heard by the court. My only concern is the absence of witnesses, if I don't count the seagulls hovering above my head and giving out piercing, almost human, shrieks: 'S-a-a-r-k! S-a-a-r-k! S-a-a-r-k!'

On the hazy horizon, I can discern the outlines of the French coast about ten miles away. I regard having to go as an infringement of my rights, for I do not want to leave the Isle of Sark, probably the happiest utopian community on earth.

Trucks in the Garden of Eden

Not part of the UK, one of Britain's overseas territories, Sark is the Commonwealth's smallest semi-independent state. It makes its own laws and manages its own money. Administered by the Seigneur, a hereditary ruler who holds the island for the British crown, Sark is the last remaining feudal community in the Western world (or was until 2008 when the islanders voted for democracy). The Seigneur still pays an inflation-free tax to the Queen of £1.79 a year—a fair sum five hundred years ago when it first came into force, constituting 'one twentieth part of a knight's fee'.

Cars are banned from Sark, and planes are not allowed to land there, or to fly over the Island under two thousand feet. The place is engulfed by a strange quiet, broken only by the wailing of the wind.

The island still abides by medieval laws, one of which says that 'unspayed bitches are not allowed to be kept on the Island, except by the Seigneur'. This law was adopted in the seventeenth century, when Chief Pleas (the island's parliament) decided that too many dogs could cause problems with sheep farming.

'Yes, our island is bitch-free,' Michael Beaumont, the 22nd Seigneur of Sark (now deceased), told me with a smile during my first visit to the island in 1996. He inherited his estate from his paternal grandmother, the Dame of Sark. Another law states that forty local family heads, including the Seigneur, are obliged to keep muskets to protect the island from invaders. A modest brochure, *Constitution of Sark*, written by Michael Beaumont himself, was destined to become one of the gems of my esoteric and ever-expanding book collection.

The defence of the island is not just an abstraction. During the Second World War, it was occupied by a garrison of three hundred Germans. The forty muskets of Sark, however, remained silent. Not a single shot was fired from either side, and the locals still refer to that period as a 'model occupation'. One of them told me how the German commandant of Sark refused to take any action against those local residents who defied the occupation authorities by keeping short-wave radios at their houses—an offence punishable by death anywhere else in occupied Europe.

In 1989, the island experienced another foreign invasion, albeit on a much smaller scale. It was taken over single-handedly by a drunken Frenchman, André Gardes, who landed on Sark with a rifle and a small cache of explosives. In a 'manifesto', written in broken English and pinned on the village noticeboard, he announced that he was taking control of the island. Having stated his intentions, he retired for a refill to a village pub, where he was apprehended and disarmed by the part-time constable (head of Sark's part-time police force) and frogmarched to the island's prison, consisting of one small windowless cell.

The Constable soon came to regret his bravery, for another island law made him responsible for feeding prison inmates, and the Frenchman proved to be voracious. Luckily, two days is the maximum jail term in Sark, and in due course the gluttonous invader was deported to his motherland, thus terminating the last recorded foreign invasion of Britain.

Not covered by the UK's social security and health schemes, the island takes good care of itself. Special community funds help young people through schools and universities, pay medical bills for the sick, and provide pensions for the old. This makes the island into a unique welfare mini-state, an exemplary utopian society.

Sark has never been part of the EU. It remains unperturbed by the 'global village' and 'unified Europe' rhetoric. It stays clear of pacts, leagues and alliances, simply because it is quite happy to be on its own in our conflict-ridden chaotic world, striving for integration and yet increasingly divided.

That is why I am always reluctant to leave this real-life island Utopia.

'*Haro! Haro! Haro!*'

7 *Stornoway, Scotland, on a Sunday*

'Only he who is familiar with the din of battle can fully appreciate quiet,' said Volodya Grishpun, the favourite Kharkiv-based poet of my youth.

There are different types of silence: a hush-hush conspiratorial whisper, a pause in a conversation, a lull before a storm, or a minute of silence in mourning or commemoration. In the USSR, all broadcasts would stop for three minutes at midnight to allow any SOS signals to be heard, three minutes of anxious, listening silence. Also, a silence à la Bill Bryson: 'It was so quiet in the pub one could hear a fly fart.'

A newspaper account of the first days of the second Gulf War began with: 'Wailing air raid sirens were drowned out as laser bombs homed in on military installations and Republican Guard strongholds.' Silence is becoming an increasingly coveted and rare commodity, a kind of a Utopia in our noise-ridden and war-torn world. Close your eyes, shut out all noises and listen to silence…

On Sunday morning, I awake in my Stornoway hotel to the shattering, deafening stillness behind the window. All habitual noises that constitute part of a quiet Sunday morning in any small town – the sounds of passing cars and human footsteps – are missing. Even dogs do not bark. The silence is such that it almost makes my teeth ache. Had I indeed had a sore tooth, there would be no chance of buying a painkiller: all pharmacies and shops on Lewis are shut for the sabbath. The best description 'the mother of all silences', as Saddam Hussein would have put it, can be found in H.V. Morton's *In Search of Scotland*:

> It is the sabbath. I lie in bed for a time listening to it. You can feel the sabbath in the Highlands of Scotland just as in cities you can feel a fall of snow: the world is wrapped in a kind of soft hush; normal early morning noises are muffled or absent.

Morton wrote this in 1929, when the sabbath was strictly observed in many rural areas of Scotland. Ninety odd years later, the Outer Hebrides were among its very last strongholds.

Thank God, water in my bathroom taps was not affected by the sabbath and kept running, as it must have done for H.V. Morton in 1929: 'I sing in my bath; then, remembering with shock that I am breaking the sabbath, stop, and feel criminal.'

At breakfast at the miraculously open and empty hotel's restaurant, the rising air-bubbles in the glass of mineral water on my table are the only things that move in the whole of Stornoway.

I walk the deserted streets of the town, where every Sunday, between 11 a.m. and midday, ninety-nine per cent of the locals attend their Sunday services. Being the only pedestrian in town at this hour of prayer does feel, if not exactly 'criminal', then definitely like a minor breach of public order.

Muffled yet synchronised singing can be heard from numerous churches. If Heaven does exist (and I am sure it does somewhere), this is how it probably sounds. And not just on a Sunday. We'll all be able to check it out one day. In the meantime, one can always come to Stornoway to get an idea...

8 Roof Gardens, Kensington, London

I first learned about the Kensington Roof Gardens on top of the former Derry &Toms department store on Kensington High Street from the book *Secret London*. Laid out by Ralph Hancock in the 1930s, those 6000-square-metre Gardens were divided into three themed areas: a Spanish Alhambra-like garden in a Moorish style, complete with palms, fountains and a chapel; a Tudor-style garden, with archways, secret corners and wisteria; and an English woodland garden, with a stream and pond with ducks and Chilean flamingos whose names were Bill, Ben, Splosh and Pecks.

And here I am, back from my travels, back in Derry Street, just 20 metres away from the hustle-and-bustle of High Street Kensington, facing an ordinary office entrance with no sign above the door. I enter a lift and press the 'Up' button. I can see the floor numbers changing slowly: 1...2...3 – and with each number I am feeling more and more relaxed...

I come out and find myself in a beautiful and totally empty utopian garden in the sky.

This is a very large garden, and I cannot see all of it at once. The bit that I can see is bathed in sunlight. It is a lovely summer day – warm but not uncomfortably hot, just right – and there is a gentle breeze blowing.

All my favourite flowers are there, and I can see colourful butterflies fluttering above them. Bees are darting from one to another collecting the pollen and making a soothing buzzing sound as they do so. I head for a small pond under a willow tree and install myself on a bench in the willow's shadow.

A graceful pink flamingo stands on one leg in the middle of the pond, its head buried in its feathers. I wonder whether it is Bill, Ben, Splosh or Pecks. It looks like a question mark in the margins of my life's book – the book that is never destined to be completed.

This bench is going to be my *starting point*, from where I can fly wherever I choose. The garden, after all, is in the sky, it is a flying garden which makes it an ideal launch pad. The bench is on the same level as the spire of a nearby church. From it I can look down at the London sprawl underneath me without lowering my head. I need to see this view telling me without a shadow of doubt that I am back in the country where I have always belonged. I spread out my hands as if they are wings, then levitate above the bench for a couple of minutes before dashing away – across the sea – to Australia (Tasmania, to be more exact), Alaska, the Faroes, the Falklands, or any other place where I felt at home and happy.

Several years ago, I was saddened to learn that the Roof Gardens, one of London's secret Utopias, closed down and were sold to a private members club which will probably limit access to them when (and if) they reopen. A limited-access 'Utopia' is a very

Soviet concept, so I'd rather keep the Gardens closed forever than make them accessible only to the privileged few.

9 Magdalene College, Cambridge

At the press of a button, the heavy iron-clad doors of the underground car park open slowly, almost reluctantly, and I, squinting at the sudden burst of bright sunlight, step into a peculiar 'bubble' having little to do with the rest of the world, an alternative universe and my life's ultimate Utopia – the perennially sun-drenched (in my eyes, at least) buildings of Magdalene College, University of Cambridge.

The first creature to greet me there is our College's resident swan – probably a fellow like me – sitting in his nest right opposite the car park entrance. He can easily be a descendant of my imaginary wagonette-pulling swans from Victorian Britain, the sweet Utopia of my childhood (see Chapter 1).

Slowly, as if savouring every step, I walk across Benson Court towards the gates. The neat gravel path is lined with bushes and flowers. Tended by a team of our staff gardeners, they appear to be blooming and blossoming all through the year – even in winter The true Garden of Eden, with no trucks in it!

I open the gates with my electronic pass, cross the narrow road trying to dodge the ubiquitous cyclists, who look as if they wouldn't mind running over an elderly university don, I enter the College's First Court and pop into the Porters' Lodge to check my pigeon hole for correspondence.

Clutching a small pile of letters, I puff up the steep stairs of the late 17th-century building to my office in the attic. The last flight of steps is so steep that it is almost vertical, and climbing up it takes some effort. I often use it as an example of bad writing during the tutorials with students: 'Good writing for a reader is smooth like the surface of my desk, and bad writing – like stairs to my office.'

The plate on the door next to mine reads 'PARADIS E'. No, I am not hallucinating. The room between my office ('DR Vitaliev') and the one of 'PROF. Raven' is occupied by Elizabeth Paradis – a francophone postgraduate student from Quebec, who asked for her name on the doorplate to be written thus. So I can state without any qualms that my Cambridge University office is right next door to 'paradise'.

It takes me a minute or so to regain my breath inside my spacious office, with beams and vaulted ceilings. One of the windows is

In The Eye of The Beholder, or My Utop Ten

facing the College's magnificent 18th-century Chapel, the domain of our Chaplain and my good friend Sarah Atkins, with whom I conducted a vigil for Ukraine in April 2022, shortly after my mother country was invaded by Russia. It was in the Chapel that I was 'anointed' a Fellow by Sir Christopher Greenwood, the College Master, who succeeded Rowan Williams, the former Archbishop of Canterbury, in that post. The ceremony was conducted in Latin.

'Do not try to understand how the College works. The only thing you need to remember is be nice to everyone,' such was the valedictory for the new Fellows from Professor Brendan Burchill, then the College President.

When in my office, I do not require a watch, I can tell the time by the Chapel's clock right opposite my window and by the chimes of its bells, albeit for me, time in its normal sense does not seem to exist in the College.

'Time flies when you're having fun' is a common English adage. Its Russian equivalent, however, is somewhat stronger. Stemming from Alexander Griboyedov's classical comedy *Gore ot Uma* ('Woe from Wit'), it can be translated word-for-word as 'Those who are happy do not hear the clocks strike.'

From my very first days as Magdalene's Fellow, I've been incredibly, almost indescribably, happy. Happy to the point when I feel tempted to pinch myself every so often to make sure I am not dreaming. When introduced to Cambridge and its colleges by Clive James during my first visit to Britain in 1988, I had pangs of painful regret at the thought that I would never be part of that breathtaking townscape, all-too-familiar from books and movies, with college spires, cobbled streets, cyclists, swans, punts on the River Cam, and cows grazing on college greens.

Thirty-three years later I did become part of my own long-time Utopia. To the point when the ever-so-observant student touts, tirelessly trying to solicit pedestrians for punting, have left me alone and pretend to ignore me when I walk past them, as if I were a local, a piece of familiar furniture, an integral and almost invisible part of the never-changing Cambridge scene.

In the intervals between tutorials, I walk to the Market Square to browse in my favourite Cambridge University Bookshop, where I want to buy and devour all the books on display and where – rather dangerously for my budget – I enjoy a 20 per cent discount, I then browse through the bookstall in the middle of the square, where my late friend Clive James told me he used to buy books that he already owned for the sheer pleasure of carrying them home.

My several years in Cambridge helped me realise how much I enjoy teaching. And it is great to know that students seem to like my talks and tutorials too. Here's a short quote from a thank-you card I received from a student at the end of the academic year: 'It has been an honour to learn, unlearn and relearn writing with you, Vitali. Truly, 'life is a literary device' (a title of one of my books) and a few lines are better than a blank page.'

I very much enjoy the college life: conversations with my fellow Fellows in the Common Room, talks, exhibitions, lunches, and of course, the frequent High Table dinners in the historic Hall, the oldest in Cambridge and the only one with no electric wires, just candlelight, enlarging and projecting on the wall long shadows of the Fellows as we slip into the Hall in two lines, and the students stand up to greet us. Candlelight dances on ceremonial old portraits on the wall and makes them come to life, particularly that of Lord Audley, a Henry VIII look-alike, who founded the College on the grounds of a Benedictine monks' hostel nearly 600 years ago and in whose honour its name is still pronounced 'Modlin'.

It feels like being a part of a film set, or like travelling several hundred years back in time.

There's a good deal of badly camouflaged jealousy in Cambridge for our magnificent Dining Hall. As *Walking Cambridge*, one of the latest guidebooks to the city, put it acerbically: '[Magdalene] College still maintains archaic traditions such as eating by candlelight.'

I love those 'archaic traditions'. After my first High Table dinner, a fellow Fellow drew my attention to a short narrow slit in the massive wooden door of the college's 'Buttery' (kitchen). 'This is where the last Fellow to leave the High Table has to drop the key to the wine cabinet. Why? 'To ensure the College porters not to drink it all during the night!'

Having said that, he ferreted out a small, battered key from under his gown and pushed it through the hole. 'We are the last to leave tonight,' he sighed.

I found it hard to imagine the present-day College porters, invariably helpful, polite and impeccably dressed, plotting to decimate the poor Fellows' wine supplies. But their medieval predecessors must have been a much more uncouth and bibulous lot! Every time I pass by the Buttery door, I stop for a short moment to look at that slit, which to me has become a portal not just back in time but also a peephole into my life's main Utopia, which will be with me for as long as I live.

In The Eye of The Beholder, or My Utop Ten

Sitting alone on a bench in one of the College's gardens of an evening and looking at the quietly flowing Cam, I often recall the essay by Vladimir Nabokov, who was himself a student in Cambridge in the early 1920s, and who might have written those words while sitting on the same bench on the river bank:

> And, gazing at the tranquil water, where subtle reflections bloom like designs on porcelain, I begin to think still more deeply, about much, about the whims of fate, about my homeland, and about the fact that my best memories grow older every day, and so far nothing can replace them.[30]

He was then 22 years of age.

10 Pegasus Cottage

My personal utopian shell is called Pegasus Cottage. My wife Christine had it built for me as a birthday present the same year we moved from North London to Letchworth. She hired a team of five workers who toiled non-stop for two weeks and created something truly incredible, Particularly for someone like myself, who – for many years – had to write in a wall closet in Moscow when living in just one room in a 'communal' flat, having to share bathroom, toilet and kitchen with several other families. I had to hide inside the closet not to wake my son, then still a baby, with the rattling of my old typewriter.

Utopia is, first and foremost, a relative concept. It takes several years of sweeping persistent black cockroaches off your impromptu desk inside a stuffy cupboard, the former abode of a radio pirate, to fully appreciate one's own fully electrified, heated and insulated garden office.

Pegasus Cottage is a small wooden house. Inside, there's one room smelling of varnished wood. It is warm and cosy, and behind the window in the autumn large red apples keep falling off the hardworking apple tree every now and then – thump, thump, thump… On the shelves along the wall are my peripatetic, long-suffering books.

I had to spend the whole day taking them out of the loft and the garden shed where they had been stored after being liberated them from their 3-year prison term in the former laundry room of Folkestone's Edwardian Metropole Hotel basement (I kept them there during my enforced Kent exile twenty years ago). Many of them must have forgotten what a proper bookshelf felt like after years of being squashed in cardboard boxes, their pages glued together by the all-permeating moisture.

The builders installed a small, but powerful, electric heater inside the hut, winking at the books with its red eye. Slowly but surely the books were warming up, their bent covers, rheumatic spines and arthritic concertina-ed pages stretching up, straightening and strengthening by the minute. To me it appeared then that the books were smiling...

Through the ornate glass door one can see a rusty horseshoe nailed to the wall above the entrance. I found it by accident on the roof of the garden shed that used to stand on the same spot. The shed's roof was leaking, and one morning I climbed up the ladder to mend it. A large rusty horseshoe lay in the middle of the roof. Horseshoes don't end up on roofs by accident. There was only one way a horseshoe could end up on the roof: if it had been dropped by Pegasus – a muse and patron of all writers! Or so I wanted to think. It was a sign that my writing abode was to be there – in Pegasus Cottage.

And here I am – having gone through many trials and writing my book number 16 (or possibly 15, I am not quite sure) on Britain's Utopias inside my own writer's shed and feeling happier than ever before – to the extent that at times it makes me feel jealous of myself.

The feeling of being jealous of oneself... My last and final definition of a Utopia!

Postscript

Several days before the final delivery deadline for the manuscript of this book, I received an email from my Cambridge University Press Bookshop: 'Dear Vitali, we have just received the book that you ordered, *Late Soviet Britain* by Abby Innes. We were unsure whether you'd like the paperback or hardback, so we have a copy of each on hold for you behind the desk.'

Talking about utopian scenarios that Cambridge, my new Avalon, keeps rewarding me with!

I couldn't wait to get hold of that book, ever since its forthcoming publication was announced in Cambridge University Press catalogues, for one simple reason – its subtitle, 'Why Materialist Utopias Fail' – which, as I thought, contained an answer to the

In The Eye of The Beholder, or My Utop Ten

largely rhetorical question it had itself posed: Because they are Materialist!

By drawing scholarly parallels between the modern British state and the 'fallacy' of the materialistically utopian Soviet system of central planning, Professor Abby Innes had effectively arrived at the same conclusion that I have reached in this thoroughly non-scholarly and largely impressionistic book: Utopias can only work on a spiritual, level, when and if they rest upon the innermost feelings, dreams and aspirations of each individual member of the society – and that in itself amounts to a Utopia in its own right!

My whole long life in different cultures and opposing, even mutually hostile, social systems has taught me that the only realistic way to change the world for the better is by changing ourselves. by making each of us a better person by all available means.

As my friend Tim Waygood put it (see above): 'With time, my ambitions have changed from changing the world to creating my own world!'

It was expressed even better by the French writer Jules Renard in his 'Journals': 'Paradise does not exist. But we must nevertheless strive to be worthy of its existence.'

'Malice in Wonderland'
Instead of an Epilogue

> A man's country is his Arcadia.
> *Utopias Old and New* by Harry Ross,
> Nicholson & Watson Limited, 1938

When I was already several chapters into this book, Russia invaded Ukraine.

War is a dystopia at its worst.

I was hit by one the very first bullets of that horrific, unexpected and totally unjustified war. Like a patient going through a near-death experience, I was vaguely aware of what was happening around me but remained irresponsive, catatonic and almost physically paralysed. The emotional paralysis was complete and felt irreversible. The most severe, unimaginable black-and white dystopia had disrupted my technicolour utopian dreams. I was temporarily unable to carry on with the book of course. Luckily, Connor Stait, my sympathetic commissioning editor, agreed to a deadline extension.

As a writer, I was subconsciously waiting for the moment when staying silent would become more unbearable than speaking out, while endlessly reliving my early-childhood dream, or rather nightmare:

Our city of Kharkiv is occupied by the Nazis. I am hiding at home, knowing that the German patrols will soon start raiding the houses one after another. Someone's heavy footsteps are heard far off. They are coming closer and getting louder and louder; I can already hear our worn-out apartment door squeaking on its rusty hinges. I scream for help… And wake up in cold sweat.

'Malice in Wonderland' Instead of an Epilogue

Sixty years on, that nightmare has become reality for many, the only difference being that the invaders are not German Nazis, but Russians, the lot I used to think I belonged to myself – spiritually and culturally, if not ethnically. The vicious zombie of the supposedly dead USSR has come back to add more victims to the many millions it had devoured between 1917 and 1991.

The morning finally came when I dragged myself to my desk and started putting my feelings and thoughts on paper in no chronological, or any other, order: just as they came.

After a weak anaesthetic of fitful sleep, the nightmare would return every morning at the press of a radio button. Something deep inside me resisted: it was probably better not to be aware of the dreadful reality that appeared entirely impossible only a couple of weeks earlier. But not knowing would mean guessing and wondering who else of my friends could have been killed, what other relic of my past had been bombed out of existence, what other parts had been torn out of Ukraine's tired heart? And out of my own heart, too.

'Kharkiv is no more,' an old friend muttered into her phone, having peeped one morning out of the basement where she had been hiding with her husband for over a week. And my exhausted brain immediately made a terrifying connection: 'Kharkiv, no more – my birthplace, no more – my childhood, no more – myself, no more.' A shortcut to deep depression, caused by the sheer inability to change the tragic course of events.

I look at the words I've written, trying to convince myself that to write about Ukraine's torment is my duty. By remembering, we bring back to life the people, the events and the buildings that are no more. It is like Schrodinger's Cat: as long as we keep picturing them alive, they are not dead yet.

For me, one of the biggest blows of the Russian aggression so far was the capture by the invaders of the Ukrainian Physico-Technical Institute (UFTI), where my late father, Vladimir Alexandrovich, a particle physicist, worked as a senior research fellow for most of his life, from the early 1950s up to his untimely death in 1982.

The Institute, thoroughly utopian in its nature, was founded in October 1928 with the aim of cracking the secrets of nuclear physics, then rightly regarded as the science of the future (unlike, say, cybernetics, which Stalin considered a 'pseudo-science'), and boasted a small nuclear reactor of its own, where the nucleus was split for the first time in 1932 and type-II superconductivity was experimentally discovered. It was located in a village with the nice-sounding Ukrainian name of Piatykhatky ('five huts'). As a child, I was a frequent visitor: for New Year dos, organised annually for the scientists' kids, or simply to see my dad. It was there that I saw a giant first-generation computer, proudly demonstrated to me by my father on the New Year's Eve of 1961 or 1962.

'Do ask the machine a question!' my father suggested with a smile.

Aged seven, the only thing I could think of was: 'Can you ask the machine how much two plus two is?'

My dad typed that unsophisticated query on a piece of yellow perforated cardboard, which he inserted into the mechanical monster that occupied several large rooms, and pressed a green button. All hell broke loose: coloured lights started blinking as the 'monster' shook and vibrated violently while emitting loud guttural noises: rattling, squeaking and, as I thought then, about ready to explode. I covered my ears and closed my eyes.

The racket suddenly stopped, the lights went out – and the dinosaur of the PC epoch spat out a small piece of perforated paper. My dad picked it up from the floor and showed to me. There was one pale number printed on it – '4'.

To say that I was stunned would be an understatement. I knew I was going to remember that moment for as long as I lived. And I was right, even if I didn't realise then that the machine had made a mistake: in our abnormal dystopian world, where 60 years on, my Ukraine was to be invaded by Russia, two and two would make anything but four. But then, in 1961-2, it would have then been easier to believe the Earth was flat and rested on five (as in 'two plus two') giant turtles.

Among the world-famous scientists who worked at the Institute was Lev Davidovich Landau (1908-1968), 'Dau' to his colleagues, and winner of the Nobel Prize for Physics – a legendary figure who recently found himself in the middle not of the bloody and purposeless Russian invasion of Ukraine, but of the monumental DAU filming project by Russian director Ilya Khrzhanovsky. The bulk of filming took place at a specially engineered life-size model of the original UFTI campus on the grounds of the Kharkiv Dynamo stadium, next to which I used to live.

The film set included (but wasn't limited to) a life-size replica of the whole of the 1930s-1960s Physico-Technical Institute campus, with loads of its fully functioning technological and scientific equipment: transformers, energy generators, the very particle accelerator on which my father used to work (then the largest in Europe), first-generation TVs and computers, and so on. It was a utopian project through and through... As if the Russian filmmakers knew that the natural set had only a few years left to live before succumbing to the Russian bombs.

The area of the Dynamo stadium was indeed destroyed by the Russian bombs and missiles (now being restored), alongside the very heart of my native city – the hub of Ukrainian science and industry – Europe's largest Freedom (formerly Dzerzhinsky) Square. A Russian Grad missile hit the Stalinist edifice of the former 'obkom' – the regional communist party committee, now the City Hall. My university nearby was also targeted, as well as the Unesco-listed Gosprom ('State Industry'), or 'Derzhprom' in Ukrainian, building – a Constructivist semi-utopian masterpiece.

According to the idea of the Gosprom's designers – Serafimov, Kravets and Felger – if viewed from the sky, the outlines of the building were to resemble the stave of the Internationale's first notes: 'Arise ye workers from your slumbers; Arise ye prisoners of want...' What could be more naively (and tragically) utopian than that?

Significantly, Gosprom came through World War Two intact, despite repeated attempts by the Nazis (the real German Nazis, not the Putin-invented Ukrainian ones) to blow it up. After failing to do so, the Germans kept animals in its towers.

From what I have been told, Gosprom is still standing – towering above the ruins of Freedom Square, the skyline of which now echoes to no music, apart perhaps from a Chopin march – just like some other parts of my beautiful native city, the utopian dream of my childhood and youth, which has already earned itself the title of the '21st-century Stalingrad'.

I do try to believe, however, that in the long term – just like with my dad's Institute – Kharkiv will be rebuilt. That 'replica' will be much more beautiful than the 'original, mercilessly destroyed by the invaders.

It is only then that the world will return to normality and two plus two will be four again. It is only then that the beautiful word 'Utopia' – a 'fight against the limits of possibility', according to one clever definition, will restore its original meaning where 'fight' would denote 'creation', and not 'destruction'.

Notes and References

1. *The utopians. Six Attempts to Build the Perfect Society* by Anna Neima, Picador, 2022, p. 7.
2. Here I am reminded of a Soviet joke. A middle-aged Jewish man applies to emigrate to Israel and is immediately summoned to his local KGB branch.

    'Well, Rabinovich, who you want to leave our great country?' A KGB Major asks him. 'Are you homeless, struggling for survival, or do not have enough to eat?'

    'No, Sir, I am actually quite well-off and have a good life,' Rabinovich replies.

    'Then perhaps you have just been misled by the proverb that life is always good wherever we happen not to be?'

    'That's right!' says Rabinovich. 'Life is much-much better wherever *you* happen not to be!'

    That, incidentally, was my own main reason for leaving the USSR.
3. Some home-grown Soviet wits deciphered the mysterious 'KVN' abbreviation (in Russian) as 'Kupil, Vkliuchil, Ne rabotayet' – 'bought, switched on, doesn't work'.
4. In his book *The Infinite City. utopian Dreams on the Streets of London* (William Collins, July 2023), Niall Kishtainy tells the story of Ada Salter's Wilson Grove – a 'pocket garden city' in the Docklands area and other utopian corners of the capital: Bertold Lubetkin's Spa Green Estate in Clerkenwell, Bevin Court in Finsbury, etc.
5. My favourite literary dystopia (as opposed to Utopia, which is *The Coming Race*) and one of my favourite books of all time is *A Scientific Romance* by Ronald Wright, a British author

now living in Canada. By genre, it is indeed a science-fiction dystopia of sorts. The plot is roughly as follows.

In 1999, in London, David Lambert, an archaeologist and reluctant curator of a museum of Victorian technology and engineering, accidentally finds out that H. G. Wells's fictitious time machine was in fact real and, having just returned from the 19th century, is ready for use after some minor repairs. 'The device somehow achieves displacement in time by producing an electrical plasma similar to ball lightning... The real machine abides by the Draconian laws of thermodynamics. The maximum range ... was a thousand years – eternity's small change.'

The time machine's peculiar 'modus operandi' for Wright is of course but a literary – and not an engineering – device to transfer his protagonist to the future. Suffering from a terminal illness and having just been dumped by his girlfriend, David thinks he's got nothing to lose and propels himself 500 years ahead to 2499. What he finds is a tropical Britain, with palm trees and monkeys but no people. To get to that stage, the place must have gone through several global conflicts, or deadly pandemics, or both. Having established a base camp under the ruined carcass of the Queen Elizabeth Bridge at Dartford, David sets off in search of humans (if any) along the remains of the A1 motorway, overgrown with grass, cacti and lianas, to the sounds of 'an uproar of parakeets and mynahs feeding in cohune palms'. On his way north, he befriends a black panther, whom he calls Graham.

David Lambert (the bulk of the book is written as his diary) comes through as passionate and erudite, a home-grown philosopher and a narrator of Nabokovian standards (to me, Wright's style was somewhat reminiscent of Nabokov's American-period prose). He is at times desperate, at times funny, but never indifferent or inhumane.

As for the landscape, it is so believable that after reading and re-reading *A Scientific Romance* (and I have done it at least five times), I started taking extra care every time I drove across the Queen Elizabeth Bridge ('two exclamation marks joined by a warped hyphen, black against a Canaletto sky'), or a stroll along the Thames: 'The river's artificial banks have long disappeared, and there's no trace of the refineries and power stations that used to greet the seaborne visitor to London like an avenue of sphinxes. Mangroves and palmettos line both shores.'

You never know behind which of the mangroves Graham the panther may be hiding.

6. Here and later in this Chapter, Rupert Brooke's poetry samples are quoted from *Rupert Brooke, Collected Poems*, Oleander Press, 2013

7. Here's an extract from an article on the utopian socialist designs of Soviet cities, published in 2021 on www.openculture.com, in which I see a number of similarities to Britain's New Towns project: 'Modernist architecture transformed the modern city in the 20th century, for good and ill. Nowhere is this transformation more evident than the former Soviet Union and its former republics. There, we find truth in the western stereotypes of the Soviet city as cold, faceless, and soul-crushingly nondescript — so much so that the plot of a 1975 Russian TV film called *The Irony of Fate*, or *Enjoy Your Bath!* hinges on a man drunkenly travelling to Leningrad by mistake and falling asleep in a stranger's apartment, thinking it's his own place in Moscow. Russians found the joke so relatable, they began a tradition of watching the film each year at Christmas. (We did watch that movie each year, but not at Christmas, which was not allowed to be celebrated in the USSR, but on New Year Eve.)

Once it had eliminated private property, the experiment of the Soviet Union began with good intentions, architecturally-speaking. Constructivism, the first form of distinctly Soviet architecture, was developed first as an art movement by Vladimir Tatlin and Alexander Rodchenko. Constructivists sought to balance the nation's need to build tons of new housing under harsh economic conditions... Many of its finest designs went unrealized, but it left a significant mark on subsequent architectural movements like Brutalism...

The synthesis of beauty and utility would fall apart, however, under the massive collectivizing drives of Stalin. When his reign ended, public housing blocks known as 'Krushchyovkas' sprang up, named after the premier who initiated their mass production in the late 1950s ... a distinctly banal architectural type' built quickly and cheaply when Moscow had twice the population its housing stock could accommodate. Five-storey Krushchovkas popped up in newly planned microdistricts...

As the popularity of *The Irony of Fate* demonstrates, Krushchovkas introduced serious problems of their own, including their grimly comic sameness... All of the housing

Notes and References

blocks were built to last 20 to 25 years and were not well-maintained, if they were maintained at all. The earliest began deteriorating in the 1970s.'

8. Andrei Sakharov, a Soviet physicist, a dissident and a Nobel Peace Prize laureate (1921–1989)
9. Here's a quote from another mindless-vandalism-relevant *Comet* news story, published on 17 August 2023: 'Stevenage: Tank smashed during Tranquil Turtle break in. A popular Stevenage restaurant's fish tank which is home to a live turtle, has been smashed along with a number of other items during a break-in.'
10. I should have touched wood when talking about the potential endlessness of my New Towns/Stevenage Chapter. On 10 October 2023, when I was in the process of final revision of the manuscript, Sir Keir Starmer, the Labour Leader, in his keynote speech at the annual Labour Party Conference unveiled his 'big build on the green belt' plan, which included building a 'new generation of New Towns like Harlow, Welwyn Garden City, Stevenage, Crawley, Basildon and Milton Keynes' – all as part of a 'decade of renewal' (he forgot to include Corby). That statement left me speechless. The only thing I can do is refer you back to Chapter 5.
11. 'Ilf and Petrov's *The Complete Adventures of Ostap Bender. The Golden Calf*, Random House, New York, 1962
12. *Paradise Planned. The Garden Suburb and the Modern City* by Robert A. M. Stern, David Fishman, and Jacob Tilove; The Monacelli Press, US, 2013
13. *The Life of Robert Owen Written by Himself. With his Preface and an Introduction by John Butt*. Charles Knight & Co. Ltd. London 1971.
14. See Note 12
15. *Portmeirion. The Place and its Meaning* by Clough Williams-Ellis; Faber & Faber, 1963
16. On the day I was writing these lines, the former grounds of that fake achievements exhibition in Moscow were hit by a Ukrainian drone. None of the showy and ugly socialist-realism exhibition buildings was damaged, unfortunately.
17. *The King of Sunlight. How William Lever Cleaned Up the World* by Adam Macqueen, Corgi, 2011
18. The Almanac's next, 1899, edition features a 'Specially Written Story by Sir Walter Besant,' an acclaimed English novelist and historian, of whose book, *History of London*, I proudly own the first edition.

19. See Note 11
20. They would actually say: 'Gde dostal? – with the verb 'dostat' implying literally 'to acquire with difficulty' – so that in direct translation from Soviet-speak to English the question would sound more like 'Where did you get it with difficulty, buddy?'
21. See Note 11
22. *Moorside. A Wartime Miracle* by Gordon L. Routledge; P3 Publications, 2020
23. See Note 13
24. *The Scottish Islands* by Hamish Haswell-Smith; Canongate, 2015
25. *Gavin Maxwell: A Life* by Douglas Botting; HarperCollins, 1993
26. *Utopia. The History of an Idea* by Gregory Claeys, Thames & Hudson, 2020
27. *The Oxford Literary Guide to the British Isles*, Clarendon Press, 1977
28. *The Quest for Rananim. D. H. Lawrence's Letters to S.S. Koteliansky*, edited by George J Zytaruk; McGill – Queen's University Press, 1970
29. *Rutland; a Shell Guide* by W.G. Hoskins, Faber & Faber, 1963
30. *Think, Write, Speak* by Vladimir Nabokov; Penguin Books, 2020

Appendix 1

Incomplete Angler

> Many men go fishing all their lives without knowing that it is not fish they are after.
>
> Henry David Thoreau

Just like ideas, communities and communes, pastimes can be utopian, too. Below is an example.

'BEE COOL, Mackerel Fishing. Reef Fishing. Boat Trips'. I spotted this sign in the small and picturesque, almost toy-like, harbour of the Cornish seaside town of Looe. We were on a short camping holiday in Cornwall and fishing – mackerel or reef – was not on the agenda. I was unable to unglue my eyes from that sun-drenched little billboard promising my favourite adventure – fishing, which I had not pursued for the last 20-odd years, having kept myself so busy that sitting on a bank or a shore with a fishing rod looked like a selfishly hedonistic waste of time. From a dedicated and almost always lucky angler, I had been slowly but surely turning into a virtual fisherman, with fishing becoming a largely utopian pastime – the domain where dreams and distant reveries reigned supreme.

I nearly forgot my once favourite quotation, attributed in Russia to Anton Chekhov and in the West to Herbert Hoover: 'The gods do not deduct from man's allotted span the hours spent in fishing.' I first heard that beautiful quote from my father when I was seven or eight years old.

'So, it means that if we keep fishing all the time, we will never die?' I enquired.

My Dad only smiled. Too busy with his beloved particle accelerator, on which he had worked most of his life, he wasn't a fisherman – that was probably why he died at the fairly young age of 56, or so I still sometimes think.

I was hooked on fishing from a pre-school age, when in summer I could often be found on the grassy bank of a small and polluted pond in the town of Liubotin, near Kharkiv, where I was often taken for holidays. In my hands, I would be holding a primitive fishing rod, made of a more or less straight tree branch. I would stand there from morning till night, causing giggles among the sun-tanned local boys. Their laughter would come to a brief stop only when I would ferret out a tiny perch or a crucian carp.

What was it that first attracted me to fishing? It must have been its sheer unpredictability in the otherwise so predictable and hence profoundly boring Soviet environment, with its ubiquitous dull slogans and equally dull people. While angling, you never know what you are going to catch. That incomparable sensation of novelty and surprise was hugely enhanced in me with the gradual emergence of the 'yar' (a 'ditch' in Ukrainian) next to our block of flats in the very centre of the huge industrial city of Kharkiv. Well, it was not a ditch but rather a crater, made by a heavy shell during the 1918-1921 Civil War.

Rain and snowfall kept extending the crater, and by the time of my birth it had turned into a long and deep ravine, overgrown with weeds and wild grass. At the bottom of the ravine was a puddle of rainwater which gradually grew into a pond fed by natural underground springs.

We boys spent hours in the ditch, which served as a rubbish dump throughout the 1950s and 1960s until some local aquarium buffs jokingly released the fry of tropical fish into the 'pond'. Mysteriously, the fish started breeding happily in the yar, and soon we were able to catch some strange aquatic mutants with our primitive bamboo fishing rods (hence that feeling of unpredictability), using sticky bread balls dipped in smelly anise drops from a local pharmacy as bait. Whenever I take a sip of a fiery Greek ouzo or a palate-burning French pastis, I am momentarily teleported to the fishing yar of my childhood.

The fish we caught were small, prickly and utterly inedible, but we enjoyed the sheer fun of fishing in the middle of a big industrial city – much to the contempt of Uncle Igor, a Second World War veteran and an inveterate fisherman who lived in our block of flats.

Uncle Igor had the character of a child. A brilliant fabricator, he'd spend hours in the courtyard entertaining children with stories of his wartime feats and his fishing achievements. He would go to

Incomplete Angler

fish in the country once a week and would come back reeking of vodka and carrying a string bag full of freshly caught fish that he proudly displayed to us.

We all adored Uncle Igor, although my parents suspected that his plentiful catches had been secretly bought at the Tempo food shop round the corner. Of course, we kept asking him to come and fish with us in the yar, but he dismissed our pleadings with a wave of his rough fisherman's hand: 'What do you take Uncle Igor for? Uncle Igor will never deign to fish in that dirty bog of yours where only small fry can be caught!'

He had a habit of referring to himself in the third person – as 'Uncle Igor', like toddlers, robots and martinets do. One day, being more tipsy than usual, he succumbed, and grudgingly went down to the yar with all his sophisticated fishing gear: spinning rods, feathers, home-made spoonbaits and whatnots. We were most impressed by his folding fisherman's chair with a tarpaulin seat.

Having unfolded his magic chair, Uncle Igor sat down and solemnly threw three spoon-baited lines into the yar's opaque, urine-coloured water. We all flocked around him, watching his performance with our mouths agape as if it was a religious rite. The fish started biting immediately, and all Uncle Igor's three floats, made of wine corks, were diving and jumping like crazy.

Uncle Igor reluctantly raised his world-weary bottom from the chair, hooked and started pulling. The fish was obviously heavy and didn't want to give in. The silk Czechoslovakian line drew like a bowstring.

'See? It only took Uncle Igor two minutes to hook the biggest fish in this bog!' Uncle Igor, ruddy-faced and puffing, announced triumphantly.

We held our breath. Soon, the top of a rusty funnel emerged from the water.

'What's that?? A bloody steam engine??' Uncle Igor cried out in disbelief.

It was not a steam engine he eventually ferreted out. It was an old, rust-eaten Tula samovar – a huge coal-heated metal urn for making tea – which had probably been dumped into the yar by its owners when electric samovars came into existence. We didn't see Uncle Igor back in the ditch ever again.

When I came back to Kharkiv from London many years later, the yar was no longer there. I was told it had been filled up after a drunk drowned there. A small park was in its place. And suddenly I felt a sharp pang of nostalgic pain for all those joyful days in the ditch, filled up by time, the days that could never be repeated. I was standing on the grave of my childhood.

During my school years, I tried to fish whenever I could. I recall ferreting out a scary and disproportionately big-headed Astrakhan bull fish during a 1960s Volga River cruise on board MV *Alexander Nevsky*, on which I was taken by my grandparents at the age of 10. I fished at every single pier we moored at, and often from the lower deck of the moving ship, too. My catches were later cooked for me at the ship's galley and solemnly served for supper at the restaurant to the applause of other passengers. Somewhere in my archives there still sits a 'Diploma' from the ship's captain, awarded to 'the most active member of the MV *Alexander Nevsky*'s fishing team'. The 'team' of course consisted of just one member.

I fished in the Dnieper River which I cruised (at the age of 16) from Kyiv (then Kiev) to Kherson with my mother. I spent long hours on the edge of a small pond deep in a thick Estonian forest where I was once approached by the still active (it was in the 1960s) unit of 'forest brothers' – the partisans fighting for Estonia's liberation from the Soviet occupation. They looked scary but were harmless (to me at least), and politely refused to take my modest catch of three small carp which I had generously (out of fear) offered them as a gift.

I fished in the swift-flowing Lithuanian River Nemunas, and – shortly before leaving the USSR – in the Siverskyi Donets River where a series of deadly battles with the Russians took place in May 2022. Then, in 1989, it was the most beautiful and peaceful fishing spot one could imagine, and I often wonder what it looks like now – pockmarked and disfigured by trenches and bomb craters.

Since coming to the West in 1990, I've only had a few attempts at fishing, all during various journalistic assignments. One of the best was probably in Port Howard (population of six) in the Falklands, in the company of a local farmer. And what wonderful fishing it was! Having barely remembered how to cast, I was able to catch five large, spangled sea trout within just 40 minutes. The Falklands fish simply could not wait to swallow my Silver Toby spoonbait. Or so it felt.

Incomplete Angler

I remember catching a strange – striped and multi-coloured – creature called a Sea Rooster from a glass-bottomed boat in Australia's Great Barrier Reef waters using just a piece of line and a hook, without any bait! The fish was so beautiful that I immediately threw it back into the ocean.

Yet my most memorable fishing – or rather non-fishing – experience was in Kachemak Bay, Alaska, where shortly before my arrival a local deckhand had reportedly hooked an orca – another name for a killer whale (and also – ironically – a nickname given by Ukrainians to the invading Russian soldiers – sorry, I simply cannot forget about the war in my native country, not even for a second), having mistaken it for a fair-sized halibut!

The story in the local *Homer News* rag was headed 'Orca Takes the Hali-Bait' (ha-ha). It was substantiated by photos taken by the skipper, in which one could clearly see a hapless angler trying to pull out a torpedo-shaped submarine-sized whale, or at least pretending to do so.

I ran to the harbour and promptly booked myself on a halibut-fishing charter the following morning. 'Remember all the fish you catch can be packaged and sent anywhere in the world,' a 'fish controller' girl told me from the window of her wooden booth on the pier. I said that I wanted my whale to be sent straight to my house in London, even if they had to charter a special cargo flight.

'Sure!' the girl replied with a smile and proceeded to compliment me on my 'lovely British accent' (it was only in Alaska and, possibly, Tasmania, that I could occasionally pass for a Brit).

But instead of hooking a whale, or even a halibut, I caught a severe bout of seasickness and spent all my time on board the *Sea Witch* supine in the boat's tiny cabin. My only consolation was that, with my environmentally friendly fishing (with no catch), I played no part in damaging Alaska's ecosystem. The boat's owners were called 'Sorry Charlie Charters', by the way. I wish I had known it before embarking.

However, I did embark on that fishing boat in Cornwall, after all. How could I not, after all those non-fishing years? Besides the weather was great, and it only cost 20 quid for two hours.

BEE COOL was a purpose-built charter boat licensed for eight anglers (there were only three of us on that trip). Cat 4-coded to 20 miles from Looe, she had all the relevant safety equipment and even a toilet. Powered by an Iveco turbo diesel engine producing 250hp and chased by a tireless squad of screaming seagulls (a good omen), she was smoothly traversing the emerald Cornwall waters. Paul Woodman, the skipper, was a fifth-generation Cornish fisherman who claimed to know every local rock, patch of rough ground, or wreck as he had 'towed the trawl or scallop dredges into most of them'.

He seemed to know for sure where the fish were likely to be and why they were there – either feeding or spawning. He provided us with super-light, almost weightless, rod-and-reel sets and showed us how to cast. All the rest was, literally, in our own hands. Here's a brief summary of that short, yet long-overdue, fishing expedition of mine.

Caught (mackerel, pilchard, pollack, whiting; Atlantic horse mackerel etc.) – 20 fish altogether

Let go – 10

Went off the hook without asking me – 5

Spotted without trying to catch – 2 mullet, 2 dolphins, 1 seal, and 27,844 hungry seagulls

Filleted (by the famous Pengelly's fishmonger in Looe's fish market) – 10

Barbecued and consumed the same evening – 10

Just like in some old fisherman's tale, my wife was waiting for me in the harbour. Had she been there all the time from 8.15 am when we set off, I wondered, as I climbed up the steep slippery steps from the landing jetty onto the pier clutching the bag with my catch?

'What time is it now?' I asked her the moment I stepped onto terra firma.

She looked at her watch. 'It's 8.15 am,' she replied.

APPENDIX 2

Utopias: an A to Z Primer

Here is a short guide to the many attempts to create perfection in an imperfect world.

Autopia

A Disneyland attraction where 'visitors of all ages' drive specially designed cars around an enclosed track. It was first set up before President Eisenhower signed development plans for the US interstate highway system back in 1955 and represented the future of American motorways. Over the years, Autopia has been updated to match the latest versions of America's never-ending automobile utopia. These days it includes a driving 'experience', where visitors watch animations of a futuristic three-dimensional city inhabited by talking cars discussing life's challenges.

Bellamy, Edward (1850-1898)

American author, best known for his writing about socialism. Despite never using this term in his works, the prevailing tone of his novels was one of resentment toward industrial society. The most successful of his books was a political, yet romantic, utopian novel called *Looking Backward* – the story of a man who falls asleep under hypnosis and wakes up in the year 2000. The book describes a utopian community with endless possibilities where people 'cooperate rather than compete'. This work launched a new political movement, with a number of 'Bellamy Clubs' set up around the country to spread his ideas. It was also read by British doctor and Labour MP Alfred Salter, who went on to attempt, albeit unsuccessfully, to recreate Bellamy's utopia in Bermondsey, London.

Celebration

A utopian settlement in Florida, US. Conceived and designed by Walt Disney and made real in 1996. Disney's idea was to create a town where people would walk or cycle everywhere. The jury is still decidedly out on whether the reality matches up to the ideal; some commentators regard it as a carefully camouflaged flop, although in 2007 Celebration was voted 'America's Dream Town of the Year'.

Defoe, Daniel (1659-1731)

Daniel Defoe's novel *Robinson Crusoe*, published in 1719, is a true literary milestone. One of the first novels written in English, it follows Robinson Crusoe as he constructs his own utopia after arriving alone on a deserted island. Crusoe's attitude pre-empts the Western capitalist economy. He is hard-working, independent and committed to business. Unlike previous works where utopian visions of modernity were static, the plot of *Robinson Crusoe* was dynamic and change was ongoing. The book went on to inspire an entire genre of novels, known as 'Robinsonade'.

Etzler, John Adolfus (1791-1846)

American technological utopianist who in 1836 published a book on 'solar paradise', with the title *The Paradise Within The Reach Of All Men, Without Labour, By Powers Of Nature And Machinery*. It contained plans for a technological utopian community where solar, wind, tidal and wave energy would be harnessed. His prophetic vision included prefab flat-roofed apartment blocks with boxes that 'move up and down' as well as piped hot and cold water, as well as gas. Among Etzler's other utopian but impractical inventions were an automated wave-powered boat, a plough-bulldozer and a machine for crystallising sugar without heat that he believed would put an end to slavery.

Fordlandia

A 5,000-square-mile tract of land in the Brazilian Amazon jungle, where American motoring tycoon Henry Ford wanted to build a rubber plantation for the needs of his car factories in 1927. He created a teetotal puritanical settlement, with rows of neat houses and straight roads. Ford's early success soon collapsed. Overcome by disease, greed and corruption, by 1945 Fordlandia was abandoned and left in ruins.

Godwin, Francis (1562-1633)

English historian and science-fiction writer. His book *The Man in the Moone* is described as a 'voyage of utopian discovery'. Published posthumously in 1638, it follows the narrator's visits to numerous societies. At one point, in a bid to escape an attack off the shore of Tenerife, he uses his flying machine to get to the Moon. He encounters the Lunars, who inhabit what appears to be a utopian paradise. Godwin was heavily influenced by the work of Galileo and took the astronomer's work a step further to conclude that there is life on the Moon.

Huxley, Aldous (1894-1963)

English novelist, essayist and critic, author of *Brave New World* (1931) a famous dystopian novel in which he satirises the idea of progress put forward by scientists, and describes a scientifically engineered technocratic hell some 600 years hence, awash with recreational drugs, consumerism, test-tube babies, 'feelie' cinemas and Neo-Pavlovian conditioning of humans. At this remove, 600 years seems an overestimate; 60 years closer. Towards the end of his life, Huxley wrote a utopian – and much less powerful – novel, *Island*, in which the horrors of *Brave New World* melt into the vision of a utopian state governed by reason and love.

Iver Diggers Colony

A group of English Protestant agricultural communalists in Iver, UK, who attempted to farm common land. Originally a movement started in 1649 by Gerrard Winstanley in Surrey, they called themselves 'True levellers'. Diggers believed in economic equality and worked to reform social order through their rural lifestyle. Winstanley aimed to build utopia on St George's Hill and later moved around the country after unsuccessful attempts to do so. Time after time defiant diggers had their homes torn down and were even taken to court by locals for trespassing.

Jordans Garden Village

A utopian rural settlement in the Chilterns, taking its name from a farmstead where Quaker farmers lived in the 17th century. Founded by Jordans Village Ltd Friendly Society in 1916 and designed by Fred Rowntree, the village initially relied on its own industries to produce the building materials, from bricks to door hinges. Started as a utopian rural community, where artisans could pursue their trades and skills to the full and under the best possible conditions, it is now a residential settlement centred around a grassed village square, with some retirement cottages at the edge. It is also a conservation area retaining the original character of the garden village.

Kurzweil, Raymond (1948-)

Renowned American author, inventor and futurist, and an advocate for technology. He often speaks of its incomprehensible potential and that progress in this field would mean advances would soon surpass the capabilities of the human brain. His favourite concept is 'singularity' – a theoretical point in time when artificial intelligence overtakes human intelligence, as reflected in a number of his books, most notably *The Singularity is Near*. Here, he forecasts 2045 as the year in which singularity will be achieved. Despite public advocacy for technology, Kurzweil makes it clear that these infinite possibilities are distinct from utopia. In an interview he said: 'I'm not a utopian and it's not a utopian vision. In fact, I've talked a lot about the intertwined promise and peril of technologies. It empowers our creative side; it also empowers our destructive side.'

Letchworth Garden City

Town in Hertfordshire, UK, population 32,000, and the world's first garden city. Started in 1903, it was based on the ideas expressed in Ebenezer Howard's book *Tomorrow: A Peaceful Path to Real Reform*, with the main aim of resettling workers from the slums of late-Victorian London by offering them cheap cottages and ideal living conditions. Designed by architects Parker and Unwin, Letchworth became the flagship of the international garden city movement and an inspiration for hundreds of garden cities, towns and villages all over the world.

Morris, William (1834-1896)

Renowned British artist and poet who developed a political strand to his work during the mid-1870s, as England was on the verge of war with Russia. Disillusioned by capitalism and inspired by Marxism, he developed a socialist vision and wrote numerous articles. *News from Nowhere* was a response to Bellamy's 'Looking Backward', which epitomised the state-socialism that Morris rejected. The narrator, William Guest, wakes up in a future utopian society, based on common ownership and democratic control, where life is pastoral and full of joy.

New Earswick

Model village for workers at the Rowntree chocolate factory in Yorkshire, where architects Parker and Unwin developed their garden city design ideas in 1902. The village was built entirely from the local materials. In the opinion of Gillian Daley, author of *Villages of Vision*, these materials, combined with imaginative planning and attention for detail, made New Earswick the most successful of all model and industrial villages.

Owen, Robert (1771-1858)

'The most important experiment for the happiness of the human race that has yet been instituted in any part of the world.' This is how Robert Owen described the work that would transform the obscure Scottish town of New Lanark into a modern-day utopian community. Owen converted an ordinary cotton-mill factory into an internationally acclaimed model town during the industrial revolution. In the community, a caring and humane attitude and use of new technologies underpinned progress and prosperity. Owen's first move was to prohibit children from working in the factories, and then to initiate reduced working hours. At the heart of Owen's vision for universal harmony was education. New Lanark was the first to open an infant s and a creche for working mothers, as well as community education centres for its workers. Owen's legacy remains apparent in the town, now awarded World Heritage Status.

Phalanstère

Originally conceived by French philosopher Charles Fourier, 19th-century phalanstère buildings were designed to house self-contained utopian communities. The buildings had a central part and two wings. The middle was for study, dining, quiet activities. One wing was for work of a noisy type – hammering, forging – and for keeping noisy kids out of the way. The other wing had ballrooms and meeting rooms. Non-resident outsiders were to pay a fee to visit phalanstère inhabitants and this income would sustain the independent economy of each community. Fourier never set up any phalanstères himself. In the 20th century, this concept inspired architect Le Corbusier, who went on to design and create a number of self-contained communes around Europe known as 'Unité d'Habitation'. The most famous of them, Cité Radieuse, was in Marseille. In the 1840s there were 30 or so Fourierist associations in the US. 'Life in the American phalanxes required hard work and self-sacrifice... The phalanxes never solved the problem of what to do about those who did not assume their share of the work.' (Carl J. Guarneri, *The utopian Alternative* (Cornell University Press, 1991).

Quakers

Members of the Society of Friends, a Christian sect founded by George Fox about 1650. According to Chris Coates, author of *Utopia Britannica*, the Quakers made the biggest impact on technological advance in the early industrial period in Britain. They provided finance for the development of Stephenson's Rocket and the Stockton-on-Tees Railway, pioneered new mining techniques and supported advances in iron smelting. If not always the actual inventors, Quakers were often a driving force behind major technological and social breakthroughs. They pushed forward the mechanisation of the weaving industry by financing Robert Owen's utopian settlement in New Lanark, with decent housing and social welfare for the workforce. Quakers had a profound influence on Ebenezer Howard, founder of the world's first Garden City, and were behind such utopian initiatives as the so-called 'steam co-operatives' (cottages located around a 'central steam engine' and surrounded by allotment gardens) and 'Q-Camps', where residents and guests were involved in gardening, farm work and various handicrafts. Famous Quakers include the Cadbury family, who set up one of the world's largest confectionary companies. Brothers Richard and George Cadbury were also renowned for their unique approach to treating their workforce. They established Bournville, a utopian village that housed workers from the Cadbury's factory in Birmingham. Their employees enjoyed beautiful houses with gardens, leisure and education facilities and pensions. Modelez International, a Kraft company, bought Cadbury in 2010, and sparked negative headlines when it discontinued the Quaker-instigated utopian Christmas tradition of sending a box of chocolates and biscuits to Cadbury's pensioners.

Rand, Ayn (1905-1982)

Novelist, philosopher and playwright who defected from Soviet Russia to the US in 1926. Her two most famous works are novels *The Fountainhead* and *Atlas Shrugged*. Written in an age of creeping global socialism, *Atlas Shrugged* is Ayn Rand's vision of what may happen to a developed technology-ridden society if the wealthiest citizens stop working, refuse to pay taxes and simply disappear. The novel shows in detail the resulting collapse of efficient production and the rise of corruption as businessmen and politicians begin to live off the labour of others. It poses the question of whether this is dystopia or utopia. For Ayn Rand, the mind is the most important tool for humanity, and reason is its greatest virtue.

The Shakers

American millenarian sect, founded in 1747 as an offshoot of the Quakers. Innovators and inventors par excellence, the Shakers had a utopian view of technology, regarding it as the main provider of social and moral benefits, which it did by 'relieving human toil or facilitation of labour' and thus creating opportunities for 'moral mechanical, scientific and intellectual improvement'. The Shakers are credited with a long list of inventions: a screw propeller, Babbitt metal, a rotary barrow, the circular saw, a silk-reeling machine, a cheese press, a revolving oven, the first metal pens and many more, none of which they patented, believing that patents 'smacked of monopoly'.

Tatlin, Vladimir (1885-1953)

Russian constructivist, the best-known member of the constructivist art community. Tatlin believed art should be pleasing to the eye as well as functional, with artworks made from organic materials that could serve people in society. One of Tatlin's models, the Monument to the Third International, was made of the usual constructivist materials of wood and wire and was the perfect example of Russian Constructivism. It was designed to serve the important purpose of housing Russian government and administration offices but was never viable from an engineering and financial points of view.

Utopia

Any real or imaginary society, place, state, settlement or technology considered to be perfect or ideal, yet not necessarily achievable. The term was coined by Sir Thomas More in 1516 as the title of his book that described an imaginary island in the New World representing the perfect society. Considering in *Journey Through Utopia* (1950) the difficulty of one all-embracing definition of utopia, Marie-Louise Berneri remarks that whereas in the *Encyclopedia Britannica* the word is defined as 'an ideal commonwealth whose inhabitants exist under perfect conditions', the *Dictionnaire General de la Langue Francaise* describes it as 'an imaginary conception of an ideal government'.

The Vrilya

An advanced human species, who live beneath the surface of the earth, as described in The Coming Race – a utopian and highly prophetic novel by Edward Bulwer Lytton (1803-73) published in 1871. The hero, a young American, falls down the shaft of a mine and finds himself in an underground world inhabited by the Vrilya, the creatures powered by a utopian energy called 'Vril', the word from which the trademark 'Bovril', a concentrated beef extract, later originated. 'Vril' combines the properties of electricity, death rays, antibiotics, ballistic missiles and much more. It powers the automata that do all mechanical tasks, fuels the Vrilya's large 'air-boats' and their inflatable wings, attached to a metal harness, which allow them to fly.

Wells, Herbert George (1866-1946)

H. G. Wells was an English writer best known for his science fiction novels and collection of utopian books. The first of these works, *Modern Utopia*, set the precedent for many modern scientific ideas. The story is set on an Earth-like planet, whose inhabitants have created the perfect society. The narrators visit this parallel land and discuss its virtues and flaws. Utopia is a world where people live healthy, happy lives, with all their needs met. Many of Wells's books inspired tropes in science fiction, including invisibility, time travel and extra-terrestrial invasions. These novels, known as 'scientific romances', include *The Time Machine, The Invisible Man* and *War of the Worlds*.

Xenophon (431-?355 BC)

Greek historian, general, disciple of Socrates and one of the first 'armchair utopists'. He led an army of 10,000 soldiers to the Black Sea to seize the throne of Persia, a campaign described in his *Anabasis*. His other works include *Hellenica*, a history of Greece, *Memorabilia* and *Symposium*, both of which contain Socratic dialogues. In a treatise *On the Revenue of Athens*, written shortly before his death, Xenophon put forward a series of utopian ideas, the main one being nationalisation – of the silver mines, of inns and lodging houses. However, he stopped short of suggesting a complete nationalisation, for which read state control, of everything.

The Year 2440

utopian novel by Louis-Sebastien Mercier (1740-1814), a best-seller of pre-Revolutionary France which went through 25 editions. The hero, a contemporary of the author, wakes in 2440 and finds Paris and the world entirely transformed. No more greed, vanity and hypocrisy. The French capital has beautiful straight streets and its residents wear simple loose clothes, with no wigs or swords. Traffic keeps to the right and is strictly regulated, but most people, including the king and his courtiers, prefer walking. There is no censorship, the press is free, and schoolchildren learn algebra, physics and astronomy.

Zamyatin, Yevgeny Ivanovich (1884-1937)

Soviet/Russian writer, a naval engineer and mathematician by education and author of *We*, considered one of the greatest dystopias ever written and an inspiration for both Huxley and Orwell. A poignant and prophetic satire on Stalinist rule, it was published in English in 1924, well before Stalin's rise to absolute power. The book prophecies the realisation of a technological Utopia in which the dictate of the state and the machine threatens the very essence of human spirit. It is set in The One State, where the citizens have numbers instead of names, buildings and furniture are all made of glass (so that nothing could be concealed from the all-seeing eyes of the ubiquitous 'guardians'. Hidden 'membranes' record all conversations in the streets of the city, surrounded with glass walls. All natural life has been destroyed, and the only food is a chemical derivative of naphtha. The Benefactor, the supreme leader, personally carries out all executions with the help of The Machine, an electric-powered contraption which transforms human tissue into chemically pure water. The One State's scientists even have a way of eradicating imagination – a scientific breakthrough, called the Grand Operation. The novel was not published in the Soviet Union until 1988.

Other Books by the Author

Special Correspondent
Dateline Freedom
Vitali's Australia
Vitali's Ireland
Little is the Light
Passport to Enclavia
Borders Up!
Dreams on Hitler's Couch
Granny Yaga
Out of the Blu
Atlas of Geographical Curiosities
Life as a Literary Device